HIGHER EDUCATION AND GRADUATE EMPLOYMENT IN EUROPE

HIGHER EDUCATION DYNAMICS

VOLUME 15

Series Editors

Peter Maassen, *University of Oslo, Norway, and University of Twente, Enschede, The Netherlands*

Johan Muller, *Graduate School of Humanities, University of Cape Town, Rondebosch, South Africa*

Editorial Board

Alberto Amaral, *Universidade do Porto, Portugal*
Akira Arimoto, *Hiroshima University, Japan*
Nico Cloete, *CHET, Pretoria, South Africa*
David Dill, *University of North Carolina at Chapel Hill, USA*
Jürgen Enders, *University of Twente, Enschede, The Netherlands*
Patricia Gumport, *Stanford University, USA*
Mary Henkel, *Brunel University, Uxbridge, United Kingdom*
Glenn Jones, *University of Toronto, Canada*

SCOPE OF THE SERIES

Higher Education Dynamics is a bookseries intending to study adaptation processes and their outcomes in higher education at all relevant levels. In addition it wants to examine the way interactions between these levels affect adaptation processes. It aims at applying general social science concepts and theories as well as testing theories in the field of higher education research. It wants to do so in a manner that is of relevance to all those professionally involved in higher education, be it as ministers, policy-makers, politicians, institutional leaders or administrators, higher education researchers, members of the academic staff of universities and colleges, or students. It will include both mature and developing systems of higher education, covering public as well as private institutions.

The titles published in this series are listed at the end of this volume.

HIGHER EDUCATION AND GRADUATE EMPLOYMENT IN EUROPE

Results from Graduate Surveys from Twelve Countries

By

HARALD SCHOMBURG

International Centre for Higher Education Research Kassel, Germany

and

ULRICH TEICHLER

International Centre for Higher Education Research Kassel, Germany

A C.I.P. Catalogue record for this book is available from the Library of Congress.

ISBN-10 1-4020-5153-0 (HB)
ISBN-13 978-1-4020-5153-1 (HB)
ISBN-10 1-4020-5154-9 (e-book)
ISBN-13 978-1-4020-5154-8 (e-book)

Published by Springer,
P.O. Box 17, 3300 AA Dordrecht, The Netherlands.

www.springer.com

Printed on acid-free paper

All Rights Reserved
© 2006 Springer
No part of this work may be reproduced, stored in a retrieval system, or transmitted
in any form or by any means, electronic, mechanical, photocopying, microfilming,
recording or otherwise, without written permission from the Publisher, with the exception
of any material supplied specifically for the purpose of being entered
and executed on a computer system, for exclusive use by the purchaser of the work.

TABLE OF CONTENTS

Introduction 1

1 Developments, Prior Research and the Concepts of this Study 3
1.1 Debates and Research 3
1.2 The Concept of the Project 8
1.3 The Contents of this Volume 19

2 Methods Used 21
2.1 Overview 21
2.2 The Research Instrument 21
2.3 The Target Group of the Study 22
2.4 The Survey Process 23
2.5 Participation in the Graduate Survey 23
2.6 The Standard Questionnaire and National Variations 25
2.7 Data Analysis 26
2.8 The Interview Studies 26
2.9 Overall Project Coordination and Cooperation 26
2.10 Survey Eight Years After Graduation 28

3 The Educational Paths and Attainments 29
3.1 Introduction 29
3.2 Gender 29
3.3 Educational Attainment of the Parents 30
3.4 Foreigners 31
3.5 Years of Schooling 31
3.6 Kind of Secondary Education 31
3.7 Activities Before First Enrolment 32
3.8 Age at the Time of Enrolment in Higher Education 33

4 Course of Study 35
4.1 Type of Degree 35
4.2 Field of Study 36
4.3 Duration of Study 38
4.4 Age at the Time of Graduation 39
4.5 Graduation Quota 40
4.6 Study Conditions and Provision 40
4.7 Rating of Study Conditions and Study Provision 42
4.8 Study Activities 45
4.9 Activities Besides Study 45
4.10 Relationship between Work Experience and Content of Study 47
4.11 Foreign Language Proficiency and Computer Knowledge 48
4.12 Study Abroad 49
4.13 Summary 50

5 Job Search, Transition to Employment and Early Career — 51

- 5.1 Job Search — 51
- 5.2 Timing of Job Search — 52
- 5.3 Length of Job Search — 53
- 5.4 Number of Contacts with Employers — 56
- 5.5 Methods of Job Search — 58
- 5.6 Time between Graduation and First Employment — 61
- 5.7 Conclusion — 63

6 Early Career — 65

- 6.1 Activities in the First 3 ½ Years After Graduation — 65
- 6.2 Predominant Activities Since Graduation — 76
- 6.3 Job Mobility — 77
- 6.4 Transition to a Permanent Job? — 78
- 6.5 Impact of First Job on Subsequent Employment — 79

7 Employment Several Years After Graduation — 81

- 7.1 Major Activity — 81
- 7.2 Unemployment — 81
- 7.3 Working Time — 83
- 7.4 Temporary Contracts — 84
- 7.5 Economic Sector of Employment — 85
- 7.6 Public or Private Sector — 88
- 7.7 Self-employment — 89
- 7.8 Job Title — 90
- 7.9 Income — 91

8 Competences and Work Assignments — 93

- 8.1 Recruitment Criteria — 93
- 8.2 Competences at Time of Graduation — 96
- 8.3 Work Requirements — 97
- 8.4 Utility of Studies — 102
- 8.5 International Competences — 102

9 Match between Education and Employment — 105

- 9.1 The Relevance of the Field of Study — 105
- 9.2 Use of Knowledge and Skills — 107
- 9.3 Appropriateness of Level of Education — 107
- 9.4 Reasons for Inappropriate Position — 108
- 9.5 Fulfilled Expectations — 109
- 9.6 The Proportion of Graduates Facing Problems — 110

10 Orientations and Job Satisfaction   113
    10.1 Life Goals   113
    10.2 Work Orientation   114
    10.3 Professional Situation   117
    10.4 Job Satisfaction   118

11 Career Relevant Aspects   119
    11.1 Initial and Continuing Professional Education   119
    11.2 International Mobility   125
    11.3 The Family Situation   128
    11.4 Regional Disparities   130

12 Major Findings and Policy Implications   133
    12.1 Aims and Methods of the Study   133
    12.2 Success in Transition, Employment and Work   135
    12.3 Studies as Preparation for Subsequent Employment and Work   137
    12.4 European and International Diversity and Disparity   139
    12.5 Strength and Limits of the Study and Prospects   141

Literature   143
Questionnaire   151

INTRODUCTION

From autumn 1998 to spring 2000, about 3,000 graduates each from nine countries in the European Union (Austria, Finland, France, Germany, Italy, the Netherlands, Spain, Sweden, United Kingdom), one EFTA country (Norway), one of the Central and Eastern European countries in transition (the Czech Republic) and one economically advanced country outside Europe (Japan) provided information through a written questionnaire on the relationship between higher education and employment three to four years after graduation. In total, over 40,000 graduates from higher education institutions answered questions on their socio-biographical background, study paths, transition from higher education to employment, early career, links between study and employment, job satisfaction and their retrospective view on higher education.

The study provided a unique opportunity to examine how far the relationships between higher education and the world of work are similar or different in the Western European countries. This became clearer through the inclusion of one country of the Central and Eastern European countries and one country outside Europe. The study also helped to understand the common elements and differences between various fields of study and occupational areas. It made it possible to analyse current salient issues of higher education, e.g. equality, the role of educational levels, the demand for specialized or general competences, the growing role of international mobility and lifelong education, the regional diversity in higher education. Last but not least, the study examined the extent to which socio-biographical backgrounds, educational experiences and achievements, as well as the transition process determined early career and links between competences and work assignments. Altogether, it offered the most thorough comparative information on graduate employment and work and the links between higher education and graduate employment and work ever provided.

In this volume, which is based on the final report to the EU, we describe the methodology of the study and present the major results in a descriptive way, mainly with respect to the differences by country. A second volume (Ulrich Teichler, ed. *Careers of University Graduates. Views and Experiences in Comparative Perspective.* Dordrecht, Springer, 2006) addresses details of the different topics of the study and uses more complex methods of analysis. A complete list of more than 200 publications and presentations of results of the study can be found at http://www.uni-kassel.de/wz1/cheers.htm.

1 DEVELOPMENTS, PRIOR RESEARCH AND THE CONCEPTS OF THIS STUDY

1.1 Debates and Research

Changes over the Last Decades

In the 1990s, the relationship between higher education and employment re-emerged as one of the major policy topics, as well as a focus of research in Europe (see the summary of debates in Teichler 1999). In the 1960s and 1970s, it had already been a key issue of higher education policy and research, but it lost momentum for some years in between (see Psachropoulos, 1987; Sanyal, 1991; Teichler, 1992).

In the 1960s, hopes had spread that the expansion of higher education might contribute significantly to economic growth and the reduction of social inequality. Economists and sociologists undertook numerous studies on the prediction of future manpower demand and supply, investigated returns on educational investments, analysed patterns of occupational mobility and identified the impact of social background and educational attainment on socio-economic status. During the 1970s, however, concern grew about growing mismatches between the slightly increasing demands for qualified labour and the rapidly growing number of higher education graduates. Pessimistic scenarios of "over-education" or "akademisches Proletariat" again fuelled interest in identifying the foreseeable problems and finding possible improvements. Some studies focused on the opportunities of graduates from non-university higher education and the impact of vocational curricular approaches on the diversification of employment prospects according to fields of study, on the role of reputational hierarchies of higher education institutions and programmes, and on the number of graduates who held positions that were considered to match their educational attainment.

During the 1980s, the relationship between higher education and employment was not high on the agenda. Faith in employment forecasts and corresponding educational planning had eroded. The warning of pending catastrophes due to the expansion of higher education had also failed. Research on graduate employment and work was not the magic tool for the provision of guidelines for curriculum development. The relationship between higher education and employment was too complex to fit into simple persuasive models.

The Debates and Research in the 1990s

The renewed debates on the relationship between higher education and employment since about 1990 cannot be characterised by single new developments or challenges. Rather, many issues are concurrently raised in this context: the increasing speed of turnover of knowledge required in jobs, the dramatic structural changes of the labour force in the wake of the introduction of new technologies and new managerial concepts, the globalization and Europeanization of the economy and society, the rapid "massification" of higher education since about the mid-eighties in many industrial societies, increasing unemployment, declining transparency and continuity of careers, etc. Obviously, the signals higher education receives as regards graduate employment and work as well as the demands of the employment system are more contradictory today and create more dilemmas than ever before.

- Despite strenuous efforts undertaken in the past to harmonize the quantitative demand and supply of highly qualified labour either through planning, information or political campaigning, *mismatch* is believed to be widespread and to have become endemic. Both the instrumental ambitions of students and their intrinsic motives regarding enrichment through knowledge and reflection reinforced a growth of enrolment in higher education beyond presumed demand from traditional areas of graduate employment.
- *Transition* to employment in the 1990s was severely hit by concurrent phenomena of economic crisis and a decline in provisions of paid work due to rationalisation and the use of new technologies. Yet, the majority of experts and key political actors in Europe tended to predict a growing long-term demand for graduates.
- Higher education institutions and students are increasingly expected to be *more responsive* in their study provisions and study activities to the needs of the employment system. Yet, these needs are more difficult to identify in times of growing uncertainty, substantial mismatches, considerable erosion of traditional occupations and employment conditions, and rapid obsolescence of knowledge. Thus, higher education and students are expected to be responsive to fuzzy demands.
- Higher education institutions are held more accountable than in the past for their contributions to the cultivation of knowledge and the utility of education and research for the economy and society. Yet, *criteria* for respective assessment are more *shaky* than ever – not only because of the uncertainties about demands quoted above, but also because research on the substance and processes of teaching and learning and their impact on employment and work has been more successful in demystifying traditional beliefs than in establishing a generally-accepted body of knowledge as regards "good practices", "quality" etc.
- In the process of growing European co-operation as well as of growing *internationalization* and globalization of higher education systems and graduate labour markets, the variety between European countries in terms of competences required as well as in work and employment settings might turn out both to be an asset and a barrier to mobility and co-operation. Diversity seems to be so bewildering that information systems are chronically insufficient.

Syntheses on the State of Knowledge and Research

The renewed debates and the state of knowledge had been documented in various publications in the course of the early and mid-1990s. These publications were valuable in preparing and in specifying the comparative graduate survey documented in this book.

First, the documents published by the Commission of the European Communities between 1990 and 1993 about the future of higher education (Commission of European Communities, 1990, 1991, 1993) clearly underscored the tensions between the high hopes set on increased student numbers on the one hand and the concern about unemployment, precarious working conditions and continuing inequalities. They also indicated rising expectations regarding responsiveness, creativity, flexibility and the social skills of graduates.

Second, in its study "From Higher Education to Employment" (OECD, 1992b, 1993a), OECD documented the potentials and pitfalls of analysing the relationship between higher education and employment in industrial societies on the basis of available statistics and large-scale surveys. Despite the impressive body of information provided by this study, problems due to different methods of information gathering and limitations of the available studies as regards the content of education and work are the most striking outcome. The study also shows that new means must be found to identify newly emerging occupations, new mixes of skills and qualifications and changes in the occupational structure.

Third, overviews on the "state of the art" of research on higher education and employment initiated by the Consortium of Higher Education Researchers called for a broadening of the research topics. Notably, analyses of the links between curricula and work assignments and of the activities of major actors to steer the relationships between higher education and employment have not received the attention they deserve (Brennan and Kogan, 1993; Brennan, Kogan and Teichler, 1995). Similarly, contributions to a conference organized by OECD's Programme on Institutional Management in Higher Education (IMHE) underlined the lack of information on curricular strategies, counselling and placement activities as well as their impact on graduate employment and work (see various articles in Higher Education Management, Vol. 6, 1994, Nos. 3 and 4).

Fourth, two issues of the *European Journal of Education* published in the mid-1990s (Vol. 30, 1995, Nos. 1 and 2) confirmed the multitude of researchers' approaches as well as the range of current issues addressed in the European countries for which information is available. Obviously, no trend towards a single major issue or paradigm is in sight.

Fifth, the research project documented in this book triggered off some accounts of the state of knowledge and debate (Teichler, 1999a, b, c; Paul, Teichler and Van der Velden, 2000). On the one hand, they showed that solid internationally comparative information was rare, and that the majority of economically advanced countries had not carried out any major surveys on graduate employment and work beyond some general statistical data. On the other hand, experts' and actors' views about graduate employment seemed to develop common dynamics and establish conventional wisdom as regards the competences required on the part of the graduates. A growing demand for highly qualified labour and graduates' increasing problems to find suitable employment can no longer be viewed as contradictory claims, but must be considered as coexisting phenomena. Higher education has to prepare students to become highly skilled specialists and to be versatile in many other domains, to increase their body of knowledge and to learn to transfer academic knowledge into practical problem solving, to be trained to cope with established job requirements and to question the established rules and tools, to foster the cognitive competences and to provide opportunities of developing socio-communicative competences and to develop work attitudes and values that are not in the domain of cognitive training. Moreover, graduates tend to spend longer periods of learning prior to employment and are increasingly expected to supplement their competences through learning on the job and continuing professional education.

Theoretical Debates and the Approach of the Study

The changing relationships between education and employment in the wake of the expansion of higher education have been one of the key areas of economics and sociology for many years. The major concepts and theoretical controversies are well documented in Karabel and Halsey (1977), Psacharapoulos (1987) and Carnoy (1995). The economic debates focused on the regulatory power of the market versus the need for infrastructural planning, the strengths of the manpower requirement approach and the human capital approach, the justification and fallacy of measuring social rates of return, the productive and screening or filter function of education, etc. The sociologists examined the persistence of inequality versus the impact of active social and educational policies, opportunities of social mobility versus the reproductive function of education, status reinforcement versus status redistribution through education, the impacts of credentials on careers and professional policies, etc. Various scholars participating in the research team undertaking the study presented in this book contributed to this theoretical debate, for example by claiming a historically growing weight of the "status distributive" function of education as compared to its qualifying function (Teichler) or by pointing out the "custodial function" of higher education (Kellermann).

The different theoretical concepts and their varied normative underpinnings have persisted and even diversified further in the last two decades. Three trends of methodological sophistication can be observed and linked to the growing complexity of theoretical models.
- In general, the range and *number of variables* taken into consideration grew. This was both the consequence of the weak explanatory power of the initial assumptions and of the growing methodological sophistication of various multivariate techniques, path analysis etc. and of the computer "revolution".

- Whereas earlier studies tended to address educational attainment in relatively broad categories, recent research pays more attention to the question of whether *minute differences* according to certain dimensions of diversity in higher education, certain conditions and provisions of study, as well as certain ways of study behaviour, have an impact on subsequent graduate careers.
- Whereas earlier studies focused on "normal careers" and often took rationales such as "homo economicus" as the guiding principles of behaviour, recent studies try to explore an almost indefinite *diversity of values* as well as careers.

The existing diversity of theoretical approaches in the area to be analysed could suggest different strategies in forming an *international research team*. We could have tried to find scholars from different countries who could form a harmonious team, as far as the major theoretical assumptions are concerned. We opted for a competing strategy, i.e. bringing together a rather diverse team, as far as theoretical approaches are concerned, but which was both very versatile in the various theories and highly experienced as far as survey research in this area is concerned.

Such a relativist *and integrative theoretical approach* to this project was taken for four reasons. First, although theories in this area differ dramatically in their conceptual basis and their normative underpinnings, they agree to a large extent as regards the variables to be taken into consideration for testing these theories. Second, theoretical preoccupations vary according to country (see the reference to different national approaches in Fulton, Gordon and Williams, 1982; Teichler, 1988b). It is not possible in this area to strive both for a theoretically harmonious and highly qualified research team in Europe. Third, the co-operation in the process of preparing this application reinforced the hope that the theoretical diversity embodied in the research team would have a strong cross-fertilizing impact on the conceptual development of the project. Fourth, the aim of establishing a basis for regular graduate surveys in Europe cannot be reached without accepting compromises in the different conceptual frameworks.

Available Statistics and Representative Surveys

In some European countries, regular complete statistical accounts are provided or representative surveys are undertaken on graduate employment. The OECD study "From Higher Education to Employment", however, clearly indicated substantial weaknesses.
- UNESCO, OECD and EUROSTAT have not succeeded in agreeing on definitions of levels and types of higher education institutions and programmes which are generally compatible with the definitions and underlying concepts in all member states of the European Union. For example, first university degrees could be grouped into bachelor-equivalent or master-equivalent or viewed as one category. Diverse approaches are found regarding graduates from short-cycle programmes.
- Different traditions of large-scale surveys and statistical data gathering have developed in the various economically advanced countries. Differences of categories or of the timing of the surveys preclude precise international comparisons.

- Many large-scale surveys provide only structural information, i.e. field of study, higher education institution, employment status, occupational category, etc. Their frequent underestimation of the extent to which graduates make use of their competences clearly suggests that a minimum number of questions regarding acquired competences, the nature of work tasks and the use of competences is indispensable for future surveys.
- Most surveys address recent graduates soon after graduation. Surveys undertaken six months after graduation (e.g. the regular British surveys) or one year after graduation (e.g. the Swedish statistics) cannot provide a more or less complete picture, for they exclude many of those who opt for a short additional study and training period on the one hand and those facing substantial employment problems on the other. In addition, they do not analyse the impact of higher education on graduate employment and work over various career stages.
- Available graduate surveys are shaped by researchers' varied concepts as well as by different national traditions in the ways competences and work tasks are defined and priorities are set regarding certain types of competences.

The available research, thus, first, suggests that a *wealth of concepts and methods* is at hand for a European and international study on the relationship between higher education and graduate employment. It remained a challenging task to develop a terminology and thus concepts of knowledge and work that were suitable for all the countries involved. Second, one had to agree on a design that *took into account the different conditions in the various countries* regarding timing of transition, career stages, regional diversity and other similar factors. Third, graduate surveys require a difficult *balance between the complexity of the theme* on the one hand and the need to *keep the length of research instruments in bounds* and to standardize questions on the other.

1.2   The Concept of the Project

Experts from eleven European countries and Japan agreed to undertake a joint study on higher education and graduate employment in the 12 participating countries. Taking into account the practical relevance of research in this area, the conceptual and methodological potentials as well as the limitations of the current state of knowledge, the following major thrusts of a joint comparative study were envisaged.

Analysis of Graduate Employment and Work

The relationship between higher education and the world of work tend to be misunderstood if surveys on graduate employment are too narrowly defined. This study, therefore, aimed to address both *the "employment" and "work"* dimensions, i.e. not only employment status, economic sector, occupational group, income etc., but also the major work tasks. This is indispensable in order to examine the wide-spread hypothesis that, a privileged status is bound to become an exception in the process of "massification of higher education", whereas the emergence of a "knowledge society" could be accompanied by an expansion of demanding job roles or at least demanding major tasks.

The study placed emphasis on *recent issues* of graduate employment and work, challenges and requirements which are generally viewed as *most important in the 1990s*. Taking into consideration the current debates and the available expertise in the project team, special attention was given to the following issues:

- *Technology*: In order to examine major technological developments and their relevance for graduates, the study paid special attention to employment and work in the technologically most advanced sectors of production and services.
- *New employment and upgrading*: As a consequence of further "massification" of higher education and a tightened labour market, a growing number of graduates is expected to be employed in sectors hitherto viewed as marginal, i.e. in positions that were traditionally not considered suitable for graduates or in newly emerging occupational roles, such as new types of flexible combinations of work tasks, new types of self-employment, new "alternative" companies, up-grading trends in occupations traditionally held by non-graduates, newly emerging job tasks, etc. The study aimed to establish the character and frequency of these positions and work tasks that were not traditionally held by higher education graduates.
- Changing and partially deteriorating *employment conditions*: The survey also aimed to establish how far graduates experienced employment conditions during the first years after graduation that lacked the comfort of regular full-time employment such as a greater number of short-term contracts, quasi-self-employment, flexible work schedules, part-time jobs, etc.
- *Graduate unemployment*: An analysis of unemployment during the first three years after graduation had to disentangle search unemployment and transitory employment from that of regular unemployment and employment. In this context, it was worth analysing the impact of both unemployment during the first years and of retraining and other counteracting measures on the subsequent career.
- *Regional disparities*: The study analysed differences in employment and work according to regions. This obviously required an analysis of mobility from or to economically and socially disadvantaged regions and its impacts.
- *Demand for general and social competences*: Employers have tended to stress in recent years a shift in recruitment criteria, where greater weight is placed on general knowledge, attitudes and social skills. The study aimed to establish the importance of these competences for the job.
- *European mobility*: Finally, attention was paid to a growing Europeanization of employment and work by establishing the frequency of cross-border mobility as well as growth of work tasks related to other countries.

The Role of Socio-biographical Background, Higher Education and Transition

Many studies on graduate employment and work measure the graduates' educational background only in broad categories of educational attainment. This could help to establish the value of investing in study in general or to show differences of employment "success" according to field of study or to individual higher education institutions. But such an approach has hardly any value as feedback for higher education, i.e. in explaining the impact of various characteristics of higher education on graduate employment and work.

The members of the CHEERS research team agreed in assuming that a thorough analysis of educational background and of the higher education path was indispensable to establish the links between higher education and graduate employment and work. Six themes were addressed: the structure of the higher education system, curricula, study behaviour, study outcomes, the socio-biographical profile of the students and the transition from higher education to employment (see Figure 1.1).

(1) *Structures of the higher education system*: Higher education aims to produce a closer match between the students' abilities and motives, the substance of study and the subsequent employment and work through structural diversity. The study intended to establish the links between types of programmes, types of higher education institutions and differences of institutional and departmental reputation on the one hand and the graduates' careers on the other.

(2) *Curricular approaches*: Similarly, the question was raised as to whether certain curricular thrusts within the major fields of study – for example the extent of general knowledge versus specialization, disciplinarity versus interdisciplinarity, academic versus professional emphasis, etc. – were relevant for graduate employment and work. Whereas the question "Does college matter?" was often the focus of attention in the past, the often neglected question "Does programme matter?" should be given attention in this study.

(3) *Study behaviour*: The survey also addressed – retrospectively – the graduates' study behaviour. Available research undertaken in the U.S., for example, suggests that the ways students make use of study conditions and provisions are more powerful in explaining study outcomes than the conditions and provisions as such (see Pascarella and Terenzini, 1991). For example, the availability of a good library is likely to contribute to students' knowledge, but the students' use of books is likely to have a stronger impact.

(4) *Study achievements:* The survey addressed former students' achievements in terms of grades and self-ratings of competences. This allowed the study to analyse the extent to which achievement in higher education predicts career success and helps to explain the discrepancies between study achievements and career success, for example competing recruitment criteria, successful search strategies or career dynamics.

(5) *Socio-biographical background:* The CHEERS study raises the question as to whether the relationships between socio-biographical background (parental education, employment and wealth, gender, and regional background), education (over various stages) and career, which were thoroughly researched in the past, changed in the 1990s in the framework of social and economic conditions of the 1980s and 1990s which, in part, tended to reinforce hierarchies and, in part, tended to, or aimed to, reduce such disparities. The study also analysed the extent to which overt links between higher education and employment were spurious and had to be attributed to the different student intake in terms of socio-biography and education preceding enrolment.

Figure 1.1: Thematic Framework of the Study

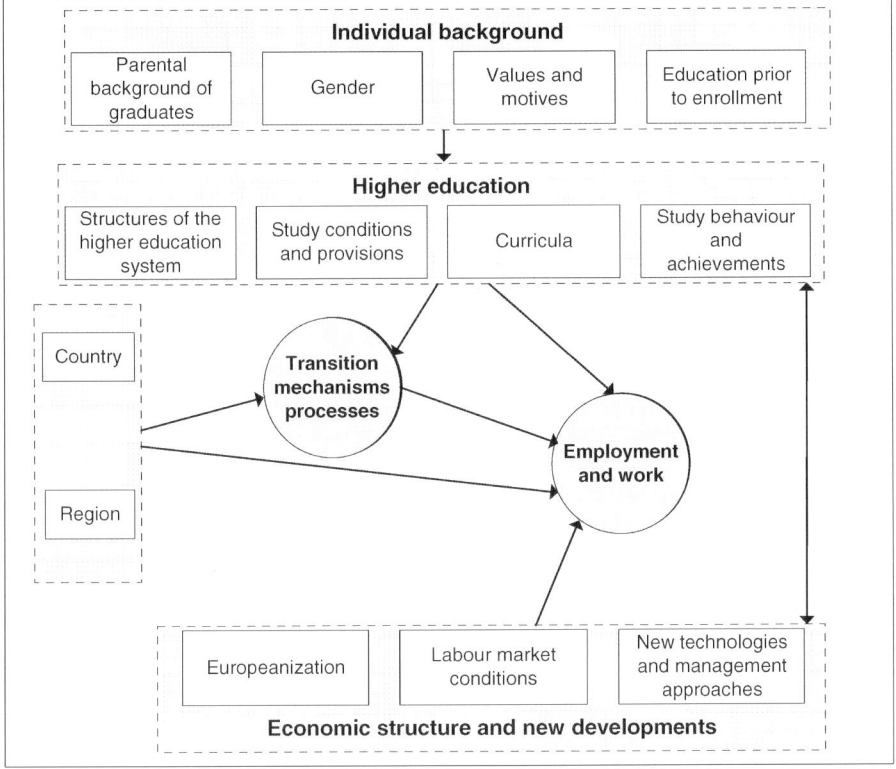

(6) *Transition to employment*: whilst past research in this domain often treated the transition from education to employment as a fairly optimal match between graduates' competences and motives on the one hand and jobs available on the other, this study analysed the internal dynamics and relative autonomy of the transition process, i.e. the extent to which search, transitory employment and unemployment etc. on the part of the graduates, guidance, counselling and assistance in job search on the part of higher education institutions and employment agencies, as well employers' recruitment policies, shaped the graduates' early career stages.

Major Themes of the Survey

As has already been pointed out, this study aimed to cover a broad range of themes: employment and work in general, recent changes of the labour market, the impact of socio-biographical backgrounds, the structural and curricular diversity of higher education and the students' study options. Some of the themes that were addressed need further explanation.

The Graduate Labour Market: Recently Changing Demands and Employment Problems

Available research suggests that any present survey of graduate employment should address the following issues:

- *New work tasks* emerge more rapidly than in the past as a consequence of the rapid obsolescence of existing knowledge and the application of new knowledge in many occupational areas (CERI/OECD, 1990; Young, 1993). The growing importance of new technologies and the growing attention paid to ecological issues were the most striking examples in the recent past. The survey had to take into account the different modes of adaptation of higher education to employment in these areas, for example the emergence of new areas of specialization in course programmes preceding corresponding professional specializations, new demands of the economy that were not systematically met by higher education, the role of continuing education and short advanced courses in this context, graduates' ability to "seize" new employment areas and to cope with the new job requirements.
- New management approaches could lead to substantial changes in the *composition and hierarchy of job roles* in individual enterprises. The gap between top positions and those of the majority of university-trained employees could grow or, on the contrary, be reduced over time.
- *New flexible ways of employment* seem to grow partly as a result of changing employment patterns introduced by companies, due to changing expectations on the part of graduates, and partly as a response to graduates' growing employment problems (OECD, 1994).
- The greater *shortage of paid employment* opportunities and the growing number of unemployed people in many European countries during the 1990s have led to increasing numbers of higher education graduates facing long periods of unemployment and/or combining unstable part-time work and advanced training and re-training activities, and to various enterprise and governmental strategies to ensure at least some kind of employment.

These issues played a role in the CHEERS project not only in terms of the background information that was useful to interpret survey findings on the distribution of graduates according to employment conditions, economic sector of employment and career progress, but also as the basis for formulating new questions regarding the specific conditions of employment and work outside the traditional domains of graduate employment.

Dimensions of Qualification and Curricular Approaches

A comparative study on higher education and work in Europe and beyond must address the variety of concepts and the situation that prevails in the different countries regarding occupationally relevant competences and their utilization on the job (Freidson, 1983; Abbott, 1988; Attewell, 1990; Vallas, 1990; Kivinen and Rinne, 1993a; Darrah, 1994; Brennan et al., 1995). This was one of the challenging tasks of the envisaged project, for we lacked a common terminology and concepts to identify and classify competences that were potentially relevant for work. Even general terms such as "qualification" have different meanings: whereas it addresses the sum of occupationally relevant competences in French and German, in English, it refers to the credentials which are necessary to access certain professions.

In studying graduates' competences and their utilization on the job, we first had to examine the *areas of knowledge emphasized in respective fields of study*. Engineering could comprise management studies in some countries, but not in others. In some countries, business studies could be linked to macro-economic studies, whilst students in other countries hardly learned macroeconomics. In some countries, students could easily combine study in different disciplines, whereas disciplinary studies could be prevalent in others.

Second, we noted different traditions in Europe with regard to the *extent to which students were expected to specialize* in the course of their studies. It was essential to examine the extent to which students acquired specialized knowledge or more open types of knowledge and how this affected both their career opportunities and the opportunity to use their competences on the job.

Third, study provisions varied substantially in Europe in terms of *the extent to which students were confronted with professional practice during the course of their studies*. In some countries, in some disciplines, and in some institutions, students could be expected to acquire merely the knowledge base, whilst in others, disciplines and institutions, a systematic confrontation of academic approaches and professional tasks and 'learning to' could be on the agenda, and they could also be expected to participate in field observations or internships.

Fourth, attention had to be paid to the role of *personal and social skills* in graduate work. In some countries, higher education institutions were expected to put a strong emphasis on developing communication skills, commitment to study and work and a miscellany of personal characteristics (e.g. adaptability, self-awareness, taking decisions and imagination), whilst in others these were not the product of deliberate educational policy. This theme deserved special attention in this project, for experts tended to agree that employers gave greater importance to personal and social skills as recruitment and promotion criteria than they did in the past.

Fifth, a study on graduate employment and work in different countries had to take into account the *different ways qualifications were certified and the role played by credentials in access to professional areas*. In some countries, curricula were highly standardized in some fields in order to guarantee expected professional competences, whereas in others, various competences were considered desirable. In some countries, access to professional activities in certain areas was exclusively reserved for graduates from a single field, whereas in others it was open for those from various fields.

Therefore, a comparative survey that only addressed categories of fields of study and of occupations would elicit artefacts. The survey had to comprise self-rating of major competences, as well as their utilisation on the job.

Utilization of Qualifications and Appropriate Careers

Mismatch between the supply of graduates in terms of their credentials and competences and the demands of the employment system in terms of available jobs and qualification requirements has been a major area of concern for several decades. Graduate surveys tended to address these issues in two ways: by comparing fields of study, competences, etc. and economic sectors, occupational areas and job tasks, and by asking the graduates to rate the extent to which their job matches their education.

Surveys of graduates dramatically differ in the way they address the latter. As was shown in an analysis of respective surveys undertaken in Europe in the 1980s (Teichler, 1988b), the share of inappropriate employment could vary in different studies between three and some 40 per cent, depending on the questions that were formulated rather than on actual differences in the links between education and employment.

Available literature suggests that questions regarding the utilization of competences must address, first, *both the horizontal and the vertical dimensions* of the link between education and work. Graduates may be in high positions but hardly make use of their competences or be in a position considered as inappropriate with respect to the level of their credential, but make substantial use of the competences acquired in the course of their studies. Second, studies produce *biased results if they only address possible under-utilization of knowledge, skills, and attitudes but not potential under-qualification*. Third, one must take into account *students' aspirations and expectations*. Fourth, *seemingly inappropriate positions are often chosen voluntarily*, for example in order not to be mobile, to live with a partner, etc. (Brennan and McGeever, 1988; Buttgereit and Teichler, 1992; Brennan et al., 1993; Kellermann et al., 1994; Wielers and Glebbeek, 1995).

Transition to Employment and First Career Stages

Transition to employment and early career could be viewed, as has already been pointed out, as a short "messy" process at the end of which a fairly optimal match between the competences of former students and their employment and work is reached. In contrast, many experts have claimed in recent years that the transition to employment and career start itself has a tremendous impact on the subsequent career.

Previous research has provided evidence that *recruitment processes and criteria varied substantially between European countries and other parts of the world* (see Roizen and Jepson, 1985; Teichler, Buttgereit and Holtkamp, 1984). In addition, higher education institutions differ substantially concerning support for students with respect to preparation and the actual job search. A comparative survey suggests that this is on the rise and that students as well as administrators favour a stronger involvement of higher education institutions in these activities (Raban, 1991). Furthermore, *the roles of public employment agencies and other intermediary bodies* in the transition from higher education to employment differ strikingly between various countries. Therefore, the aim of the CHEERS study was, first, to analyse the search strategies and institutional support, and, second, to establish whether this was crucial for initial employment and the subsequent career.

In the past, little attention was paid to the *characteristics and the impact of transitory employment, unemployment and other activities*. With the expansion of higher education and the rising unemployment problems in many countries, however, flexible employment increased, with more temporary and part-time jobs. This has had a great impact on the early career stages of graduates and has led to more interrupted and more "uncommon" career paths. The transition from education to work has become a process in which periods of unemployment could be followed by periods of employment and further studies. For some graduates, their first job is the beginning of a career that matches their educational background, and for others it is a step in the job search process (see Veum and Weiss, 1993; Klerman and Karoly, 1994).

Therefore, it was important to have a better understanding of whether an untraditional career start is common amongst graduates, and whether these problems are restricted to certain fields of study or constitute a more general pattern for all graduates. If the latter is true, this could be viewed as an indication that the labour market has gone through structural changes and that what we have called untraditional early career paths will in future be described as one of several "natural" career paths.

Second, the CHEERS study aimed to establish the links between the various activities immediately after graduation and the employment and work situation some four years after graduation. This shows whether the protracted transition period opens up opportunities for a trial and error search or whether employment shortly after graduation is already a valid indicator of a successful career.

Traditions as regards the timing of major graduate surveys in Europe differ substantially. Whilst annual British graduate surveys are undertaken some six months after graduation, French representative surveys on the insertion of graduates into the employment system are conducted 33 months after graduation (see Martinelli, 1994). Although the practice of the British survey needs to be reconsidered because it only provides information about the early employment of about half the graduates (see Mason, 1995), the varying practices reflect different lengths of the transition period which varies considerably according to country.

Career

A survey that addresses the links between higher education and the world of work provides a more complete picture if several years of occupational experiences are analysed. First, competences acquired during the course of studies do not only serve the career start, but are relevant for *several years of employment*. Second, the consequences of transitional experiences and initial career steps on later stages can be made visible if the survey also addresses the time at which careers tend to stabilize.

Traditionally, career has been associated with vertical mobility or several stages of promotion ("job ladders"). For a person with higher education a typical career has traditionally started with a professional job followed by a transition to an administrative or managerial job. For some fields of study, such as engineering, the switch from a technical to a managerial job tends to be the most direct if not the only path to higher earnings and status (Biddle and Roberts, 1994). However, the definition of a "successful" career seems to have changed over time. The trend to more horizontal labour organization has reduced the number of levels in the hierarchy (Esland, 1990). There is also an increasing tendency to build career paths that are professional and not administrative or managerial. A career for a person with higher education does not necessarily consist only of vertical job mobility, but can consist of several horizontal steps. Therefore, it is worth tracing different "career paths".

There is a vast range of literature on the topics of career and job mobility. Most analyses on career tend to focus on promotion or vertical mobility and factors that encourage or hinder promotion. As the labour market and career paths have become more complex, these studies need to be complemented. We need analyses of careers that take into account both vertical and horizontal job mobility, thus enabling us to trace different career typologies.

The Institute for Studies in Research and Higher Education (Oslo) therefore undertook a study eight years after graduation. The Centre for Research on Higher Education and Work (Kassel) surveyed graduates some ten years after graduation in the framework of a longitudinal study. Obviously, such time spans are necessary to measure the stability or change in early careers. Unfortunately, the CHEERS project had no funds to undertake graduate surveys at an advanced stage of career in all the participating countries. A survey with a cohort 7-10 years after graduation was conducted only in the Netherlands and Japan.

The Impact of the Diversity of Higher Education and Study Options

In most countries, higher education has become diversified in the last few decades in terms of its research functions and the nature of its study provision. Diversification is generally considered to be essential to meet the growing diversity of students' talents and aspirations, of the financial conditions of the higher education system and of graduates' employment prospects. However, the patterns of institutions and degree programmes, as well as the curricular thrusts, vary strikingly between the European and other economically advanced countries (see OECD, 1973; Teichler, 1988a; OECD, 1991; Gellert, 1993; Kivinen *et al.*, 1996).

In this framework, the survey may shed light on the issues *of whether varied formal elements of diversification* in the European countries *serve similar functions*, as far as preparation for employment and work are concerned, and whether they achieve their respective national goals. Is there, for example, a more visible link between study and work tasks for graduates of non-university higher education institutions with a strong vocational emphasis (e.g. graduates of German *Fachhochschulen* and Dutch *hogescholen*) than for those from lower-ranking universities in unitary higher education systems, i.e. Italy and recently the United Kingdom (see Brennan *et al.*, 1994). The comparative study, could therefore contribute to an assessment of the success of different models of differentiation.

Second, the survey addressed European diversity, as far *as links between fields of study and segments of the employment system* are concerned. Many generalizations about the growing employability of graduates enrolled in professional fields and substantial problems of graduates from academic fields turned out to be misleading in the past, if examined in detail. Employment and work for graduates from individual fields of study must be compared more precisely and be interpreted in terms of the size of the respective employment sectors, the modes of access and professional control, the labour market conditions, and the academic and professional thrusts of the curricula.

Third, the CHEERS study aimed to establish the extent to *which curricular approaches are relevant for subsequent employment and work*. In the past, many surveys neglected the fact that the curricular dimension had a substantial impact on the vertical components of higher education (type of institution, level of degree, reputation of the institution). It could be argued, though, that the role of vertical differences was overestimated because their role in comparison to horizontal diversity was not measured at all. The studies undertaken by De Weert (1993, 1994), however, suggest that a generalized concept of major curricular thrusts can be used across fields of study and can be assessed by various groups of actors in higher education.

Socio-biographical Background, Study and Employment

Educational policies in many countries aim to reduce inequalities in the educational and social opportunities of traditionally disadvantaged social groups. Also, the European Community has placed a strong emphasis on education to counteract social disparities. Available research does not provide consistent results as to which inequalities, as measured by equality of results, according to socio-economic background, gender, ethnicity and region, have been reduced over time (see Husén, 1987; Shavit and Blossfeld, 1993).

It is obvious, though, that inequalities have not completely vanished. Some experts point out that the growing emphasis on social skills and personality in graduate recruitment could reinforce social inequality. Others claim that we may overestimate the opportunities for previously disadvantaged groups by analysing only transition to employment and entry positions, since disadvantages become more salient in the course of professional careers.

The CHEERS study does not only provide *information about the extent to which inequalities are prevalent* in early career stages. It also aims to show the role they play in different stages of education and employment. This helps to establish the extent to which these inequalities are manifest at the time of access to higher education, at the time of transition to employment and a few years after graduation and to get a more realistic picture of the role of higher education in social selection.

Regional Differences in Higher Education and Employment

There are great regional differences in the relationship between higher education and employment in some European countries, as a study on Italy suggests (Moscati and Pugliese, 1995). In contrast, they tend to be viewed as almost negligible in others, e.g. in the Netherlands.

Regional disparities are relevant for graduate surveys in three respects. First, one must take into consideration the *regional function of higher education* (see Kellermann, 1982, 1994a). Do higher education institutions address explicitly the specific needs of their region, by, for example, analysing the culture, social environment, economic or natural resources of the region and by training graduates specifically to serve these regional needs? How is this regional function related to other functions of higher education in the country? Do certain institutions primarily serve the region, whereas others pursue a more universal, international or national thrust? Is there a regional emphasis in curricula and research, or are institutions only regional by virtue of recruitment catchments and location?

Second, *regional social and economic disparities* affect graduates' job opportunities. For example, unemployment ratios varied in Europe according to region between three and 35 percent in the late 1990s. Views differ as regards the extent to which higher education in disadvantaged regions helps to counteract regional disparities or, on the contrary, reinforce inequalities. The latter could occur by offering lower quality education and research or by providing the talented youth of the respective regions with the skills needed to leave the regions and find employment in richer regions instead of contributing to the social and economic improvement of the disadvantaged area (Eurostat, 1994; ISTAT, 1994).

Third, *equality of opportunity according to region* of origin is an important political goal: how do people who were living in relatively poor regions during the first few years of their life compare with those from other regions in terms of education and career? Parity of education and career is more likely to be achieved if education is similar in all regions and if mobility from the poorer to the richer region is made easy.

Therefore, the CHEERS survey addressed four regional issues: (a) employment and work of graduates according to the location of the higher education institution from which they graduated ; (b) employment and work of graduates according to region of destination; (c) pattern of regional mobility at different stages of the life course (birth, school, higher education institution, first employment, subsequent employment); (d) links between the specific thrusts of the higher education institutions and the employment of graduates who found employment in the region.

In analysing the relationship between higher education and employment/work in Europe, various definitions of regions had to be used. First, we referred to the Nomenclature of Territorial Units used in European statistics. Second, we addressed regional differences in terms of economic and social wealth in all countries analysed. Third, we analysed the differences between higher education and employment in the metropolitan area as against other areas. Finally, we took into account the wealth and vicinity of study provision in order to analyse the impact of regional dispersion of higher education on education and career opportunities.

Europeanization and Internationalization of Higher Education and Employment

The European Community promotes co-operation among European higher education institutions in order to increase student mobility and encourage curriculum development, both of which will eventually strengthen the European dimension in higher education. Developing such activities is considered essential because of the growing number of job roles which require European competences.

Up until the late 1990s, the number of graduates who found employment abroad was estimated at three per cent in the countries addressed in the CHEERS study. Also, available research shows that many employers are still reluctant to employ graduates from other countries (see List, 1996; Stein *et al.*, 1996); on the other hand, students opting for an international dimension in their studies are likely to be internationally mobile upon graduation. For example, a survey showed that 18 per cent of former ERASMUS students, i.e. students spending a study period abroad in another European country with the support of a supplementary fellowship provided by the European Commission, lived abroad some five years after their study period abroad, and, of these, about a half lived in the host country of their ERASMUS-supported study period (Maiworm and Teichler, 1996). An increase in European graduate mobility is predicted by many experts.

The debate on internationalization or Europeanization lacks precision. For example, definitions of the "European dimension" of employment and work tend to be vague. Moreover, the information base is weak. Most surveys of employers' expectations ask about expected competences in general rather than about expectations regarding the – still – minority of jobs for which international and European competences are crucial. Few surveys have been undertaken of graduates who were enrolled in programmes that emphasized European and international competences. A comparative survey on graduate employment could help to redress this.

The CHEERS study revealed the extent to which the most *obvious European and international dimensions* of employment and work *actually played a role*. It showed, first, the number of graduates
– employed in another country,
– who used foreign languages frequently on the job,
– who co-operated frequently with persons and institutions of other countries, and
– made use of knowledge of European and international institutions, regulations, international organizations, global markets, etc.

Second, the survey aimed to establish *the extent to which higher education contributed to respective competences*. For example, we compared employment and work of graduates of programmes that put strong emphasis on European and international dimensions or who had spent a study period abroad with those of other graduates. We also took into account learning and other experiences prior to enrolment.

1.3   The Contents of this Volume

As already pointed out in the Introduction, the analysis of the findings of the CHEERS project was divided into many steps and stages. This volume comprises the revised text of the final report submitted to the key sponsor of the project, the European Commission, at the time the financial support for this project came to an end. It aims to describe the major findings across all areas of graduate employment and work addressed in the study.

Subsequently, many analyses have been undertaken as regards specific issues, countries, fields of study, etc. Detailed analyses were published on graduate employment and work in Germany, Japan, Spain and the United Kingdom. All major thematic areas were analysed more thoroughly in the second volume. And several subsequent essays focus on the impact of various dimensions of higher education on graduate employment and work. In the meantime, the European Commission also decided to support a similar successor study, the REFLEX project, that analysed employment and work of graduates of the academic year 1999/2000 some five years later across a similar range of countries. Thus, the information base underlying this volume has already had an impact on improving the knowledge base on graduate employment and work so far – and even in the future.

2 METHODS USED

2.1 Overview

In the project, researchers from 12 countries cooperated in developing concepts, questionnaires and survey approaches that were suitable for an internationally comparative analysis and surveying representative samples of higher education institution graduates in their respective countries.

The representative samples were based on those who had graduated between autumn 1994 and summer 1995 in the 12 countries. Altogether, some 40,000 graduates participated. The questionnaire addressed their socio-biographical profile, their study experiences and (self-perceived) competences acquired their employment, work and careers since graduation and the links they perceived between education and work.

This representative questionnaire survey was supplemented by *interview surveys with graduates and employers*, thus allowing for a more comprehensive understanding of the relationships between education and work. Graduates' perceptions and interpretations of their competences, job roles and life goals should be analyzed in selected areas, notably those undergoing the most rapid and most challenging changes. Similarly, employers were asked to present their views on changing job requirements and the graduates' skills.

2.2 The Research Instrument

The objectives of the survey required the use of a *standardized mail questionnaire* as the core research instrument in order to include a high number of graduates in an efficient way and elicit comparable and representative information on graduate employment and work. The elaboration of the questionnaires was based partly on the approaches and experiences of previous surveys conducted in the European countries and partly on newly developed questions that aimed to overcome the pitfalls of prevailing terminologies and research approaches in individual countries.

The research teams in each country contributed to the conceptualisation of the study and the elaboration of the questionnaires and were responsible for the translation of the "master questionnaire" into their respective language. The major themes of the questionnaire survey were:
− socio-biographical and early education background,
− enrolment, as well as study conditions and provisions,
− the individual course of study and study behaviour,
− study achievements,
− job search and transition period,
− employment during the first three to four years after graduation,
− regional and international mobility,

- work content and use of qualifications,
- work motivation and job satisfaction,
- further professional education/training,
- career prospects.

A broad scope of questions was selected which resulted in a 16-page master questionnaire (English language) with about 80 questions and 600 variables.

2.3 The Target Group of the Study

The target group for the representative sample of graduates in each country was defined according to the following criteria:
- national citizens and foreigners graduating in that country;
- graduates from higher education institutions according to the national definition of the higher education system;
- graduates from the academic year 1994/95; persons graduating between autumn 1994 and summer 1995);
- only graduates who were awarded their first degrees in the academic year 1994/95 (graduates who were awarded a second degree at that time were only included if the first degree typically did not lead to employment);
- the national samples should take into account the distribution of the national population of graduates by field of study, gender, region and other relevant factors, if any.

Most graduates were surveyed in the first half of the year 1999, i.e. some four years after graduation.

Some four years after graduation the timing took into account the fact that professional training periods after graduation, as required or customary in some countries in some professional areas, could last up to two years. It also allowed us to analyse the transition to employment of those graduates who – after the award of a degree that was equivalent to a bachelor's – continued academic study towards an advanced degree. This timing enabled us to identify the first regular employment of graduates even after a protracted transition period. Last some early career stages of those had who transferred to employment shortly after graduation could be analysed.

The study initially comprised nine European countries: Austria, Finland, France, Germany, Italy, Norway, Spain, the Netherlands, and United Kingdom. The Czech Republic, Sweden and Japan conducted almost identical studies without EU funds.

A broad range of higher education institutions was addressed in order to ensure a representative distribution of graduates. Students were surveyed after having been awarded a first degree requiring between 3 and 6 years of study.

2.4 The Survey Process

The procedures for collecting the addresses of the graduates varied according to the local conditions. In some countries the addresses were available from a current central database, whilst in others only addresses at the time of graduation were available from the higher education institutions.

The survey process (collection and updating of addresses, mailing, checking of questionnaires, coding, documentation of the coding and data editing) was handled by the local research teams. Two reminders were sent in most countries. National and international classifications were used for the open questions regarding job title, economic sector, field of study and region.

2.5 Participation in the Graduate Survey

The individual countries defined the sample size according to anticipated return rates in order to ensure that some 3,000 responses would be available. Assuming, for example, that the average response rate was about 40 per cent, it was considered necessary to mail the questionnaire to almost 7,500 graduates.

During the period from October 1998 to September 1999, altogether 117,000 graduates were sent questionnaires. In Italy, the survey was personally administered. In almost all other countries, two reminders followed the initial mailing. In Spain and Japan, only one reminder was sent.

The large sample size was chosen because low return rates were anticipated in some countries. Moreover, the researchers in some countries aimed to extend the major study. For example, specific groups were included which did not correspond to the general definition of the target group (e.g. graduates from 2-year programmes), or large numbers of graduates from individual higher education institutions were included.

Altogether, more than 40,000 responded. On average, the return rate was 39 per cent. It varied from 50 per cent in Norway to slightly over 30 per cent in a few countries and 15 per cent in Spain (see Figure 2.1).

Figure 2.1: Return Rates of Questionnaires, by Country (per cent)

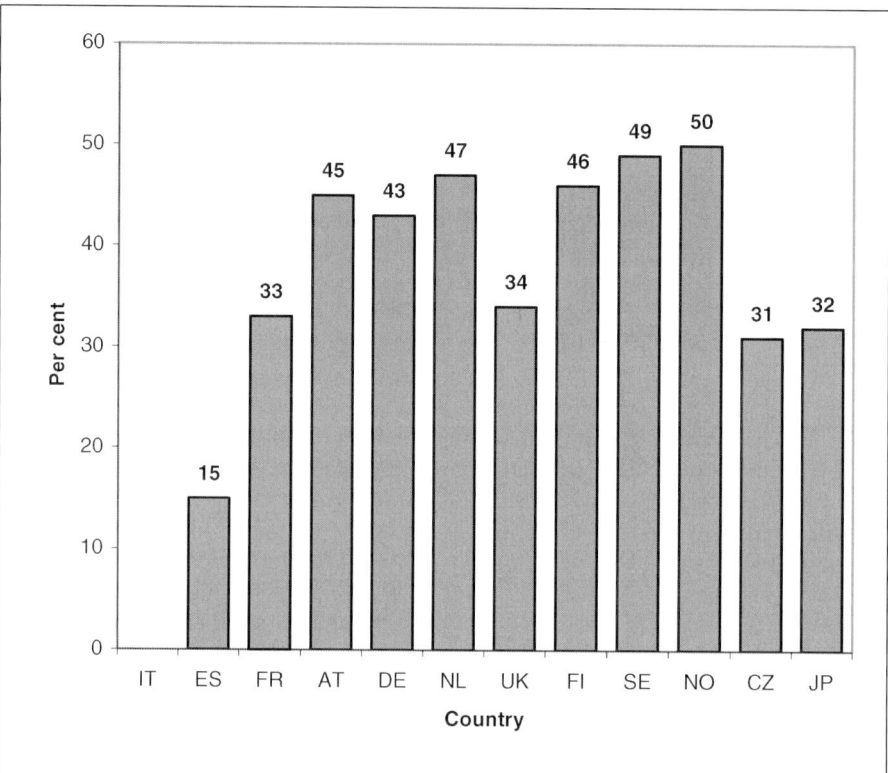

* In Italy, the questionnaires were administered personally.
Source: CHEERS survey data.

The profile of the respondents was compared with that of all 1994/95 graduates according to national statistics in the 12 countries. Accordingly, a final weighing was undertaken so that the respondents in the final database were represented according to type of institution and degree, field of study and gender. 36,694 graduates from the 12 countries were included in the representative "final database" (see Figure 2.2) on which the subsequent analysis is based.

According to the national reports of the field phase, the quality of the returned questionnaires seems to be high. Most students accepted the standardized structure of the questionnaire and responded to almost all the questions that were applicable.

Figure 2.2: Absolute Numbers of Graduates Included in the International Database, by Country

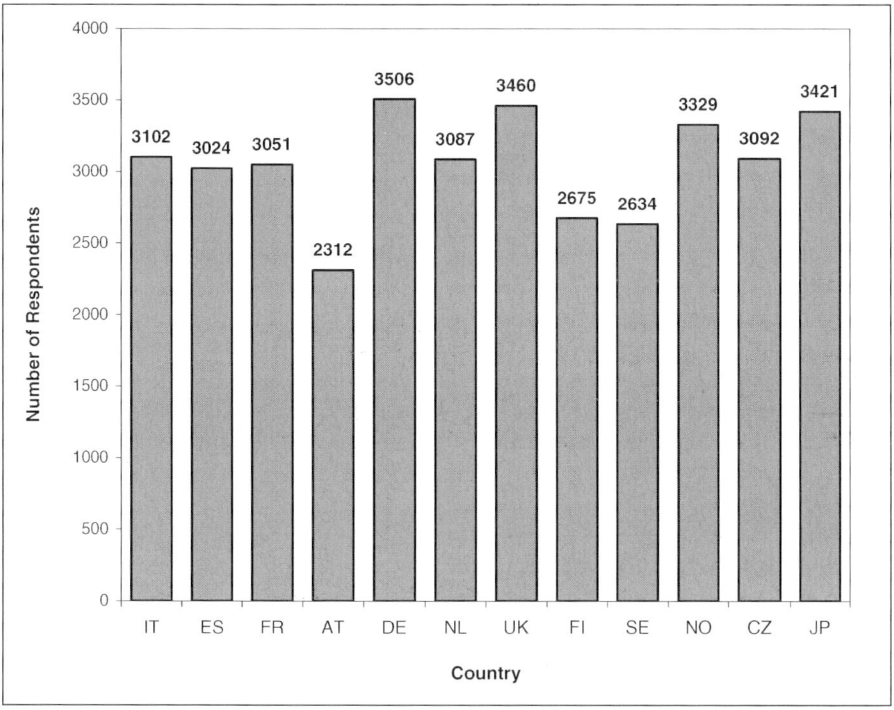

Country	Number of Respondents
IT	3102
ES	3024
FR	3051
AT	2312
DE	3506
NL	3087
UK	3460
FI	2675
SE	2634
NO	3329
CZ	3092
JP	3421

Source: CHEERS survey data.

2.6 The Standard Questionnaire and National Variations

The project aimed to develop a joint questionnaire for all countries insofar as an agreement could be reached. It was obvious, however, that
- national categories had to be used in some cases for types of schooling, higher education institutions, occupations etc.,
- different concepts of education and work prevailed in countries which could not be met by simple translation,
- the researchers participating in the project might prefer different concepts and thus would not be able to agree on a common questionnaire,
- views varied on the length of the questionnaire accepted by graduates.

These problems notwithstanding, the participating research teams largely agreed on a 16 page-questionnaire with about 80 questions and 600 variables. In the 9 countries supported by the EU, about 95 per cent of the questionnaires were identical except for national categories. The questionnaires of the other three additional countries matched the master questionnaire to about 80 per cent. Notably, they were somewhat shorter.

2.7 Data Analysis

The data analysis was to a great extent undertaken centrally at the institutional base of the project coordinator who also developed the international data file (SPSS system file). However, all partners were provided with complete data sets, thus being in a position to pursue more detailed studies regarding their respective areas of specialisation and their country in a comparative perspective. Special emphasis was placed on procedures of multivariate analysis.

2.8 The Interview Studies

The graduate survey was supplemented by in-depth case-studies through interviews with graduates and employers. First, these interviews enabled the research team to investigate rationales and motives more efficiently because people could describe their views in more complex oral statements. Second, the open structure of interviews was chosen because it was more suitable for addressing certain issues which were not well-known. The overall picture of the relationships between higher education and employment/work was enriched with information from employers.

2.9 Overall Project Coordination and Cooperation

The *coordination* rested with the Centre for Research on Higher Education and Work of the University of Kassel (Wissenschaftliches Zentrum für Berufs- und Hochschulforschung der Universität Kassel). Professor Ulrich Teichler and Harald Schomburg were the coordinators of the project both in terms of its administration and the research process, notably the graduate survey.

As regards the *additional studies*, they were coordinated by Dr. Egbert de Weert (CHEPS, University of Twente) who was responsible for the employer interviews and Professor Paul Kellermann (University of Klagenfurt) who was responsible for the graduate interviews. The interviews were conducted in each country by the respective members of the research teams.

The researchers of the participating 12 countries (see Table 2.1) were in charge of analysing the theories and methods employed for certain thematic areas, for example the impact of diversification, regional differences in higher education, or changing relationships between higher education and employment/work in the wake of Europeanization. The details of the research design and the survey instruments (questionnaires and interview guidelines) were based on close cooperation and joint agreement.

Four workshops were organised in order to provide the opportunity for face-to-face communication in the most crucial stages of the project.

Table 2.1: Countries Involved in the Project, Participating Institutions and Project Directors

Austria	Prof. Paul Kellermann	Institut für Soziologie, Universität Klagenfurt
Finland	Prof. Osmo Kivinen	Research Unit for the Sociology of Education (RUSE), University of Turku
France	Prof. Jean-Jacques Paul	Institut de Recherche sur l'Economie de l'Education (IREDU), Université de Bourgogne
Germany	Prof. Ulrich Teichler and Harald Schomburg (Co-ordinators)	Wissenschaftliches Zentrum für Berufs- und Hochschulforschung, Universität Kassel
Italy	Prof. Roberto Moscati	IARD Istituto di Ricerca, Milano
Norway	Dr. Per Olaf Aamodt	Norwegian Institute for Studies in Research and Higher Education (NIFU), Oslo
The Netherlands	Dr. Egbert de Weert	Centre for Higher Education Policy Studies (CHEPS), University of Twente
	Dr. Rolf van der Velden	Research Centre for Education and the Labour Market (ROA), Limburg Institute for Business and Economic Research, Maastricht
Spain	Prof. José-Ginés Mora Ruiz	Instituto Valenciano de Investigaciones Economicas (IVIE), Valencia, and Universidad de Valencia
United Kingdom	Prof. John Brennan	Quality Support Centre, The Open University (OU), London
Japan*	Prof. Keiichi Yoshimoto	Faculty of Education, Kyushu University, and Japan Institute of Labour
Czech Republic*	Dr. Pavel Kuchar	Institute of Sociological Studies, Charles University, Prag
Sweden*	Dr. Gunilla Bornmalm-Jardeloew	Dept. of Economics, Göteborg University

* Not funded by the European Union.

Most of the researchers who were involved in this research project have already cooperated for several years in the framework of the Consortium of Higher Education Researchers (CHER), i.e. the Europe-based association of researchers in the area of higher education who are interested in comparative research. Regular cooperation in conferences, training seminars and joint publications has led to a common basis of knowledge in this area as well as to mutual trust in creative cooperation.

2.10 Survey Eight Years After Graduation

In the Netherlands and Japan, a representative study was also undertaken on graduates from higher education institutions 8 years after graduation. Although a cross-sectional design was chosen, i.e. simultaneous surveying of a previous cohort, this study provides an overview of the change in the relationships between higher education and graduate employment during the 1990s in two countries. The results of this survey are published separately.

3 THE EDUCATIONAL PATHS AND ATTAINMENTS

3.1   Introduction

The educational paths and attainments of the graduates, including their parental background, are not the key focus of this study. But this information is relevant for a better understanding of their subsequent course of study and career. It also provides helpful insights into the differences between the education systems of the 12 countries regarding such factors as the age at the time of obtaining the entry qualification to higher education, the number of years of schooling, and the students' experiences before enrolment in higher education.

3.2   Gender

About half the graduates who were surveyed were women (see Figure 3.1). Their share is below 50 per cent in three of the 11 European countries (Germany 41%, Austria 45% and Czech Republic 44%). In Japan, only 32 per cent of the graduates were women.

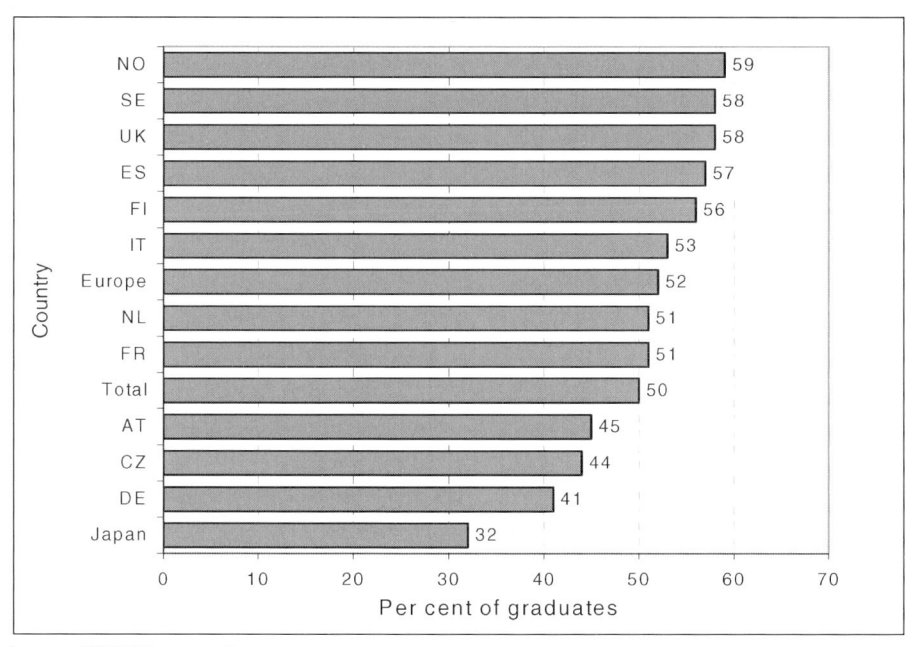

Figure 3.1: Female Graduates, by Country (per cent)

Country	Per cent of graduates
NO	59
SE	58
UK	58
ES	57
FI	56
IT	53
Europe	52
NL	51
FR	51
Total	50
AT	45
CZ	44
DE	41
Japan	32

Source: CHEERS survey data.

Women succeeded more frequently than men in secondary education. They also started studying more frequently without any major activity outside the regular education track. But the average age of men and women was almost identical at the time of graduation.

3.3 Educational Attainment of the Parents

Parents of the majority of graduates surveyed had not graduated from higher education. According to the information provided by the graduates, only 45 per cent of their fathers completed compulsory school or less. The differences between the European countries are substantial: compulsory school or less as father's highest level of education was reported by 64 per cent of the graduates in Spain, but only by 30 per cent of the graduates in the Netherlands.

Table 3.1: Parents' Highest Level of Education, by Country (per cent)

	Country													Total
	IT	ES	FR	AT	DE	NL	UK	SE	FI	NO	CZ	EUR	JP	
Father														
Compulsory education or less	36	64	51	52	43	30	46	52	m	34	m	45	m	45
Completed (upper) secondary education	37	16	16	23	23	32	20	24	m	22	m	24	m	24
Higher education diploma/degree	27	20	33	25	35	38	34	24	m	44	m	32	m	32
Total	100	100	100	100	100	100	100	100	m	100	m	100	m	100
Count	3030	2919	2967	2235	3425	2920	3283	2627	m	3192	m	26599	m	26599
Mother														
Compulsory education or less	46	78	54	67	49	45	48	54	m	39	m	53	m	53
Completed (upper) secondary education	38	11	21	26	37	37	28	29	m	29	m	29	m	29
Higher education diploma/degree	16	11	25	7	14	18	24	16	m	32	m	19	m	19
Total	100	100	100	100	100	100	100	100	m	100	m	100	m	100
Count	3041	2928	2987	2226	3433	2872	3318	2644	m	3202	m	26652	m	26652

Question I5: Parent's and partners highest level of education.
m = missing (the question was not asked in Sweden, Czech Republic and Japan).
Source: CHEERS survey data.

35 per cent of the graduates who were surveyed reported that at least one of their parents graduated from higher education. This was true for almost one third of the fathers and about one fifth of the mothers. This was about twice as high as the proportion of higher education trained persons in the typical age group of their parents (see Table 3.1). The data confirm the conventional wisdom that – despite efforts to

increase equality of opportunity – the children of higher education trained parents continue to be more likely to be enrolled and to graduate than those of other parents.

The proportion of parents who had not been educated beyond compulsory schooling is strikingly high in Spain. This can be explained by the fact that the major expansion of education occurred in only in the 1980s and 1990s, i.e. substantially later than in almost all other countries of this study.

3.4 Foreigners

About two per cent of the graduates in the countries surveyed were foreigners. A further two per cent had a different nationality at the date of birth; most of the latter moved to the country where they graduated at an early age and obtained their secondary education qualifications in the country where they were citizens at the time of graduation.

3.5 Years of Schooling

Almost half the graduates surveyed had attended 12 or 13 years of schooling prior to enrolment in higher education (see Table 3.2). In some countries, 12 or 13 years is the common pattern for all types of programmes that give access to higher education, in some countries the required duration varies according to the type of higher education.

Table 3.2: Years of Schooling to Acquire Entry Qualification, by Country (median)

	Country												Total
	IT	ES	FR	AT	DE	NL	UK	FI	SE	NO	CZ	EUR	JP
Years (median)	13	12	12	12	13	13	13	12	12	12	12	12	12

Question A4: How many years of (primary plus secondary) schooling did you spend altogether before acquiring the entry qualification to higher education (include years of repeating classes)?
Source: CHEERS survey data.

3.6 Kind of Secondary Education

Over three quarters of the respondents had successfully completed academic secondary education. This was true for more than 90 per cent of respondents from Finland, France and Spain, as well as Japan. In contrast, almost half the Dutch graduates had followed other paths in order to qualify for entry to non-university higher education (see Table 3.3).

Table 3.3: Type of Entry Qualification at Time of First Enrolment, by Country (per cent)

	Country												Total
	IT	ES	FR	AT	DE	NL	UK	FI	SE	NO	CZ	EUR	JP
Academic secondary education	69	92	91	70	78	51	81	97	75	74	65	76	95	78
Other secondary education (e.g. vocational)	31	5	8	26	20	47	10	2	5	6	32	17	3	16
Exceptional (2nd chance etc.)	0	0	2	1	2	0	7	0	9	10	3	3	0	3
No qualification	0	2	0	0	0	0	2	0	6	0	1	1	0	1
Other	0	1	0	3	1	2	0	0	5	11	0	2	2	2
Total*	100	100	100	100	100	100	100	100	100	100	100	100	100	100

Question A1: What were your entry qualifications when you entered higher education (full or part-time) for the first time?
* Count by Country: IT (3091); ES (3009); FR (3032); AT (2305); DE (3500); NL (3069); UK (3322); FI (2654); SE (2623); NO (3312); CZ (3092); EUR (33011); JP (3400); Total (36411).
Source: CHEERS survey data.

3.7 Activities Before First Enrolment

An immediate transition from secondary to higher education is not common across all countries surveyed. As Table 3.4 shows, only a clear majority of Japanese respondents and about half the respondents in the Netherlands and the United Kingdom began to study shortly after secondary education. About half of all the persons surveyed reported a time gap of at least 10 months. In the Nordic countries and Germany, over one third enrolled more than two years after secondary education.

Table 3.4: Time Gap Between Acquisition of Entry Qualifications and Entry in Higher Education, by Country (per cent)

	Country												Total
	IT	ES	FR	AT	DE	NL	UK	FI	SE	NO	CZ	EUR	JP
0-3 months	33	40	42	15	15	54	47	6	29	34	0	28	70	32
4-9 months	42	37	20	45	22	8	12	22	6	2	0	19	0	17
10-24 months	13	8	6	24	27	12	16	27	18	20	69	23	21	22
25-48 months	6	7	24	8	22	9	10	26	29	24	16	17	8	16
49 months or more	6	8	9	8	14	18	16	20	18	21	15	14	2	13
Total	100	100	100	100	100	100	100	100	100	100	100	100	100	100
Count	2918	2560	2730	2139	3426	2418	2518	2461	2339	3105	3089	29703	3269	32972

Question A5: How many months did you spend on the following activities between obtaining the entry qualification and your first enrolment in higher education?
Source: CHEERS survey data.

The most frequent interim activities mentioned were (see Table 3.5)
– employment,
– education or training not required for entry to higher education, and
– military or similar services.

Table 3.5: Kind of Other Education/Training/Apprenticeship Before First Enrolment, by Country (per cent; multiple responses)

	IT	ES	FR	AT	DE	NL	UK	FI	SE	NO	CZ	EUR	JP	Total
Employment/self-employment	15	6	13	36	39	38	16	77	m	57	m	32	23	31
Education/training/apprenticeship	5	5	4	5	22	11	9	19	m	25	m	12	33	14
Military or civilian service	3	1	1	21	38	3	0	24	m	17	m	12	0	11
Child rearing, family care	2	1	2	2	2	1	2	5	m	9	m	3	0	3
Not employed, seeking employment	4	0	1	19	15	2	3	11	m	5	m	6	0	6
Other	10	3	2	27	24	21	6	18	m	12	m	13	1	12
No answer	68	86	81	19	7	38	77	11	m	17	m	46	50	46
Total	106	103	104	128	147	115	113	165	m	142	m	124	107	122
Count	3102	3024	3051	2312	3506	3087	3460	2675	m	3329	m	27547	3421	30967

m = missing (the question was not asked in Sweden and the Czech Republic).
Source: CHEERS survey data.

3.8 Age at the Time of Enrolment in Higher Education

The entry age to education, the years of schooling and the time gap between the end of secondary education and entry in higher education are the major factors in explaining the age differences at the time of enrolment in higher education.

Of all respondents,
- 49 per cent enrolled in higher education when they were under 20,
- 42 per cent at the age of 20-25, and
- 9 per cent were over 25.

The proportion of very young students entering higher education was 70 per cent or more in Italy and Spain as well as in the Czech Republic and Japan. In contrast, it was only a quarter or less in Finland, Germany, Sweden and Norway (see Table 3.6).

In the United Kingdom, many students enroll very early; on the other hand, we also note the highest proportion of students taking up study when they are over 30. It should be noted that many of the latter were enrolled at the Open University.

The proportion of women entering higher education at a very young age is slightly higher than that of men. On the other hand, slightly more women than men begin to study when they are over 30.

Table 3.6: Respondents' Age at Entry to Higher Education, by Country and Gender (per cent)

							Country							Total
	IT	ES	FR	AT	DE	NL	UK	FI	SE	NO	CZ	EUR	JP	
Male														
19 or under	68	73	53	52	7	45	51	25	13	24	77	44	64	47
20-25	28	23	43	42	83	48	28	65	73	62	18	47	35	46
26-30	2	3	2	3	8	3	6	4	7	9	1	5	0	4
31 and more	2	2	2	2	2	4	14	6	6	6	4	4	0	4
Female														
19 or under	75	76	62	64	27	55	57	24	17	16	80	49	83	51
20-25	23	20	34	29	64	37	22	59	63	58	16	39	16	38
26-30	1	2	1	3	6	3	5	5	8	10	2	4	0	4
31 and more	1	2	3	4	3	5	16	11	12	16	2	7	0	7
Total														
19 or under	71	74	58	58	15	50	54	25	15	19	78	47	70	49
20-25	26	21	38	36	75	42	25	62	68	60	17	43	29	42
26-30	2	3	2	3	7	3	6	5	8	9	2	4	0	4
31 and more	1	2	2	3	2	5	15	9	9	12	3	6	0	5
Total	100	100	100	100	100	100	100	100	100	100	100	100	100	100
Count	2965	2614	2950	2241	3476	2954	3233	2608	2560	3182	3090	31873	3361	35234

Question B1: Please, provide information about all higher education courses you have followed (including part-time, post-graduate, and courses not completed)
Note: The age at entry was calculated by subtracting the graduate's year of birth from the entry year to higher education.
Source: CHEERS survey data.

4   COURSE OF STUDY

The study addressed students graduating from three- to six-year higher education programmes in 1994/95. It did not include two-year programmes at higher education institutions, tertiary education programmes that were not considered to be part of "higher education" in the respective countries and graduates of advanced programmes requiring more than 6 years of study (e.g. the Finnish Licentiate) and those awarded a Ph.D. However, the study might also include persons awarded those advanced and doctoral degrees during the first four years after graduation which formed the basis of the survey.

This chapter provides information on the course of study of the graduates in the different countries: the type of degree, the field of study, the duration of studies and the time spent on study related activities and work experience. Besides this objective information, the graduates were also asked to describe and to evaluate the conditions and provisions of study.

4.1   Type of Degree

The type of degree awarded was largely an outcome of the sampling strategy which aimed to describe the characteristics of the respective countries (see Table 4.1):
– Only university graduates of long (master-equivalent) programmes were surveyed in Austria and Finland (the newly established Austrian *Fachhochschulen* and Finnish *Ammattikorkeakoulu (AMK)* did not yet have any graduates in 1994/95) and Italy.
– Only university graduates were surveyed in Sweden, where study in some fields is short (bachelor-equivalent) and in most fields long (master-equivalent).
– Only university graduates of mostly four-year programmes were surveyed in Japan, where the degree is considered equivalent to a Bachelor.
– More than 90 per cent of the British graduates who were included were awarded a bachelor degree and only a small minority a master degree.
– In contrast, over 90 per cent of Czech respondents were graduates of long university programmes and only a minority were graduates of bachelor-equivalent programmes.
– Around sixty per cent of the graduates included in the study were awarded a long university degree in France, Germany and Spain, whilst graduates with a licence, a *Fachhochschul*-degree or a short university degree represented about 40 per cent.
– Finally, the number of university graduates was the lowest in the Netherlands and in Norway.

Table 4.1: Type of Degree Obtained 1994/95, by Country (per cent)

Country	Degree	Per cent	Country	Degree	Per cent
IT	Laurea	100	NL	HBO	58
				Post-HBO	2
ES	Short cycle	30		Doctoraal	22
	Long cycle	53		Meester	5
	Doctorate	11		Ingenieur	8
	Others	5		Basisarts	1
				Other	1
FR	Licence	42			
	Maîtrise	27			
	DEA	8	UK	BA/BSc/BEd etc (Hons)	76
	DESS	8		BA/BSc/BEd etc	9
	Engineering school	8		Postgraduate certificate/diploma	3
	Business school dipl	6		Taught master's	2
				Other	3
AT	Mag. (Dipl)	59		No answer	5
	Mag. (LA)	9			
	Dipl.Ing.	20	FI	Master degree	100
	Dipl.Tierarzt	2			
	Dr	10	SE	Bachelor degree	52
				Master degree	47
DE	Uni-Diplom	33			
	FH-Diplom	37	NO	Higher level degree (5Y)	35
	Uni-Magister	5		Lower level degree (3Y)	65
	Uni-Teacher examination	12			
	Uni-other state examinations	11	CZ	Bachelor degree	9
	Uni-Doctorate	1		Magister degree	91
	Other	1			
			JP	Bachelor	99
				Master	1

Question B1: Please, provide information about all higher education courses you have followed (including part-time, post-graduate, and courses not completed).
Source: CHEERS survey data.

4.2 Field of Study

Fields of study varied substantially between the countries included in the survey (see Table 4.2):

- Education came very high in the Czech Republic (19%) and Sweden (18%), whereas it was not included in France because teacher training takes place after a degree;
- Humanities comprised by far the highest number in the United Kingdom (26%) with only 6 per cent in Norway as the other extreme;
- Social sciences were most frequently chosen in France, the Netherlands and Japan (35% or more);
- Legal studies had a relatively high number of graduates in Italy (15%);

Table 4.2: Field of Study, by Country (per cent)

	IT	ES	FR	AT	DE	NL	UK	FI	SE	NO	CZ	EUR	JP	Total
Education	2	10	0	13	6	15	6	14	18	14	19	10	6	10
Humanities	17	10	19	8	11	9	26	17	8	6	7	13	18	13
Social sciences	27	33	36	26	30	35	26	26	32	17	28	29	36	29
Law	15	11	12	12	7	5	4	4	4	5	5	8	10	8
Natural sciences	8	3	17	4	8	2	10	7	3	5	6	7	4	7
Mathematics, computing.	3	5	9	6	5	4	6	4	3	3	0	4	1	4
Engineering	17	18	8	17	25	21	12	21	20	25	29	20	21	20
Medical science, health	11	10	0	13	7	9	8	7	10	26	6	10	4	10
Total*	100	100	100	100	100	100	100	100	100	100	100	100	100	100

Question B1: Please, provide information about all higher education courses you have followed (including part-time, post graduate, and courses not completed).
* Count by Country: IT (3102); ES (2993); FR (3022); AT (2270); DE (3489); NL (3053); UK (3003); FI (2674); SE (2627); NO (3329); CZ (3070); EUR (32633); JP (3421); Total (36054).
Source: CHEERS survey data.

- Natural sciences had the largest share by far in France with 17 per cent, compared to only 2 per cent in the Netherlands, 3 per cent in Spain and Sweden and 4 per cent in Japan;
- Mathematics/computing were chosen most frequently in France (9%);
- Engineering fields comprised the highest proportion in Finland (29%), Germany and the Czech Republic (25% respectively).
- Medical studies (including nursing) were very prominent in Norway (26%), because more para-medical professions were included than in other countries.

Figure 4.1: Female Graduates' Field of Study (per cent)

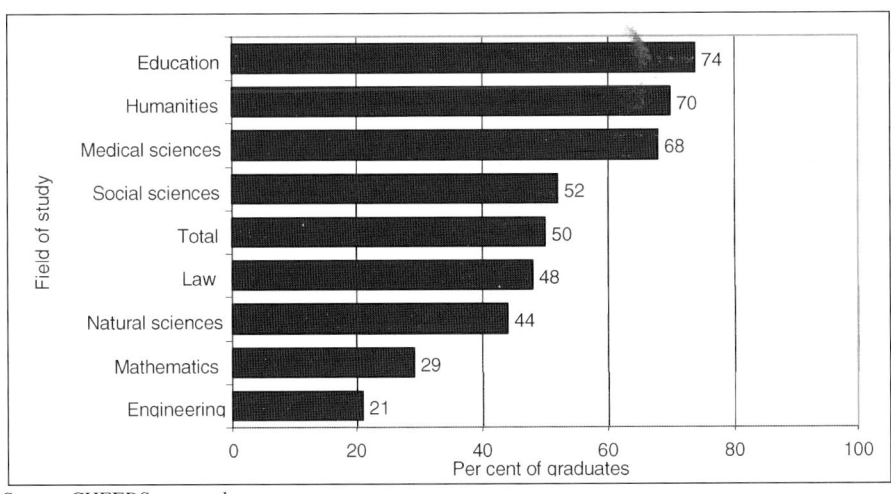

Field of study	Per cent of graduates
Education	74
Humanities	70
Medical sciences	68
Social sciences	52
Total	50
Law	48
Natural sciences	44
Mathematics	29
Engineering	21

Source: CHEERS survey data.

As one might expect, women were more strongly represented in humanities, social sciences and health fields. On the other hand, they were underrepresented in engineering and natural sciences (see Figure 4.1).

The patterns vary, however, according to country, as can be seen in Table 5.3. The proportion of women in mathematics/computing in Italy is remarkably high (46%) compared to only 13 per cent in Japan, and 15 per cent in Norway. In engineering, we find a very large proportion of women in the United Kingdom (52%), whilst in Austria, Germany and Japan they only represent 14 per cent (see Table 4.3).

Table 4.3: Proportion of Female Graduates, by Field of Study and Country (per cent)

	Country												Total	
	IT	ES	FR	AT	DE	NL	UK	FI	SE	NO	CZ	EUR	JP	
Education	80	73	65	69	76	70	60	78	79	85	67	74	65	73
Humanities	82	70	67	71	66	66	64	73	74	55	58	69	69	69
Social sciences	50	62	58	48	48	55	60	61	59	62	48	55	22	52
Law	56	59	58	41	45	56	56	49	53	50	42	52	21	49
Natural sciences	57	58	41	39	34	41	57	57	71	43	33	47	24	46
Mathematics, computing	46	33	23	16	33	14	52	36	42	15	0	31	13	31
Engineering	25	29	24	14	14	19	52	23	25	25	21	24	14	23
Medical science, health	52	69	72	58	47	75	56	66	69	84	59	67	48	66
Total	53	57	51	45	41	51	58	56	58	59	44	52	32	50

Question B1: Please, provide information about all higher education courses you have followed (including part-time, post-graduate, and courses not completed).
Source: CHEERS survey data.

4.3 Duration of Study

The study period required in the programmes the respondents graduated from was less than four years on average in the United Kingdom and France, but four years or more in all other countries.

The actual period of study was almost one year longer on average than the period required:

- Prolongation of about two years on average could be observed in Austria and Italy,
- some prolongation (between half a year and one and a half years) on average in Finland, France, Germany, the Netherlands, and Spain, as well as the Czech Republic,
- hardly any prolongation could be found in Norway, the United Kingdom and Japan (see Table 4.4).

Table 4.4: *Required and Actual Period of Study, by Country (means; years)*

	Country												Total
	IT	ES	FR	AT	DE	NL	UK	FI	SE	NO	CZ	EUR	JP
Actual study period													
Arithmetic mean	7.2	5.0	5.0	7.0	5.2	4.6	3.4	5.1	4.7	4.2	5.5	5.1	4.1	5.0
Median	6.7	5.0	5.0	6.5	5.0	4.3	3.0	5.0	4.4	3.0	5.0	5.0	4.0	5.0
Required study period													
Arithmetic mean	4.4	4.2	3.8	4.6	4.2	4.0	3.5	4.5	m	4.0	m	4.1	4.0	4.1
Median	4.0	5.0	4.0	4.5	4.0	4.0	3.0	4.0	m	3.0	m	4.0	4.0	4.0

Question B5: How long did you study to obtain the degree you were awarded in 1994 or 1995 and what period is required normally/by law (including lower level diplomas and degrees in higher education and including mandatory periods of work placements/internships; excluding other studies, periods of other activities, etc.? m = data missing

Source: CHEERS survey data.

4.4 Age at the Time of Graduation

At the time of graduation, the average age of the graduates who were surveyed was about 26 years (see Figure 4.2). It shows a very large spectrum: on average the Finnish graduates were 29 years old, i.e. almost six years older than the other extreme, i.e. Japanese graduates with an average age of 23.4 years, and graduates from France (23.9 years), the Czech Republic (24.4 years) and Spain (24.5 years).

Figure 4.2: *Age at the Time of Graduation 1994/1995, by Country (arithmetic means; years)*

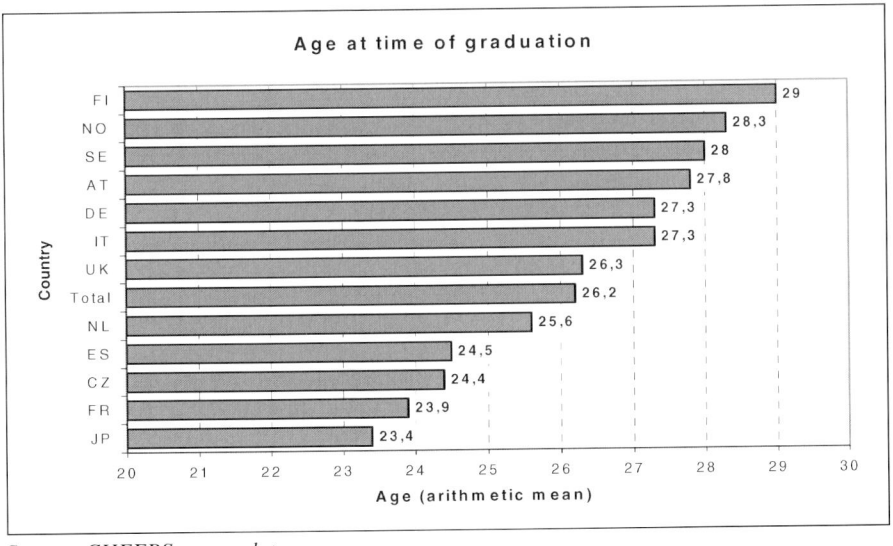

Country	Age (arithmetic mean)
FI	29
NO	28,3
SE	28
AT	27,8
DE	27,3
IT	27,3
UK	26,3
Total	26,2
NL	25,6
ES	24,5
CZ	24,4
FR	23,9
JP	23,4

Source: CHEERS survey data.

4.5 Graduation Quota

It should be noted that higher education graduates in the countries surveyed comprised quite different proportions of the respective age groups in these countries. Available data from OECD and national statistics suggest that those who had obtained a higher education degree that was at least equivalent to a bachelor comprised
- about one quarter of the respective age group in Norway, Spain, the United Kingdom, and Japan,
- between about 15 and over 20 per cent in Finland, France, Germany, the Netherlands, and Sweden,
- less than 15 per cent in Austria, Italy, and the Czech Republic.

Thus, they form quite different potential shares of the overall labour market.

4.6 Study Conditions and Provision

Graduates differ, as far as employment opportunities are concerned, not only with respect to their socio-biographical background and the formal elements of their course of study, i.e. field of study, duration, type of degree etc., but also according to the conditions and provisions of study and their ways of making use of the study period. The questionnaire, therefore, laid strong emphasis on the conditions and provisions of study as well as on the options chosen by students regarding life and study while enrolled in higher education.

For example, the prevailing modes of teaching and learning, as perceived by the graduates, differed substantially by country (see Table 4.5):
- According to their former students, Italian higher education institutions laid a relatively strong emphasis on independent learning. Little is done for problem-based learning and direct acquisition of work experience.
- Spanish higher education institutions conceived the teacher as the main source of information and put emphasis on theory. Like Italian institutions, problem-based learning and practical experience did not play a major role.
- French graduates noted an above-average emphasis on out-of-class communication between teachers and students and little regard for regular class attendance.
- Austrian and German higher education institutions were similar in the eyes of their graduates in underscoring factual knowledge and showing little regard for attitudes and socio-communicative skills.
- Dutch graduates pointed out that their institutions were interested in fostering attitudes and socio-communicative skills and in the direct acquisition of work experience.
- British higher education institutions were seen as fostering socio-communicative skills, providing opportunities for out-of-class communication with staff and emphasising regular class attendance.
- Finnish higher education institutions seemed to lay great emphasis on theory and less emphasis on out-of-class communication between teachers and students.
- Swedish institutions seemed to highly regard the value of facts and instrumental knowledge.

- Norwegian graduates underscored their higher education institutions' emphasis on theory as well as on socio-communicative skills and problem-based learning and practical experience. They had few opportunities to choose their courses.
- Czech graduates believed that their higher education institutions underscored theory, but were not very concerned with problem-based learning or practical work experience.
- Japanese graduates often believed that their higher education institutions laid strong emphasis on regular class attendance, but did not encourage independent learning.

Table 4.5: Emphasis on Modes of Teaching and Learning, by Country
(per cent of all graduates responding 'to a very high' or 'high extent'*)

	Country**												Total
	IT	ES	FR	AT	DE	NL	UK	FI	SE	NO	CZ	EUR	JP
Theories, concepts or paradigms	71	85	67	75	67	64	72	88	76	84	89	76	71	76
Writing a thesis	100	15	59	44	52	72	76	64	56	46	39	57	66	58
Independent learning	66	29	55	58	60	67	68	67	63	68	49	59	33	57
Facts and instrumental knowledge	20	18	46	79	72	55	68	45	74	60	19	50	50	50
Regular class attendance	52	52	28	32	41	48	63	30	36	40	35	42	61	44
Freedom to choose courses and areas of specialisation	42	35	42	45	40	37	53	53	30	28	35	40	58	41
Teacher as the main source of information and understanding	38	49	30	35	29	35	32	39	27	35	34	35	22	34
Project and problem-based learning	15	20	31	19	21	27	53	25	33	45	6	27	36	28
Attitudes and socio-communicative skills	21	14	25	15	15	49	40	24	29	45	22	28	23	27
Detailed regular assessment of academic progress	10	14	19	7	25	21	49	14	80	17	25	26	33	26
Direct acquisition of work experience	9	9	15	8	14	38	23	18	25	34	8	19	8	18
Out-of-class communication between students and staff	12	16	30	8	13	16	27	8	15	16	10	16	17	16

Question B8: If you look back to the course of study you graduated from in 1994 or 1995: to what extent were the following modes of teaching and learning emphasised by your higher education institution and its teachers?
* 1 and 2 on a scale of responses from 1 = 'To a very high extent' to 5 = 'Not at all'.
** Count by Country: IT (3102); ES (3009); FR (3017); AT (2291); DE (3497); NL (3047); UK (3418); FI (2657); SE (2621); NO (3311); CZ (3090); EUR (33059); JP (3407); Total (36466).
Source: CHEERS survey data.

A factor analysis suggests that the graduates note four major areas of modes of teaching and learning:
- practical learning,

- free choice,
- teacher and teaching orientation,
- theory orientation.

4.7 Rating of Study Conditions and Study Provision

The graduates had been asked to rate the study conditions and provision at their higher education institution on a scale from 1 = very good to 5 = very bad (see Figure 4.3).

Figure 4.3: Rating of Study Provisions and Conditions (per cent of all graduates responding 'very good' and 'good'*)

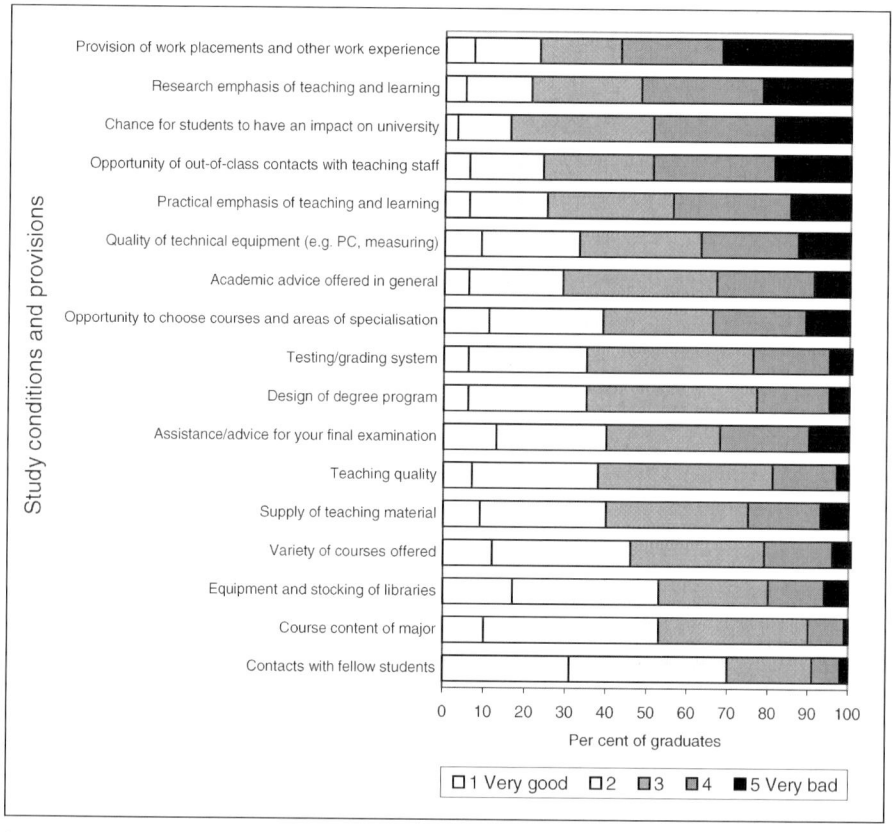

Question B9: How do you rate the study provision and study conditions you experienced in the course of study you graduated from in 1994 or 1995?
* Scale of answers from 1 = 'Very good' to 5 = 'Very bad'.
Source: CHEERS survey data.

Altogether, many students rated the course content and the modes of teaching as good. They were less satisfied, however, with the links to research and to practice, they often considered out-of-class-communication with teaching staff as too limited, and they noted little chance for students to have an impact on the institution.

Figure 4.4: Rating of Study Provision and Conditions in Europe and Japan (arithmetic mean)

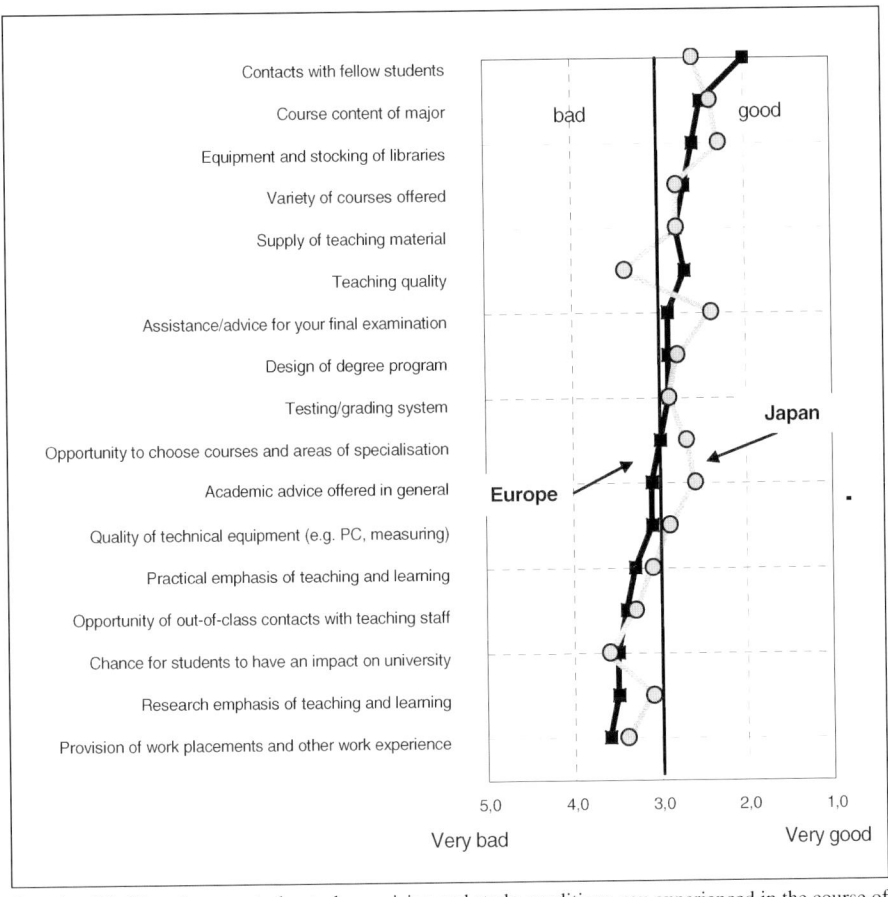

Question B9: How do you rate the study provision and study conditions you experienced in the course of study you graduated from in 1994 or 1995?
Scale of answers from 1 = 'Very good' to 5 = 'Very bad'.
Source: CHEERS survey data.

It is interesting to note the difference between the ratings of the European and the Japanese graduates. Figure 4.4 shows that they both had a similar view of the conditions and provision of study in some respects. However, the Japanese graduates viewed the assistance and the advice they received more positively in various respects. But, they rated the quality of teaching less well than their European counterparts, and they were less satisfied with contacts with fellow students.

Major differences exist between the different countries in the emphasis on practical teaching and learning. The Northwestern countries of Europe (the Nordic countries, the Netherlands and the United Kingdom) seem to stress particular practical aspects such as practical learning, practical experience, communication and equipment. Italy and to a lesser extent the Czech Republic seem to have an opposite mode of functioning. Notably, less emphasis is placed on practical experience, communication and equipment.

Table 4.6: Rating of Study Provisions and Conditions, by Country (per cent of all graduates responding 'very good' or 'good'*)

	Country**													Total
	IT	ES	FR	AT	DE	NL	UK	FI	SE	NO	CZ	EUR	JP	
Contacts with fellow students	62	71	62	73	75	71	71	74	79	85	72	72	48	70
Library Equipment and stock	32	45	45	56	46	59	57	68	60	69	33	51	65	53
Course content of major	38	35	58	48	40	60	71	58	62	45	51	51	60	52
Variety of courses offered	42	39	57	55	46	67	59	47	24	40	34	46	43	46
Assistance/advice for your final examination	39	10	18	23	36	38	51	45	44	47	62	38	60	40
Supply of teaching material	23	38	27	34	34	48	41	56	54	58	29	40	39	40
Opportunity to choose courses and areas of specialisation	38	22	40	47	42	45	53	41	26	29	37	38	49	39
Quality of teaching	38	25	40	44	40	42	60	39	38	31	48	40	15	38
Design of degree programme	22	18	47	31	37	31	53	43	39	35	34	36	35	36
Testing/grading system	19	20	33	37	30	37	51	20	47	49	48	36	26	35
Quality of technical equipment (e.g. PC, measuring instruments, etc.)	15	20	32	28	31	44	40	49	35	39	28	33	40	33
Academic advice offered in general	10	14	25	20	25	14	50	36	16	30	55	27	46	29
Practical emphasis of teaching and learning	8	15	22	15	20	41	46	25	29	36	20	26	26	26
Opportunity of out-of-class contacts with teaching staff	14	25	41	12	17	29	29	26	28	25	13	24	26	24
Provision of work placements and other work experience	4	8	19	18	26	52	25	26	35	28	12	23	23	23
Research emphasis of teaching and learning	11	6	30	21	18	27	30	37	23	21	7	21	23	21
Chances to participate in research projects	9	6	24	17	16	30	23	22	14	12	9	16	13	16
Chance for students to have an impact on university policies	8	14	10	12	11	32	17	22	25	15	14	16	12	16

Question B9: How do you rate the study provision and study conditions you experienced in the course of study you graduated from in 1994 or 1995?
* Scale of answers from 1 = 'Very good' to 5 = 'Very bad'.
** Count by Country: IT (3071); ES (2997); FR (3026); AT (2291); DE (3491); NL (3049); UK (3429); FI (2661); SE (2624); NO (3307); CZ (3079); EUR (33025); JP (3408); Total (36434).
Source: CHEERS survey data.

Autonomy in organising one's studies plays a somewhat different role. This aspect, addressed above in the themes of "free choice" and "content", seems to be most strongly emphasised by Italian and British higher education institutions (see Table 4.6).

4.8 Study Activities

The graduates also vary substantially by country according to the time they devote to attending courses and self-study during the lecture periods. According to their estimates, the average time they spend per week on study was:
- slightly more than 40 hours in Italy, Spain and Sweden,
- around 35 hours in France, Germany and Norway,
- around 30 hours in Austria, Finland, the Netherlands and the United Kingdom, and
- only 27 hours in Japan.

One must bear in mind that the graduates spent about five hours per week on average during the lecture period on earning money and on practical activities (16 hours outside the lecture period) and about four hours on extra-curricular activities which were partly related to the study activities (see Table 4.7).

Table 4.7: Activities During Lecture Period by Country (arithmetic mean[1]; hours)

	Country*												Total
	IT	ES	FR	AT	DE	NL	UK	FI	SE	NO	EUR	JP	
Major subjects: attending lectures	17.7	23.5	21.6	11.6	21.7	15.7	15.7	11.5	19.8	18.2	16.3	21.4	16.7
Major subjects: other study activities**	23.2	16.4	11.9	17.2	12.3	13.1	14.6	12.5	18.6	15.9	14.0	5.2	13.2
Other subjects	.0	2.4	.8	1.7	1.1	3.5	1.5	5.4	3.7	.2	1.7	-	1.7
Extra-curricular activities***	6.6	4.2	4.2	5.8	5.4	4.9	5.2	2.4	1.1	4.1	4.0	6.9	4.3
Employment/work****	4.8	4.5	4.4	7.5	5.6	7.0	5.8	5.7	2.0	4.8	4.7	12.1	5.4
Other	.6	.9	1.2	1.6	.7	.7	1.2	.9	-	.9	1.0	-	1.0
Total activities	54.4	52.3	45.1	46.7	47.4	46.2	45.2	41.8	46.0	45.4	47.2	46.2	47.1

Question B6: How many hours per week during your study (that you graduated from in 1994 or 1995) did you spend on average on each of the following activities? Please estimate.

[1] The means include graduates stating "0".

* Count by Country: IT (3022); ES (2999); FR (2981); AT (2245); DE (3469); NL (3001); UK (3372); FI (2461); SE (2584); NO (3225); EUR (29359); JP (3372); Total (32731).

** Incl. self studies etc.

*** E.g. societies, drama, sport, student union.

**** Excluding work placements/internships.

Czech Republic: data missing

Source: CHEERS survey data.

4.9 Activities Besides Study

Obviously, students do not consider their study period as a period merely providing them with learning opportunities by attending classes at their home higher education institution and self-study related to classes and exams. Rather, most students consider it as a phase in life that offers wider opportunities for activities and learning.

Table 4.8: Activities During Study Period by Country (per cent; multiple responses, and arithmetic mean*; months)

	IT	ES	FR	AT	DE	NL	UK	FI	SE	NO	CZ	EUR	JP	Total
Activities (per cent)														
Employment/work not related to study or possible future work	38	39	48	56	44	46	65	59	60	52	58	51	1	46
Employment/work related to study or possible future work	22	26	15	54	40	26	23	69	42	46	45	36	0	33
Work placement, internship (as part of degree course)	7	30	40	26	55	68	25	34	33	40	0	33	1	30
Child rearing, family care	9	5	5	7	4	3	5	9	8	11	6	6	0	6
Military or civilian service	15	6	6	9	3	3	0	9	6	6	0	6	0	5
Not employed, seeking employment	5	9	4	8	2	3	11	6	7	4	0	5	0	5
Other	7	8	4	9	5	8	5	5	7	6	0	6	1	5
No answer	32	23	22	8	10	11	13	7	8	9	22	15	97	23
Total activities	135	146	144	179	163	168	146	197	172	175	131	159	100	153
Duration of activities (months)														
Employment/work not related to study or possible future work	8.9	6.3	6.8	9.5	6.0	8.6	8.8	8.5	6.0	7.9	7.2	7.6	.1	6.9
Employment/work related to study or possible future work	5.3	4.5	2.6	9.5	6.1	5.4	3.3	14.1	4.0	6.5	7.0	6.0	.0	5.5
Work placement, internship (as part of degree course)	.7	2.1	2.4	1.7	4.0	6.0	2.4	1.7	1.7	3.1	.0	2.4	.0	2.2
Child rearing, family care	2.4	1.2	.6	1.8	.8	1.0	1.6	1.5	1.4	3.0	1.2	1.5	.0	1.3
Military or civilian service	1.7	.6	.7	.7	.3	.4	.0	1.0	.5	.7	.0	.6	.0	.5
Not employed, seeking employment	.6	1.5	.7	3.0	.4	.3	1.3	.3	.4	.3	.0	.8	.0	.7
Other	2.2	1.7	.7	1.7	.7	1.3	.6	.6	.8	1.1	.0	1.0	.1	.9
Total activities														
Arithmetic mean	21.8	17.9	14.5	27.9	18.5	23.1	18.0	27.7	14.8	22.6	15.5	20.0	.3	18.1
Median	10.0	9.0	7.0	16.0	12.0	13.0	10.0	18.0	10.0	12.0	8.0	12.0	.0	10.0

Question B4: How many months between first enrolment in higher education and graduation 1994 or 1995 did you spend predominantly on...
* Including those stating "0".
** Count by Country: IT (3102); ES (3024); FR (3051); AT (2312); DE (3506); NL (3087); UK (3460); FI (2675); SE (2634); NO (3329); CZ (3092); EUR (33273); JP (3421); Total (36694).
Source: CHEERS survey data.

As Table 4.8 shows, graduates reported that they had spent more than five hours on paid employment on average per week during the lecture period as well as over four hours on extra-curricular activities. Both activities were most frequently undertaken by Japanese students and least frequently by Swedish students.

In addition, more than three quarters of the former students stated that, during the course of study, they spent extended periods on organised activities outside higher education. These comprised on average about 1 ½ years per student, as Table 4.8 shows, among them notably
- employment not related to study (almost 7 months on average),
- employment and work related to study (over 5 months),
- work placement and internships (over 2 months),
- child rearing and family care (over 1 month), and
- other activities (about two months).

The activities varied substantially by country, as Table 4.8 shows.

Notably, Finnish and Austrian graduates had spent substantial periods on being employed in activities that were related to their field of study. Dutch graduates spent the longest internship periods. Japanese students hardly spent any periods on work or other non-study activities. However, they spent an exceptionally high share of their time during the lecture period on paid employment work in order to earn money.

4.10 Relationship between Work Experience and Content of Study

Altogether, 35 per cent of the graduates believe that the work experience they acquired during the course of study was closely linked to the content of their studies. 30 per cent participated in internships, and 33 per cent reported that they took jobs during the course of study which were related to their future employment (see Table 4.9).

Table 4.9: Relationship Between Work Experience and Content of Reference Study, by Country (per cent and arithmetic mean)

	Country											EUR	Total JP
	IT	ES	FR	AT	DE	NL	UK	FI	SE	NO	CZ	EUR	JP
1 To a very high degree	10	19	16	20	17	14	15	23	m	31	8	18	3	16
2	13	13	20	21	23	34	9	25	m	15	17	20	15	19
3	18	12	18	22	26	24	10	18	m	15	26	19	8	18
4	16	12	14	18	20	13	10	18	m	17	36	18	21	18
5 Not at all	43	43	31	18	14	14	56	16	m	23	13	26	52	29
Total*	100	100	100	100	100	100	100	100	m	100	100	100	100	100
Arithmetic mean	3.7	3.5	3.2	2.9	2.9	2.8	3.8	2.8	m	2.9	3.3	3.1	4.0	3.2

Question B7: To what degree was your work experience (employment, internships etc. during study) linked to the content of your studies (you graduated from in 1994 or 1995)?
Scale of answers from 1 = 'To a very high degree' to 5 = 'Not at all'.
* Count by Country: IT (1750); ES (1582); FR (2505); AT (2163); DE (3311); NL (2872); UK (2584); FI (2618); SE (m); NO (2897); CZ (2638); EUR (25021); JP (3264); Total (28285).
m = data missing
Source: CHEERS survey data.

4.11 Foreign Language Proficiency and Computer Knowledge

Students could also acquire supplementary skills during the course of study which were not necessarily included in the course programmes. Foreign language proficiency and computer knowledge were often quoted as important supplementary areas of knowledge of that kind.

Asked about foreign language proficiency,

- 60 per cent of the non-native speakers considered themselves able to read professionally relevant texts in the English language at the end of the study period,
- respective figures were 16 per cent for French, and about 20 per cent for German.

Table 4.10: Ability to Read Professionally Relevant Texts in Foreign Language at the Time of Graduation 1994/1995, by Country (per cent; multiple responses)

Language	Country													Total
	IT	ES	FR	AT	DE	NL	UK	FI	SE	NO	CZ	EUR	JP	
English	56	68	78	76	77	56	m	89	m	m	30	66	20	60
French	31	26	m	34	18	22	12	8	m	m	2	18	0	16
German	6	31	20	m	m	56	5	34	m	m	13	24	0	20

Question B11: How do you rate your language proficiency at the time of graduation 1994 or 1995?
Here: able to read professionally relevant texts.
m = data missing
Source: CHEERS survey data.

Almost half the graduates remembered that they had expertise in as the use of word processors at the time of graduation. Twenty per cent felt well qualified in the use of spread sheets, and about 10 per cent each regarding programming languages, data base and subject-related software.

Table 4.11: Self-rating of Expertise in Selected Software Areas at the Time of Graduation 1994/1995, by Country (per cent of all graduates responding 'very good' and 'good'*)

	Country													Total
	IT	ES	FR	AT	DE	NL	UK	FI	SE	NO	CZ	EUR	JP	
Word processor	26	23	31	61	44	58	49	58	52	m	m	44	m	44
Programming languages	7	7	11	13	13	11	9	10	14	m	m	10	m	10
Spread sheet	9	10	18	33	18	27	23	23	21	m	m	20	m	20
Data base	6	8	9	14	7	14	13	11	9	m	m	10	m	10
Subject-related software**	6	7	9	14	12	21	16	13	12	m	m	12	m	12

Question B10: How do you rate your expertise in selected software areas at the time of graduation 1994 or 1995 and now?
* Scale of answers from 1 = 'Very good' to 5 = 'No expertise at all'.
** E.g. CAD for engineers, SPSS for social scientists.
m = data missing
Source: CHEERS survey data.

For both foreign language proficiency and computer knowledge, the questionnaire did not address the timing and location of learning, but merely the degree of proficiency upon graduation. It could well be that students acquired this knowledge in the framework of the course programme, on their own initiative outside the programme or prior to enrolling in higher education.

4.12 Study Abroad

22 per cent of the respondents reported that they spent a study period abroad. The proportion ranged from 30 per cent of those graduating in the Netherlands and Sweden to 14 per cent in Spain and 11 per cent in Japan, as can be seen in Table 4.12.

The graduates studied at a time when the EU ERASMUS programme covered more than five per cent of the students' support to spend a temporary period in another European country. The findings suggest that three times as many students went abroad by other means.

Table 4.12: Graduates Having Spent Time Abroad During Study Period, by Country (per cent)

	Country												Total
	IT	ES	FR	AT	DE	NL	UK	FI	SE	NO	CZ	EUR	JP	
Yes	21	14	18	28	19	30	25	28	30	17	27	23	11	22
No	79	86	82	72	81	70	75	72	70	83	73	77	89	78
Total	100	100	100	100	100	100	100	100	100	100	100	100	100	100
Count	2901	3013	2952	2240	3477	3058	3345	2619	2610	3289	3092	32596	3401	35997

Question B2: Did you spend any time abroad during your period of study (in order to work or to study)?
Source: CHEERS survey data.

Of those spending a study-related period abroad, almost two-thirds studied, more than 40 per cent worked (internship etc.), and less than one fifth undertook other activities (preparation for examination, language courses, etc.) abroad (see Table 4.13).

Table 4.13: Major Activities Abroad, by Country (per cent of graduates with a period abroad; multiple responses)

	Country												Total
	IT	ES	FR	AT	DE	NL	UK	FI	SE	NO	CZ	EUR	JP	
Study	81	79	66	54	57	81	56	58	57	79	39	63	81	64
Work (internship etc.)	12	30	43	39	47	71	46	53	39	24	60	45	3	43
Other*	20	14	17	22	17	21	23	5	27	14	14	18	25	18
Total	113	123	126	115	121	173	125	116	124	117	113	126	109	125
Count	619	417	538	611	669	907	787	729	783	542	816	7418	345	7763

Question B3: If you stayed abroad: please state (for each period abroad, if you have spent more than one) the countries, the duration and the activities.
* Preparation for examination, language courses, etc.
Source: CHEERS survey data.

4.13   Summary

All available information suggests that the graduates who were surveyed considered their experience during their study period abroad richer and more diversified than that provided by their home higher education institution. In many countries, targeted teaching and learning, additional communication and extra-curricular activities linked to higher education, internships, paid employment and other off-campus experiences jointly contributed in one way or another to the employability and work-relevant competences acquired at the time of graduation. There are, however, striking differences by country regarding the extent to which the higher education institutions actively contributed to learning and socialisation outside the classroom, and the extent to which the students made use of those learning opportunities and employers seemed to appreciate these kinds of learning and competences.

The extent to which such an extended concept of socialisation and learning during the study period took root in various European countries becomes evident in comparison to Japan. Japanese students are among those who undertook "efficient" studies in terms of low drop-out rates and low proportion of prolongation. They quoted fewer additional activities during the course of study which could broaden their potentially employment-relevant competences. However, as will be pointed out below, they considered their competences upon graduation as considerably more limited than those of European graduates. They see the substantial amount of time spent on paid work as occasional activities with hardly any relevance for their professional competences.

Thus, prolongation of study beyond the required period must be seen to be caused primarily by two interrelated factors: paid employment in order to cover part of the costs of study and living and additional activities to broaden one's competences. Slow learning or insufficient time and energy or other elements of "wastage" must only be seen as the third most important factor in explaining prolongation of study.

5 JOB SEARCH, TRANSITION TO EMPLOYMENT AND EARLY CAREER

Traditionally, analyses of the relationship between higher education and the world of work did not put much emphasis on the period and the processes of transition from study to employment. It was taken for granted that the labour market was rather rational and shared the workforce according to job requirements. In recent years, however, more attention is paid to the transition processes and mechanisms, which may be more or less smooth. The transition period is now often seen as a stage with dynamics of its own. Problems may occur even for highly talented students if they were not well prepared for handling the search process. On the other side, those who had not been very successful students might get another chance if they perform as "smart managers" of this process.

5.1 Job Search

One should bear in mind that not all graduates seek jobs. About a quarter of the graduates who were surveyed were not seeking employment. A substantial number
- obtained a job without seeking; for example they were made an offer by the company where they had worked occasionally or had undertaken an internship during their course of study, they took over a family business, etc. (11%),
- were employed during their course of study and continued this activity (7%), or
- continued their studies (9%).

Some started their own business (2%) and a few (3%) mentioned other reasons for not seeking employment (family care, illness, etc.) (see Table 5.1).

Table 5.1: Job Search Since Graduation, by Country (per cent; multiple responses)

	Country												Total
	IT	ES	FR	AT	DE	NL	UK	FI	SE	NO	CZ	EUR	JP	
Yes, I sought a job after graduation	73	72	78	68	70	73	88	69	85	80	54	74	80	74
No, I obtained work without searching	8	7	5	18	18	13	4	12	12	7	22	11	4	11
No, I continued to study	11	12	20	12	9	6	5	2	5	5	4	8	12	9
No, I continued the job I had before graduation	9	7	7	10	4	5	6	17	3	4	14	8	1	7
No, I set up my own business/self-employment	4	3	1	2	2	2	1	2	1	1	3	2	0	2
Other	5	1	2	7	5	2	2	1	1	3	3	3	2	3
Total	110	102	112	117	108	100	107	103	107	100	100	106	100	105
Count	3048	2978	3027	2278	3334	3064	3433	2656	2630	3303	3092	32844	3403	36247

Question C1: Did you seek a job after you graduated in 1994 or 1995? Exclude applications for casual and vacation jobs.
Source: CHEERS survey data.

5.2 Timing of Job Search

Also, the timing of the job search differs strikingly according to country. Almost all Japanese respondents started their job search over six months before graduation; as a rule, they had their places in the employment system several months before graduation. In the European countries, over one third of British students started their job search more than three months before graduation. At the other extreme, more than half the French graduates and almost half the Italian and Spanish graduates waited until graduation before they started their job search (see Figure 5.1).

In some countries, an early search is customary. In Japan, for example, students who had not been offered a reasonable employment opportunity six months before graduation had reasons to believe that they would be the "losers". Altogether, early search is more likely when the universities are strongly involved in the placement process and if the final examinations and the grades awarded in these play a small role in the overall assessment of the graduates' competences.

The beginning of the search varies between of fields of study, but consistent patterns across countries are rare (see Figure 5.2). By and large, health and engineering graduates often start their search early. Law graduates, in contrast, often start late, notably in Austria and Germany. In France, business studies graduates show a much stronger propensity to start their job search prior to graduation than other graduates. In Italy, Spain and Austria as well as in Japan, the differences between fields of study are relatively small with respect to the start of the job search.

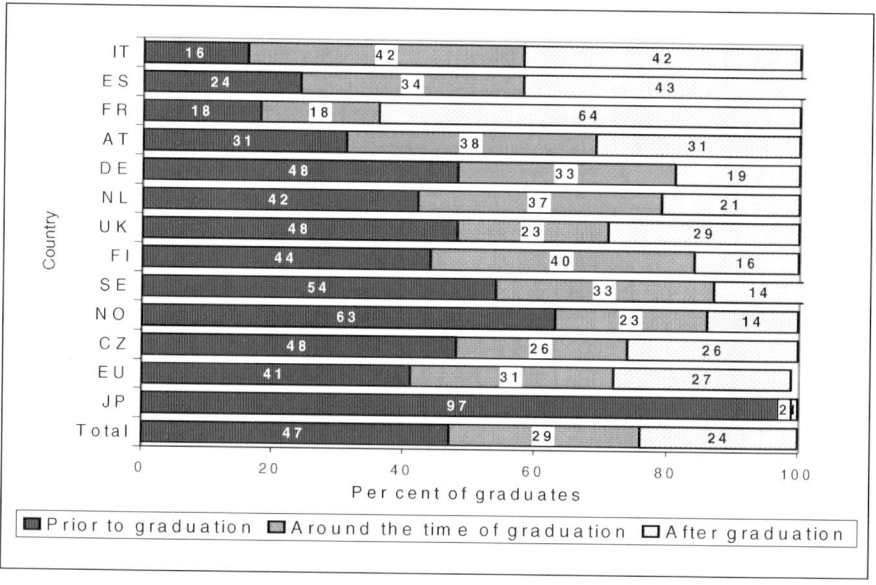

Figure 5.1: Time of Starting Job Search, by Country (per cent of graduates seeking for a job)

Country	Prior to graduation	Around the time of graduation	After graduation
IT	16	42	42
ES	24	34	43
FR	18	18	64
AT	31	38	31
DE	48	33	19
NL	42	37	21
UK	48	23	29
FI	44	40	16
SE	54	33	14
NO	63	23	14
CZ	48	26	26
EU	41	31	27
JP	97		2
Total	47	29	24

Question C2: When did you start looking for a job? Exclude search for casual and vacation jobs.
Source: CHEERS survey data.

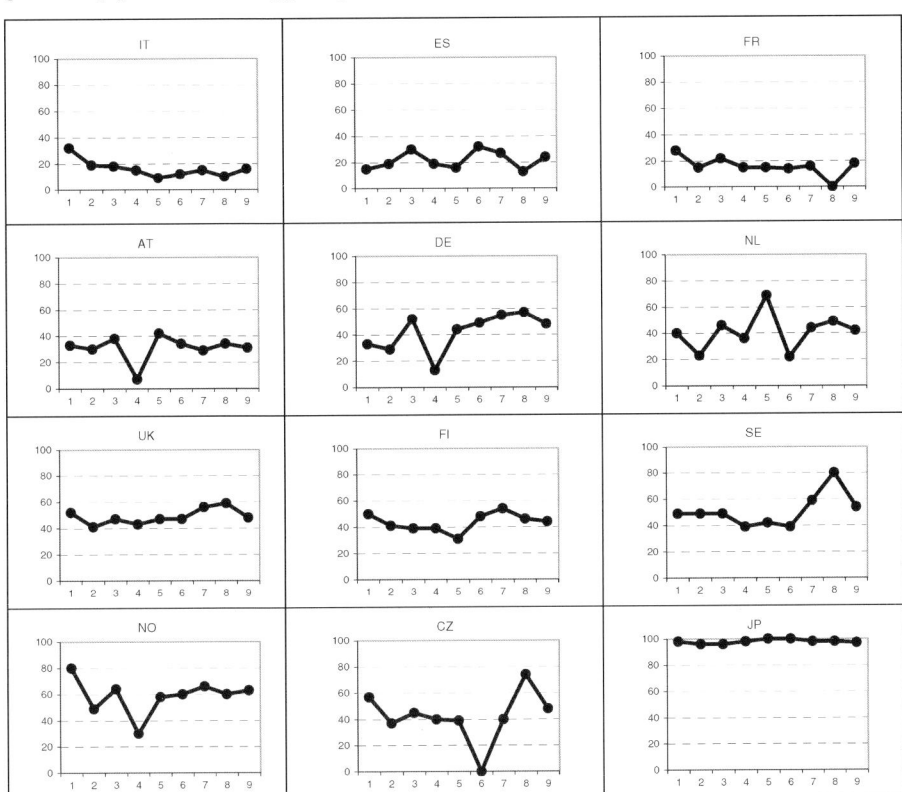

Figure 5.2: Job Search Started Before Graduation, by Country and Field of Study (per cent of graduates seeking for a job)

Question C2: When did you start looking for a job? Exclude search for casual and vacation jobs.
Field of study: 1 Education; 2 Humanities; 3 Social Sciences; 4 Law; 5 Natural Sciences; 6 Mathematics; Computer Science; 7 Engineering; 8 Health/Medicine; 9 Total
Source: CHEERS survey data.

5.3 Length of Job Search

The length of the search for first employment after graduation is often seen as a key indicator of the labour market conditions for graduates. A long job search can be a sign of objective difficulties to obtain a job in accordance with the graduates' expectations because of labour market conditions as well as job seekers' "employability". On the other hand, a certain time span is needed for the graduates to explore their chances on the labour market. Those who seek for only a short time may too easily accept a job that is not the most promising for them.

The graduates in this study were asked to state the length of their search (before or after graduation) for their first official job. On average, it was 6 months; 66 per cent of the graduates who responded did not seek for more than 3 months. Only 7 per cent sought for more than year.

The duration of the job search varies substantially by country. It is about 6 months on average, with Czech and Norwegian graduates only seeking for about three months on average, as compared to Spanish graduates seeking for almost a year on average (see Table 5.2).

Table 5.2: *Length of Job Search for the First Job After Graduation in 1994/1995, by Country (per cent and means of graduates seeking for a job)*

	Country												Total
	IT	ES	FR	AT	DE	NL	UK	FI	SE	NO	CZ	EUR	JP	
0 months	21	19	24	37	31	31	33	42	47	38	39	33	8	31
1-3 months	27	22	31	30	33	41	40	35	33	43	45	35	29	35
4-6 months	18	16	19	16	21	16	15	11	11	12	11	15	37	17
7-12 months	17	20	15	11	11	8	9	6	6	5	4	10	21	11
13-24 months	13	14	9	5	4	4	3	3	2	1	1	5	4	5
25+ months	4	9	2	1	1	1	0	2	1	0	0	2	1	2
Total	100	100	100	100	100	100	100	100	100	100	100	100	100	100
Count	2069	2042	1176	1682	2754	2571	2830	2043	2239	2792	2287	24484	2694	27178
Arithmetic mean	8.9	11.6	7.1	6.0	5.5	4.7	4.4	5.1	4.9	3.3	2.9	5.8	6.0	5.9
Median	6.0	8.0	5.0	4.0	4.0	3.0	3.0	3.0	3.0	2.0	2.0	3.0	5.0	3.0

Question C7: For how many months did you seek altogether (before or after graduation) for your first official job after graduation in 1994 or 1995?
Source: CHEERS survey data.

43 per cent of the graduates in Spain and 34 per cent of the graduates in Italy sought for more than six months, as compared to 9 per cent in Sweden, 6 per cent in Norway and 5 per cent in the Czech Republic.

Despite the substantial differences between countries, there are some fairly systematic differences between fields of study which apply across most of the countries. Many graduates in the humanities and social sciences seem to search for a long period before obtaining their first job. This in contrast, is relatively rare for those in the fields of engineering, health, natural sciences and business studies, although there are some exceptions to this rule. In particular, graduates from health fields seek for a long period in Spain. The search period for law graduates varies most substantially between countries (see Figure 5.3).

In combining the information on the beginning of the job search and the period it lasts, we could determine the timing of the terminations of the job search with respect to the time of graduation. On average, graduates ended their job search about six months after graduation. This, however, differed substantially by country:
- Japanese graduates ended their job search on average five months before graduation, and

- Norwegian and Czech graduates shortly after graduation, whereas
- Italian and Spanish graduates knew on average almost only one year after graduation where they would be employed.

Japanese graduates started their job search very early, while the period of job search was close to the average of all graduates surveyed. In contrast, Italian and Spanish graduates started their job search relatively late on average and, in addition, searched for a long time before accepting a job.

Figure 5.3: Length of Job Search for the First Job After Graduation, by Country and Field of Study (in months; arithmetic mean of graduates seeking for a job)

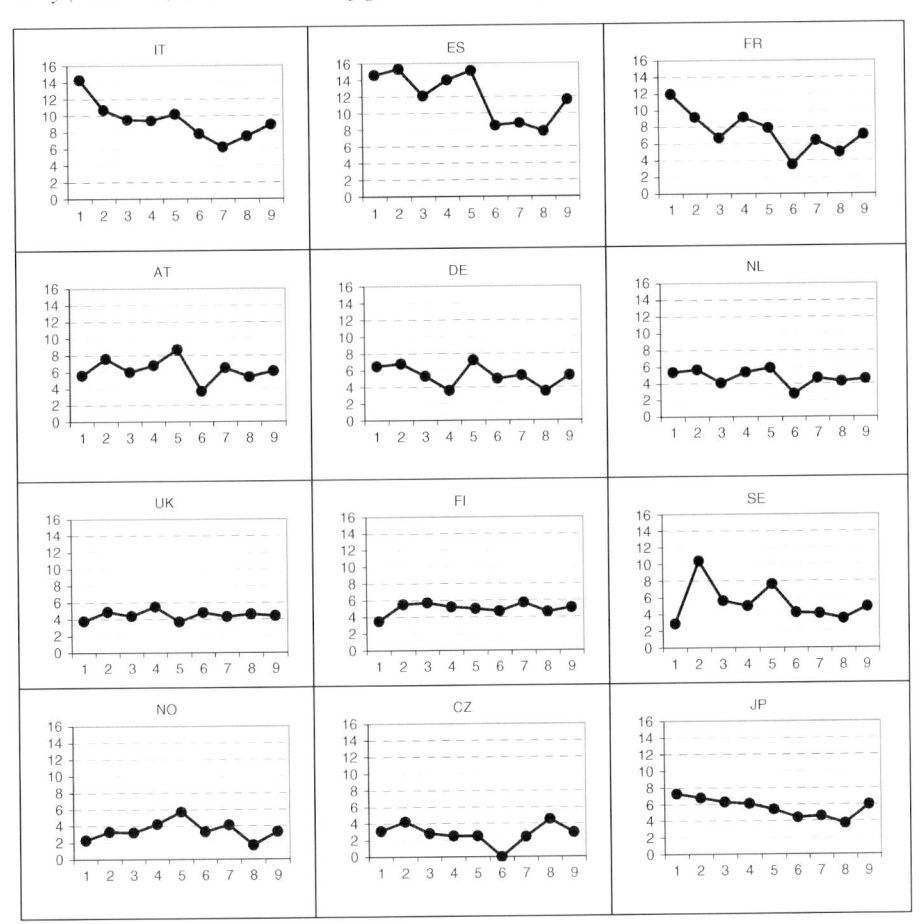

Question C7: How many months did you search altogether (before or after graduation) for your first official job after graduation in 1994 or 1995?

Field of study: 1 Education; 2 Humanities; 3 Social Sciences; 4 Law; 5 Natural Sciences; 6 Mathematics; Computer Science; 7 Engineering; 8 Health/Medicine; 9 Total.

Source: CHEERS survey data.

5.4 Number of Contacts with Employers

The respondents seeking employment contacted on average about 25 employers before they decided upon their first regular job. French and Spanish graduates contacted on average over 50 employers (see Table 5.3).

In some countries, those who seek for a longer period are likely to contact substantially more employers. This holds true for French and Norwegian graduates. French graduates with a job search period of more than six months contact on average over 100 employers. In contrast, Japanese graduates who seek for a long period do not contact more employers: obviously some students just stretch the period of contacting employers more than others.

Table 5.3: *Number of Employers Contacted in the Search for the First Job After Graduation (per cent and means)*

	\multicolumn{12}{c}{Country}	Total
	IT	ES	FR	AT	DE	NL	UK	FI	SE	NO	CZ	JP	EUR
0 employer	15	15	7	9	8	9	7	12	8	6	9	3	9	3
1-3 employers	27	17	12	26	22	39	24	40	35	44	44	24	31	24
4-10 employers	33	20	15	28	27	27	26	31	34	28	36	35	28	35
11-20 employers	9	13	12	12	15	11	15	8	12	10	7	15	11	15
21-50 employers	10	16	21	15	17	10	16	8	9	8	3	16	12	16
51+ employers	5	19	33	10	12	3	12	2	2	4	0	7	8	7
Total	100	100	100	100	100	100	100	100	100	100	100	100	100	100
Count	1841	1837	1023	1275	2164	2180	2718	1715	1941	2552	1620	2546	20865	2546
Arithmetic mean	17.3	46.0	70.4	22.9	24.5	11.9	27.7	10.2	11.0	11.6	6.2	20.2	21.5	20.2
Median	5.0	20.0	40.0	10.0	10.0	5.0	10.0	4.0	5.0	4.0	4.0	10.0	6.0	10.0

Question C6: How many employers did you contact (by e.g. letter) before you took up your first job after graduation in 1994 or 1995?
Source: CHEERS survey data.

In many countries, the number of graduates who contact employers varies substantially by field of study. As a rule, a large number of employers are contacted by graduates from fields that typically prepare for the private sector, i. e. social sciences, natural sciences, computer sciences and engineering. In Austria, Norway and Japan, law graduates contact a large number of employers on average (see Figure 5.4).

Figure 5.4: Number of Employers Contacted in the Search for the First Job After Graduation, by Country and Field of Study (arithmetic means)

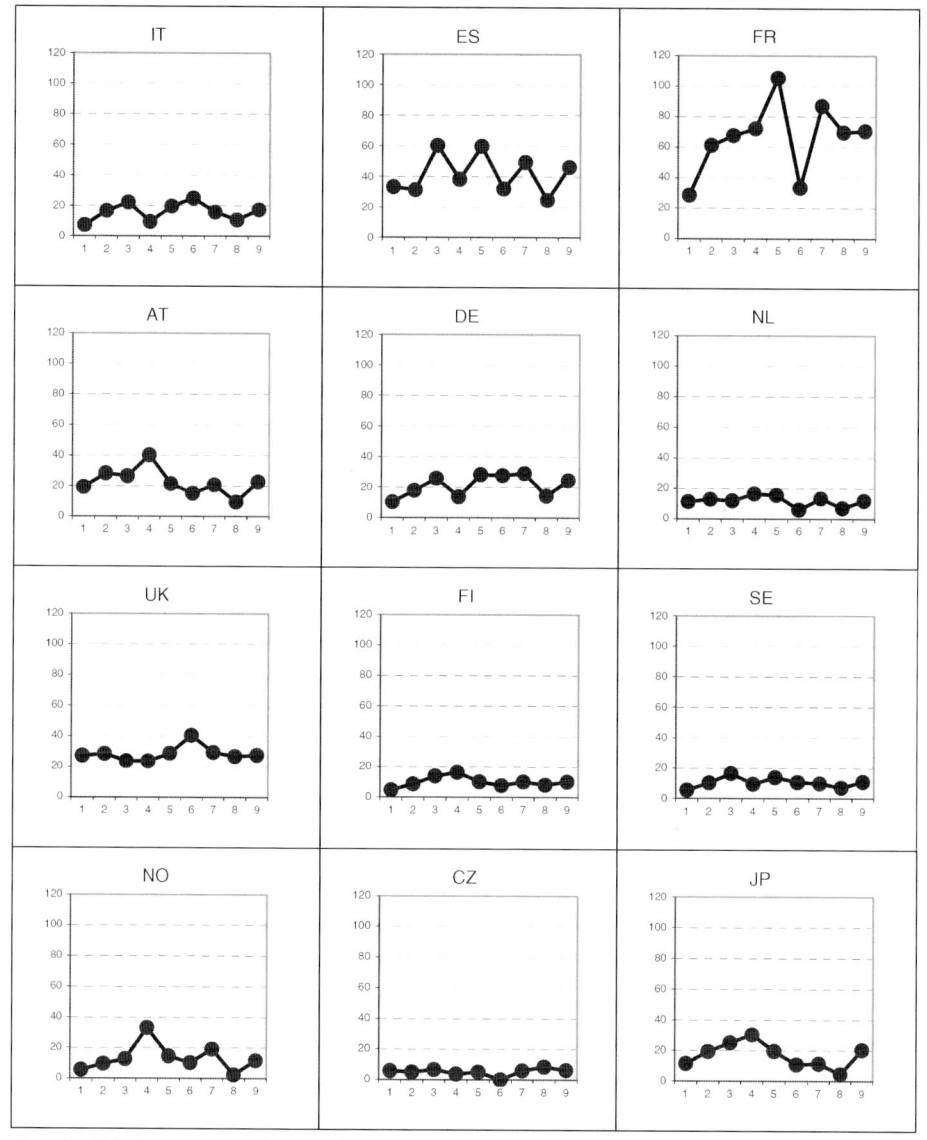

Question C6: How many employers did you contact (by e.g. letter) before you took up your first job after graduation in 1994 or 1995?

Field of study: 1 Education; 2 Humanities; 3 Social Sciences; 4 Law; 5 Natural Sciences; 6 Mathematics; Computer Science; 7 Engineering; 8 Health/Medicine; 9 Total.

Source: CHEERS survey data.

5.5 Methods of Job Search

Most graduates applied various methods in seeking for their first regular employment
- Almost three quarters applied for advertised vacancies,
- about half contacted employers on their own initiative without knowing about a vacancy,
- more than one third contacted the public employment agency, and
- almost one third used private contacts in the job search.

Other modes of search were quoted less frequently (see Figure 5.5).

Figure 5.5: Methods of Job Search (per cent of graduates seeking for a job; multiple responses)

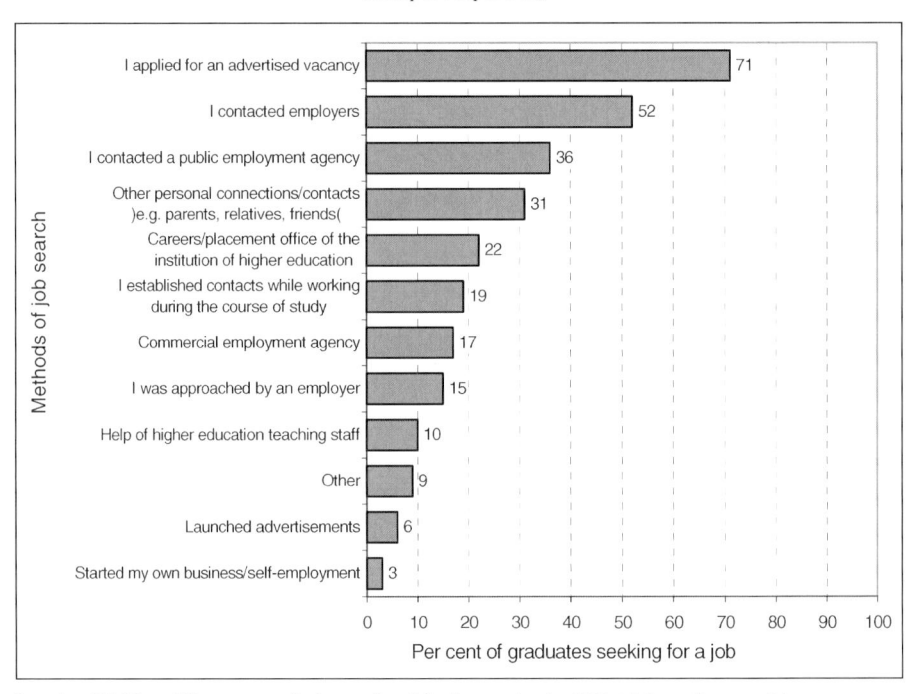

Methods of job search	Per cent
I applied for an advertised vacancy	71
I contacted employers	52
I contacted a public employment agency	36
Other personal connections/contacts (e.g. parents, relatives, friends)	31
Careers/placement office of the institution of higher education	22
I established contacts while working during the course of study	19
Commercial employment agency	17
I was approached by an employer	15
Help of higher education teaching staff	10
Other	9
Launched advertisements	6
Started my own business/self-employment	3

Question C4: How did you try to find your first job after graduation? Multiple replies possible.
Source: CHEERS survey data.

The mode of job search varied substantially by country, as can be seen in Table 5.4.
- Italian graduates often relied on private contacts.
- The same holds true for Spanish graduates who were also often helped by the career office of their university and the public employment agency and who relatively seldom contacted employers on their own initiative.
- French graduates mostly used the public employment agencies.
- Finnish and German graduates often established contacts with employers during the course of study.

- This also holds true for Dutch graduates who, in addition, much more frequently requested the help of commercial employment agencies.
- British graduates often relied on the help of the career office of their higher education institution. Relatively few contacted employers on their own initiative or made use of the public employment agencies.
- Japanese graduates clearly differed from European graduates in that they depended more often on the placement office of their university and the help of professors and seldom contacted employers without knowing about a vacancy.

Table 5.4: Methods of Job Search, by Country (per cent of graduates seeking for a job; multiple responses)

	Country*													Total
	IT	ES	FR	AT	DE	NL	UK	FI	SE	NO	CZ	EUR	JP	
I applied for an advertised vacancy	48	61	75	64	74	84	68	73	78	84	62	71	73	71
I contacted employers without knowing about a vacancy	70	43	79	65	60	69	40	62	61	40	63	57	13	52
I used other personal connections/contacts (e.g. parents, relatives, friends)	54	49	38	36	26	37	27	20	25	15	38	32	21	31
I contacted a public employment agency	40	52	63	32	40	42	26	43	48	23	38	39	13	36
I asked for the help of the careers/placement office of my higher education institution	10	40	14	13	7	12	37	26	3	3	19	17	63	22
I established contacts while working during the course of study	11	12	21	24	28	31	17	28	20	21	20	21	3	19
I contacted a commercial employment agency	14	33	16	13	4	54	27	4	0	6	21	18	13	17
I was approached by an employer	19	8	10	4	12	19	9	21	18	19	26	15	14	15
I asked for the help of teaching staff of the higher education institution	13	8	6	11	8	12	9	9	5	6	10	9	23	10
I launched advertisements by myself	10	10	24	13	11	1	1	11	1	1	7	7	1	6
I started my own business/ self-employment	9	3	2	6	6	2	2	3	0	1	3	3	0	3
Other	8	39	12	7	9	5	7	4	5	4	4	9	10	9
Total*	305	358	361	288	284	369	268	305	265	224	311	298	246	293

Question C4: How did you try to find the first job after graduation? Multiple replies possible.
* Count by Country: IT (2143); ES (2106); FR (1122); AT (1487); DE (2284); NL (2238); UK (2889); FI (1791); SE (2181); NO (2626); CZ (1672); EUR (22539); JP (2671); Total (25210).
Source: CHEERS survey data.

The patterns change, if one takes into account the methods which turned out to be most important in actually finding the first regular employment. Application for an advertised vacancy and self-search are on average the most successful methods, i.e. leading to success by almost one third and almost one-fifth of the graduates respectively, and private contacts played a decisive role in one-seventh of the cases. In contrast, search with the help of a public employment agency, though employed by 36 per cent of the job-seeking graduates, turned out to be decisive only for about one-tenth of them; actually for about 4 per cent of the job-seeking graduates. Table 5.5 shows the role the various methods employed actually played for getting the first job after graduation.

Table 5.5: *Most Important Method for Getting the First Job After Graduation, by Country (per cent of graduates seeking for a job)*

	Country*												Total	
	IT	ES	FR	AT	DE	NL	UK	FI	SE	NO	CZ	EUR	JP
I applied for an advertised vacancy	11	20	17	25	33	24	40	31	40	55	18	31	31	31
I contacted employers without knowing about a vacancy	20	14	29	33	25	15	12	25	24	13	31	20	3	19
I used other personal connections/contacts (e.g. parents, relatives)	31	28	19	16	11	8	12	7	7	6	20	14	13	14
I established contacts while working during the course of study	4	4	7	10	10	11	7	11	5	10	7	8	1	7
I was approached by an employer	8	3	3	2	4	7	3	8	12	7	6	6	6	6
I contacted a commercial employment agency	1	4	1	1	0	21	11	1	0	1	2	5	5	5
I enlisted the help of the careers/placement office of my university	2	4	3	2	1	1	6	2	0	1	5	2	21	5
I contacted a public employment agency	0	5	11	2	3	4	2	6	5	2	4	4	2	4
I enlisted the help of teaching staff of the institution of higher education	3	1	1	2	3	3	1	4	1	2	2	2	9	3
I started my own business/ self-employment	4	2	1	1	2	1	1	1	0	1	1	1	0	1
I launched advertisements by myself	1	2	1	1	1	0	0	1	0	0	1	1	0	1
Other	14	13	8	4	8	4	4	3	6	2	2	6	8	6
Total*	100	100	100	100	100	100	100	100	100	100	100	100	100	100

Question C5: Which method was the most important one for getting your first job after graduation in 1994 or 1995?
* Count by Country: IT (1841); ES (1837); FR (1023); AT (1275); DE (2164); NL (2180); UK (2718); FI (1715); SE (1941); NO (2552); CZ (1620); EUR (20865); JP (2546); Total (23411).
Source: CHEERS survey data.

Applying for an advertised vacancy turned out to be the most frequent method of job search in the more Northern countries of Europe (the Nordic countries, Germany, the Netherlands and the United Kingdom) as well as in Japan. Individual search was the single most successful job search method in Austria, the Czech Republic and France, while private contacts played the most prominent role in Italy and Spain. Two other findings stood out: Dutch graduates often obtained their first job with the help of commercial employment agencies and Japanese graduates with the help of the placement offices of their university.

Altogether, contacts between employers and job seekers were crucial for employment in more than 70 per cent of the cases. Amongst the intermediate actors, parents, relatives and others played a more frequent role than employment agencies and higher education institutions. However, these patterns varied by country. Most strikingly, support on the part of the higher education institution, i.e. either the teachers or the career offices, was crucial for some 30 per cent of Japanese graduates. This held true for only four per cent of the European graduates on average.

5.6   Time between Graduation and First Employment

In discussions concerning the transition from school to work, a central role is understandably assigned to the length of time it takes after graduation to obtain one's first regular employment in an acceptable job (e.g. excluding occasional employment or even regular employment in a job considered by the graduates themselves as an opportunity to earn money to fund the search period). It may be considered a smooth process of transition if the period of search starts early, does not take long and does not demand strenuous efforts, and it may be considered as limited "friction" or "wastage" if the graduates embark on employment shortly after graduation.

39 per cent of the graduates who were eventually employed began their first employment prior or immediately after (at most one month after) graduation. A further 25 per cent found employment between the second and the sixth month after graduation. A further 10 per cent needed up to one year, whilst about a quarter found regular employment more than one year after graduation (see Table 5.6).

In considering the period up to three months after graduation as a rapid transition to employment we note that rapid transition was the case for

- about three quarters of Japanese, Norwegian and Finnish graduates,
- almost two-thirds of the Dutch and Czech graduates,
- about half or somewhat more German, British and Swedish graduates,
- one third or more of Spanish, Italian and Austrian graduates, and
- only one fifth of the French graduates.

Table 5.6: Time Between Graduation and First Employment, by Country (per cent of employed graduates)

	Country*												Total
	IT	ES	FR	AT	DE	NL	UK	FI	SE	NO	CZ	EUR	JP
Before end of study	13	7	7	13	6	13	9	21	9	13	14	11	2	10
Up to about one month after the end of study	13	17	7	16	29	29	22	35	27	41	18	24	76	29
2-3 months	12	10	5	14	16	18	25	17	19	24	31	18	2	16
4-6 months	12	10	4	15	14	13	11	9	10	6	10	10	2	9
7-9 months	8	9	4	7	7	7	6	5	8	4	3	6	1	6
10-12 months	6	8	5	7	4	5	4	4	5	3	2	4	1	4
13 - 24 months	21	21	28	18	9	10	15	6	10	6	13	14	4	13
25 and more months	15	18	40	10	14	6	8	3	13	4	9	12	12	12
Total*	100	100	100	100	100	100	100	100	100	100	100	100	100	100

Question C10: Please inform us about your current major activity. Question C11: If your major activity has changed since graduation in 1994 or 1995 (e.g. from 'unemployed' to 'employed') or if you experienced a substantial change in your job (e.g. new employer, new position, new work tasks), please provide further information in the following table.

* Count by Country: IT (2537); ES (1957); FR (2231); AT (2128); DE (3230); NL (2836); UK (2999); FI (2395); SE (2222); NO (3109); CZ (2921); EUR (28566); JP (3252); Total (31817).

Source: CHEERS survey data.

Figure 5.6 shows the pattern of transition over time. Most Japanese graduates find employment immediately after graduation, but those who are not immediately employed may have relatively long transition periods. In other countries, we note that a high number of graduates rapidly find a job. France is the only exception: the proportion of graduates embarking on a job is more or less regular spread over a period of more than three years.

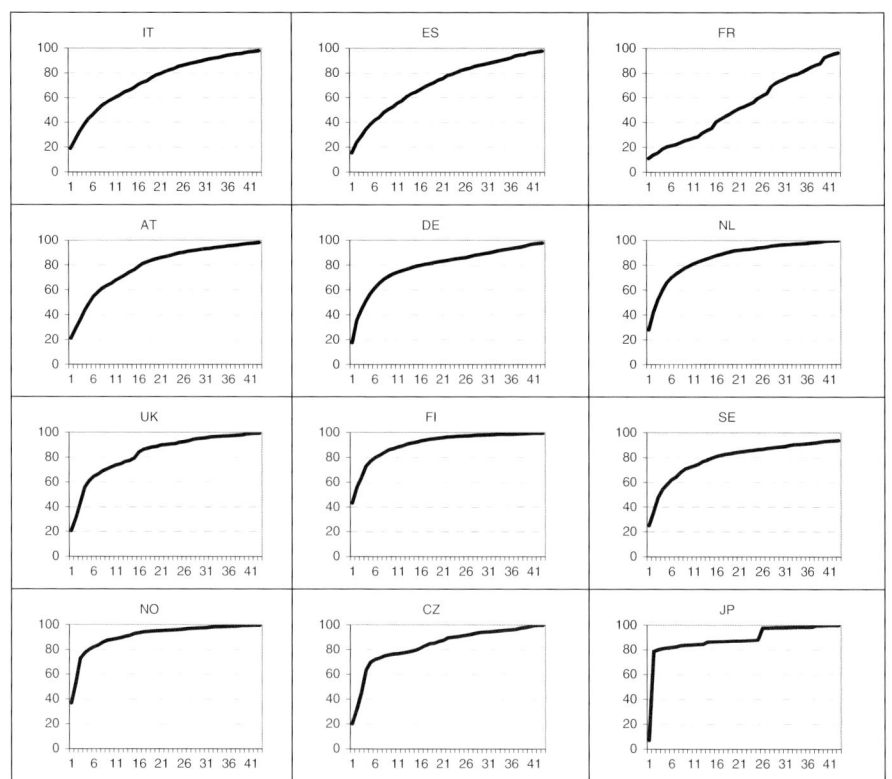

Figure 5.6: Duration Between Graduation and First Employment in the First 42 Months After Graduation*, by Country (per cent of employed graduates)

Question C10: Please inform us about your current major activity. Question C11: If your major activity has changed since graduation in 1994 or 1995 (e.g. from 'unemployed' to 'employed') or if you experienced a substantial change in your job (e.g. new employer, new position, new work tasks), please provide further information in the following table.

* Accumulated per cent of employed graduates already employed for the first time from the first to the 42nd month after graduation.

Source: CHEERS survey data.

5.7   Conclusion

Altogether, the findings suggest that the degree of smoothness of the transition process for recent graduates cannot be merely explained by demand-supply interaction on the labour market. Rather, different social norms in the transition process and related practices play a major role: for example, whether universities are involved in the placement process, whether employers rate highly the graduates' final achievements and whether long search and alternative activities for some period after graduation are viewed as acceptable. Both the culture of transition period and the labour market configuration have to be taken into consideration when explaining the differences in timing, duration, efforts and modes of recruitment and search.

6 EARLY CAREER

The survey was undertaken some three to four years after graduation. This moment in time was chosen for various reasons. On the one hand, some time should have elapsed since graduation in order to include the transition to employment of those who had to go through special training periods prior to regular employment and observe the transition of those who faced substantial problems in finding employment and first career steps of those who rapidly found work. On the other, the time span between graduation and the administering of the survey should not be too long in order to provide feedback to higher education that is not completely out of date. Therefore, those who were addressed in the surveys had graduated three to somewhat more than four years before.

The subsequent analysis of the early career on a month-by-month basis was undertaken for the first 3½ years. This cut-off point was chosen because a substantial number of graduates had responded to the questionnaire between three and 3 ½ years after graduation.

One should bear in mind, though, that some graduates do not provide information on there whereabouts. This is true for the majority of respondents immediately after graduation, for about one quarter half a year after graduation and for about 10 per cent 3½ years after graduation. Respondents who did not provide any information on this question were also included. Some were not employed and were seeking a job. Others had opted for full-time educational activities. Others just happened not to provide any detailed information. Therefore, these data must be viewed with some caution.

6.1   *Activities in the First 3 ½ Years After Graduation*

As Figure 6.1 shows for all respondents who provided information, about 20 per cent were already employed in the first month after graduation. This percentage rose to over 50 per cent six months after graduation. Thereafter, the increase levelled off. The employment quota of all respondents was below 60 per cent one year after graduation, slightly less than 70 per cent two years after graduation and about 80 per cent 3 ½ years after graduation. Those who were not employed represented about 15 per cent some six months after graduation and gradually levelled off to about 10 per cent. Finally, the quota of those reporting that they were unemployed remained more or less constant at about 2 per cent over the period under study.

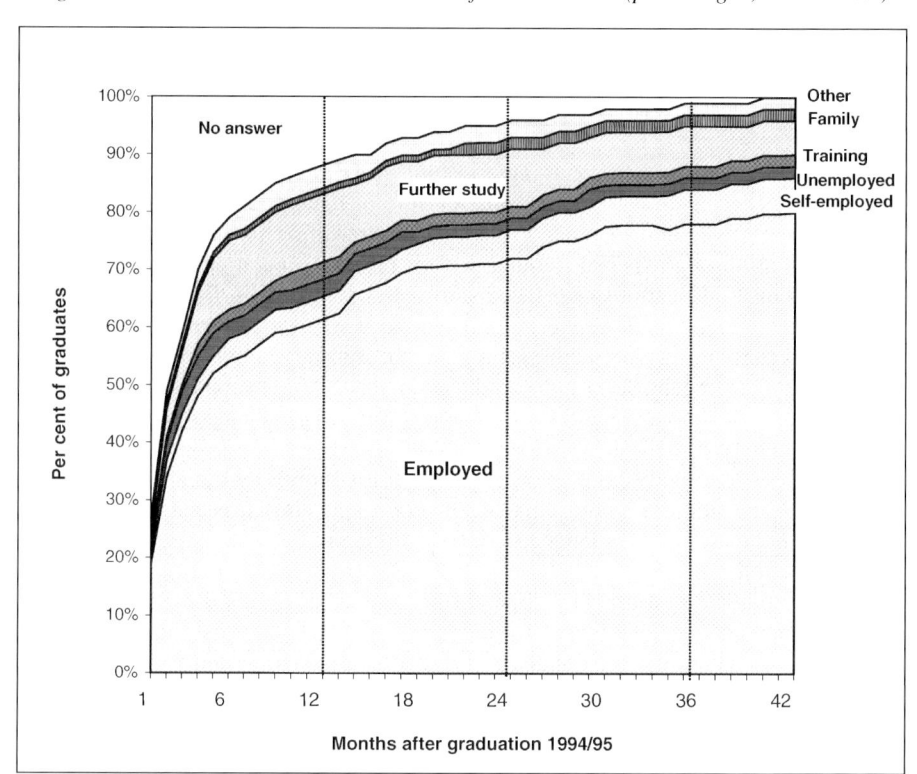

Figure 6.1: Activities in the First 42 Months After Graduation (percentage*; 12 countries)

[Figure: Stacked area chart showing percentage of graduates by activity (No answer, Further study, Employed, Self-employed, Unemployed, Training, Family, Other) over months after graduation 1994/95, from 1 to 42 months. Y-axis: Per cent of graduates, 0% to 100%.]

* Not included are graduates who did not provide any information at all.
Source: CHEERS survey data.

Gender: The proportions of male and female graduates in employment evolved in a similar way during the first two years (see Figure 6.2 and Figure 6.3). Thereafter, a gap emerged and grew. After 3 ½ years, the share of women employed was 74 per cent, as compared to 83 per cent for men, i.e. 9 per cent less. Obviously, an increasing number of women chose to discontinue employment a few years after graduation in order to care for children and family. The paths of men and women were not only quite similar for the first two years, but the difference in the third and at the beginning of the fourth year after graduation can be viewed as surprisingly small, even though there is an indication of a "divided track" for some of them.

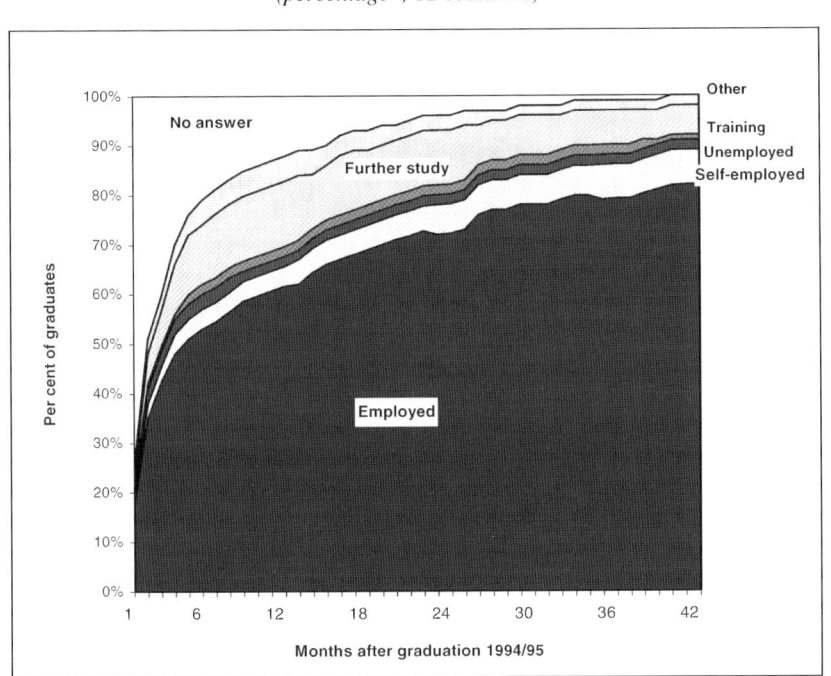

Figure 6.2: Activities of Male Graduates in the First 42 Months After Graduation (percentage*; 12 countries)

* Not included are graduates who did not provide any information at all.
Source: CHEERS survey data.

Country: The differences by country are fairly large, as can be seen in Figures 6.4 to 6.15. This can be seen in the cases of Italy on the one hand (Figure 7.4) and of Finland on the other (Figure 6.11). In Italy, less than 40 per cent stated that they were employed six months after graduation. The share rose to 47 per cent one year after graduation, 63 per cent two years after graduation and 75 per cent 3 ½ years after graduation. Transition to employment begins slowly in Italy and then becomes more rapid over several years. In Italy, we note the highest number of self-employed graduates and the proportion increases over time (see Figure 6.4).

In contrast, the employment quota in Finland reached 70 per cent already six month after graduation. Then, the growth was less than a third of that observed in Italy, but remained at 83 per cent 3 ½ years after graduation, which is higher than in Italy.

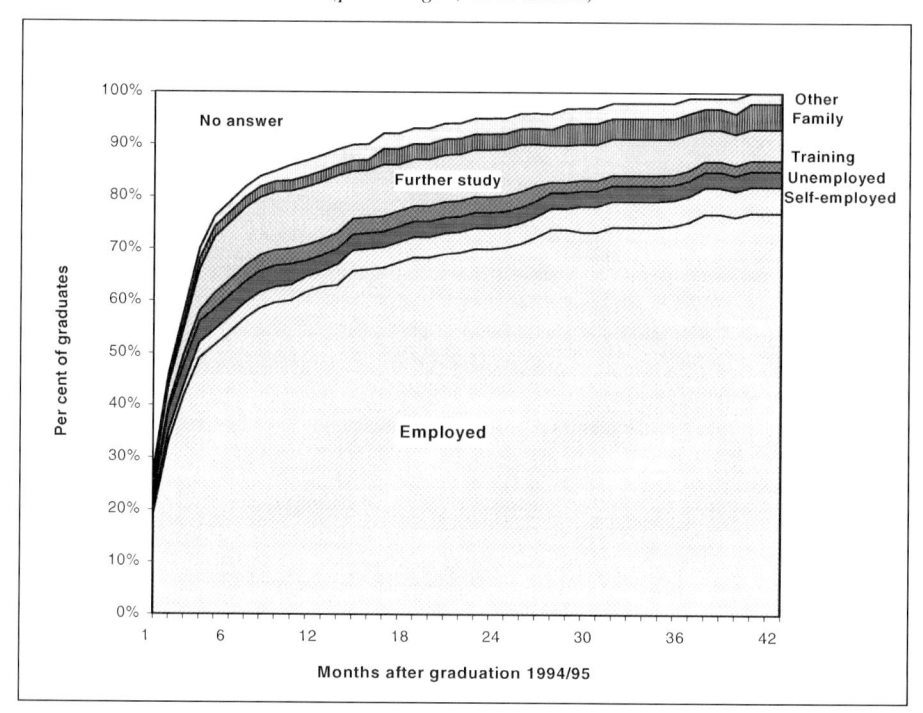

Figure 6.3: Activities of Female Graduates in the First 42 Months After Graduation (percentage*; 12 countries)

* Not included are graduates who did not provide any information at all.
Source: CHEERS survey data.

In Spain, the number of unemployed graduates is rather high during the whole period, as is the number of graduates who started further study (see Figure 6.5). The curves indicate substantial problems of transition to employment.

The situation for graduates in France was completely different. Most graduates continued their studies, and 12 months after graduation less than 20 per cent were employed. Even two years after graduation, less than 50 per cent were employed. Self-employment does not play a visible role in France. Very few graduates stated that they were self-employed in this period, and family activities were rare (see Figure 6.6). One must bear in mind that French graduates graduating with a "licence" degree, which is often seen as transitory for the award of a "maîtrise" degree had also been surveyed. This notwithstanding, transition to employment cannot be viewed as smooth in France as in most countries included in this study.

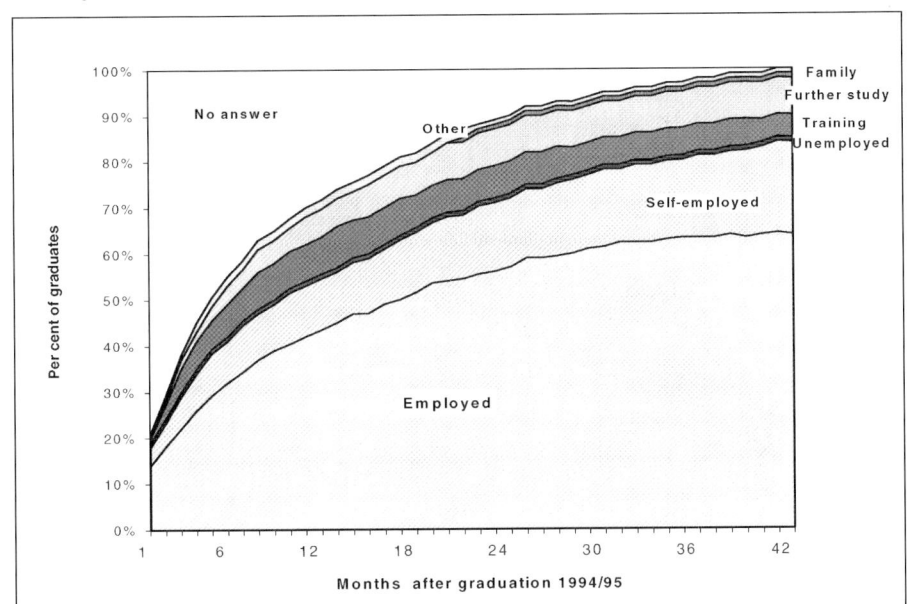

Figure 6.4: Activities in the First 42 Months After Graduation – Italy (percentage*)

[Figure: Stacked area chart showing percentage of graduates by activity (Employed, Self-employed, Other, No answer, Training, Further study, Family, Unemployed) over months after graduation 1994/95, from 1 to 42 months. Y-axis: Per cent of graduates, 0% to 100%.]

* Not included are graduates who did not provide any information at all.
Source: CHEERS survey data.

The transition pattern for Austria, Germany, Netherlands, United Kingdom, Finland, Sweden, Norway and Czech Republic is fairly similar. A somewhat smooth transition to employment is the dominant pattern.

Japan shows a completely different transition pattern (see Figure 6.15): employment immediately after graduation or further study is customary if graduates do not opt for graduate education. There was hardly any friction in the transition from higher education to employment at the time when the respondents had graduated.

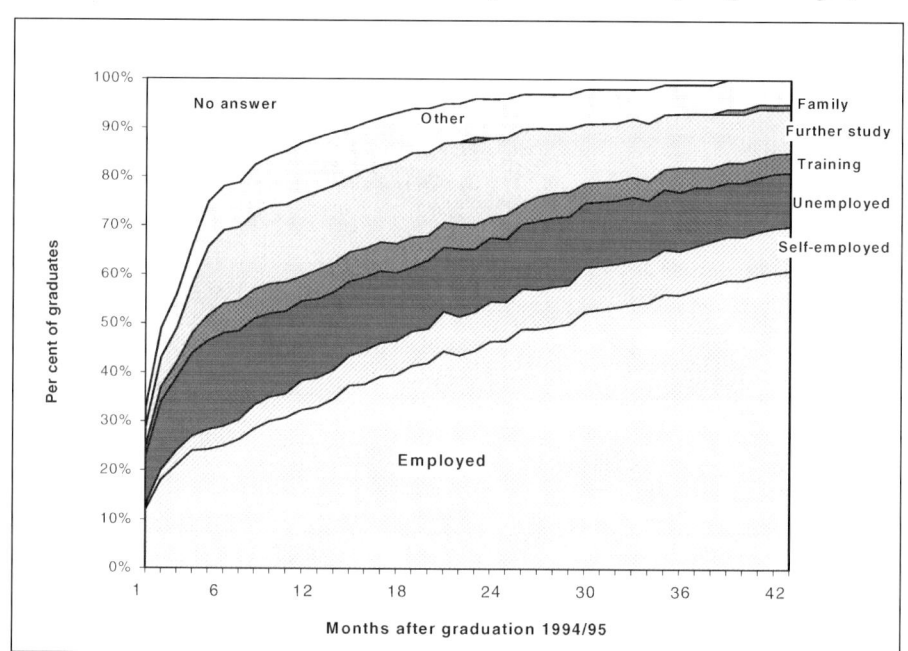

Figure 6.5: Activities in the First 42 Months After Graduation – Spain (percentage*)

* Not included are graduates who did not provide any information at all.
Source: CHEERS survey data.

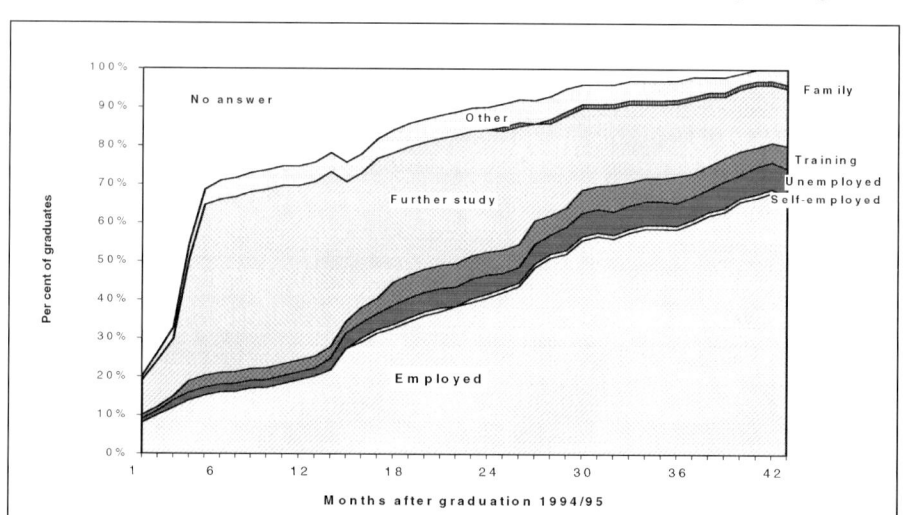

Figure 6.6: Activities in the First 42 Months After Graduation – France (percentage*)

* Not included are graduates who did not provide any information at all.
Source: CHEERS survey data.

6 EARLY CAREER

Figure 6.7: Activities in the First 42 Months After Graduation – Austria (percentage*)

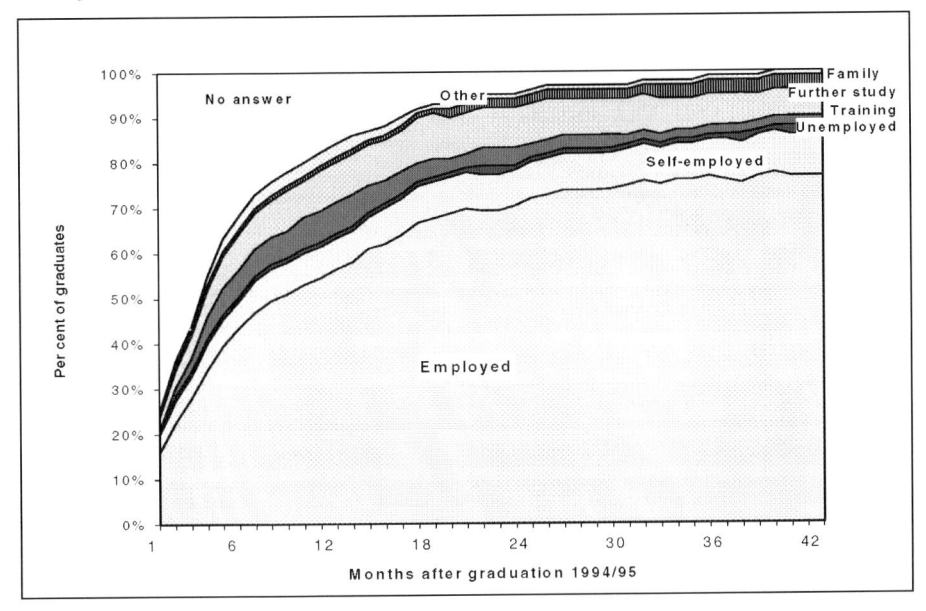

* Not included are graduates who did not provide any information at all.
Source: CHEERS survey data.

Figure 6.8: Activities in the First 42 Months After Graduation – Germany (percentage*)

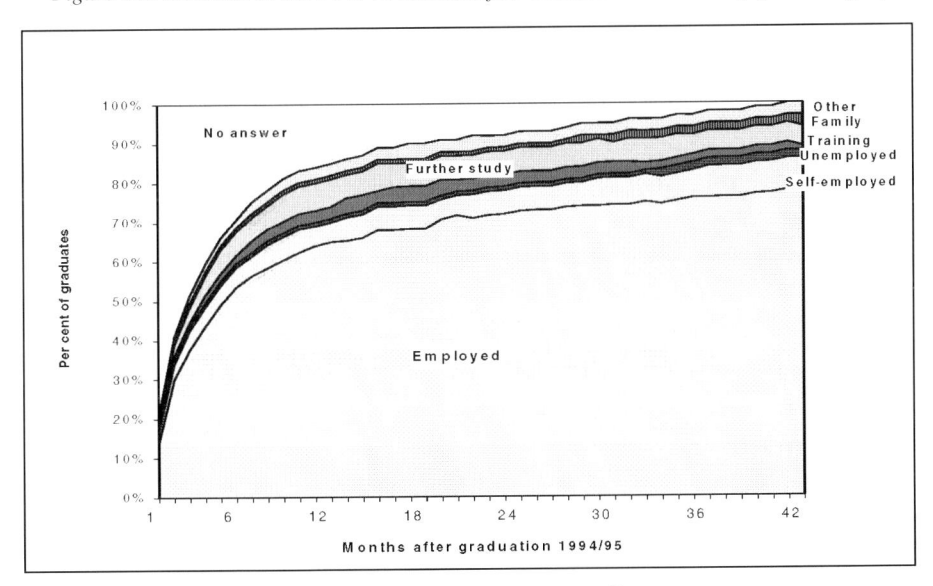

* Not included are graduates who did not provide any information at all.
Source: CHEERS survey data.

Figure 6.9: Activities in the First 42 Months After Graduation – the Netherlands (percentage*)

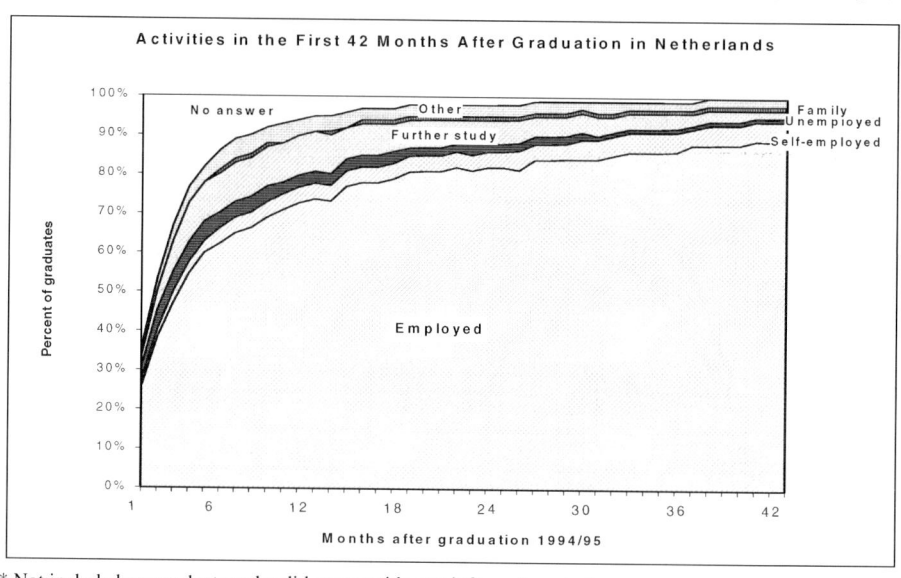

* Not included are graduates who did not provide any information at all.
Source: CHEERS survey data.

Figure 6.10: Activities in the First 42 Months After Graduation – United Kingdom (percentage*)

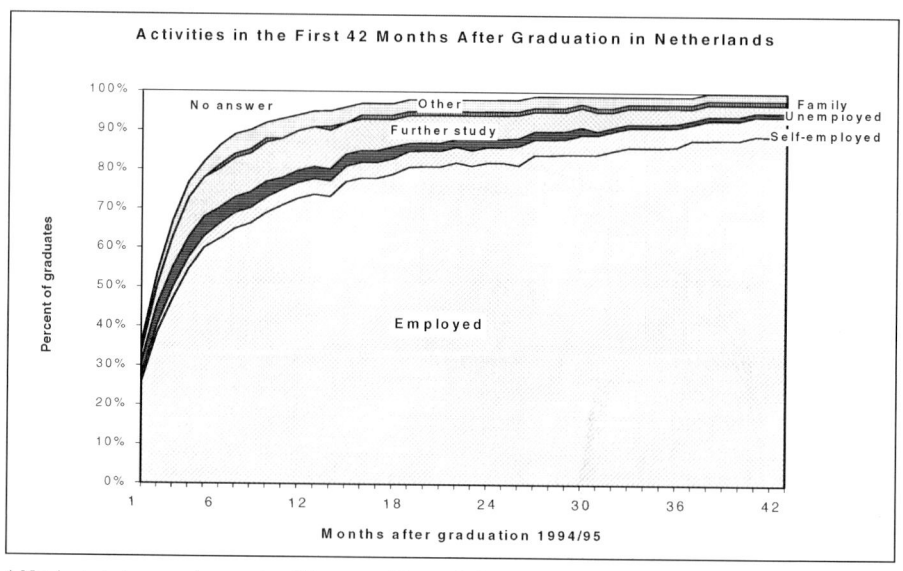

* Not included are graduates who did not provide any information at all.
Source: CHEERS survey data.

Figure 6.11: Activities in the First 42 Months After Graduation – Finland (percentage*)

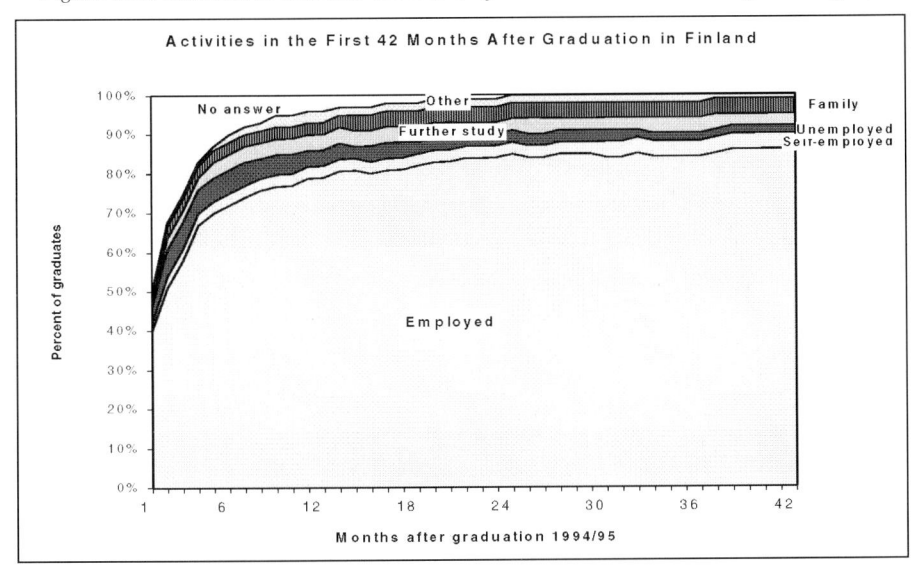

* Not included are graduates who did not provide any information at all.
Source: CHEERS survey data.

Figure 6.12: Activities in the First 42 Months After Graduation – Sweden (percentage*)

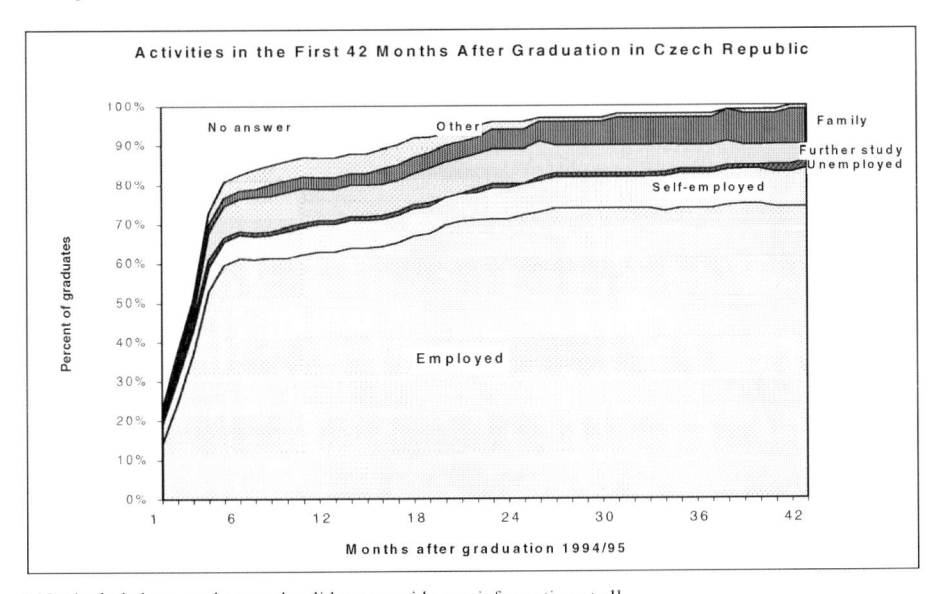

* Not included are graduates who did not provide any information at all.
Source: CHEERS survey data.

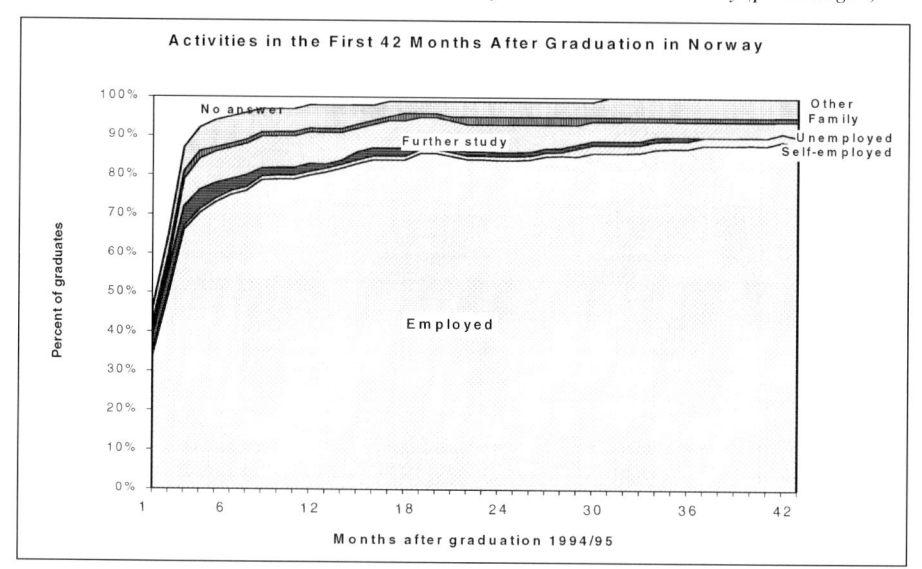

Figure 6.13: Activities in the First 42 Months After Graduation – Norway (percentage*)

[Chart: Activities in the First 42 Months After Graduation in Norway. Categories shown: No answer, Other, Family, Further study, Unemployed, Self-employed, Employed. X-axis: Months after graduation 1994/95 (1 to 42). Y-axis: Percent of graduates (0% to 100%).]

* Not included are graduates who did not provide any information at all.
Source: CHEERS survey data.

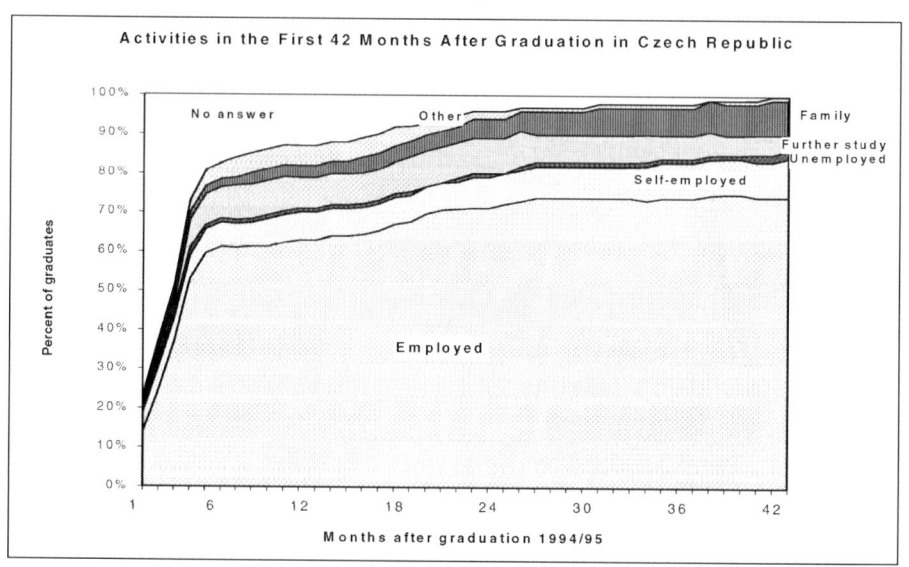

Figure 6.14: Activities in the First 42 Months After Graduation – Czech Republic (percentage*)

[Chart: Activities in the First 42 Months After Graduation in Czech Republic. Categories shown: No answer, Other, Family, Further study, Unemployed, Self-employed, Employed. X-axis: Months after graduation 1994/95 (1 to 42). Y-axis: Percent of graduates (0% to 100%).]

* Not included are graduates who did not provide any information at all.
Source: CHEERS survey data.

Figure 6.15: Activities in the First 42 Months After Graduation – Japan (percentage*)

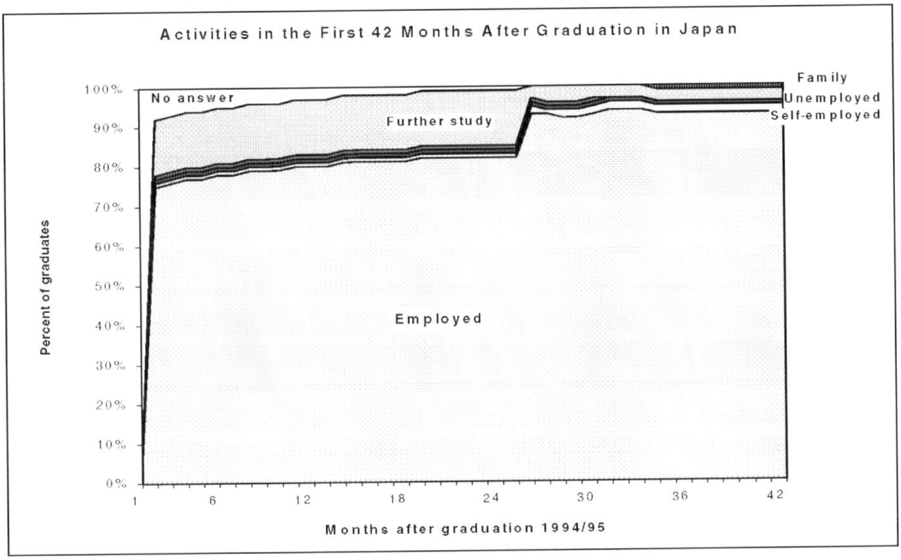

[Figure: Area chart titled "Activities in the First 42 Months After Graduation in Japan". X-axis: Months after graduation 1994/95 (1 to 42). Y-axis: Percent of graduates (0% to 100%). Categories from top: No answer, Family, Unemployed, Self-employed, Further study, Employed.]

* Not included are graduates who did not provide any information at all.
Source: CHEERS survey data.

Field of Study: Figure 6.16 shows the employment quotas during the first 42 months after graduation according to field of study. The curve is relatively low for graduates in natural sciences, where many opt for advanced studies. This also holds true for graduates in humanities who relatively often face employment problems and comprise a large proportion of women, some opting out of the labour market to rear children. Altogether, the curves differ to a lesser extent by field of study than one may have expected on the basis of public debates about the varying demands for graduates in different fields.

Figure 6.16: Employment in the First 42 Months After Graduation, by Field of Study (per

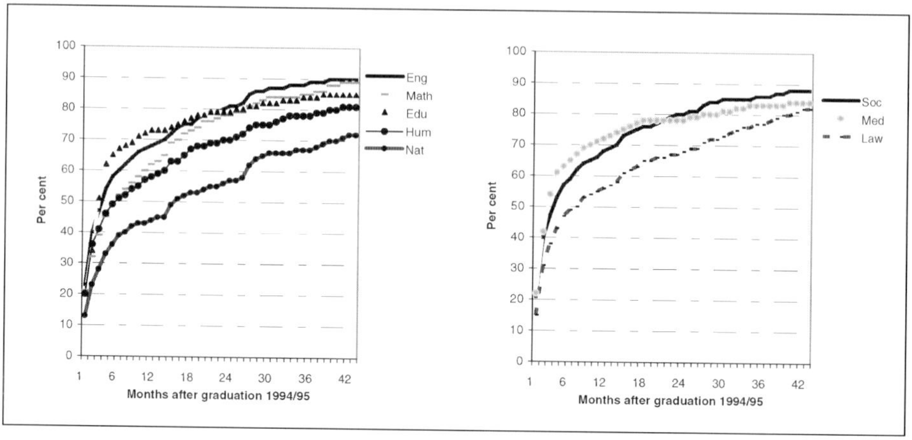

Source: CHEERS survey data.

6.2 Predominant Activities Since Graduation

Graduates were asked to report their predominant activity during the period from graduation until the time the survey was conducted, i.e. three to four years. Altogether, almost one quarter stated more than a single activity as characteristic for the early years after graduation.

Regular employment was the predominant activity for more than two thirds of the graduates (69%) in the 12 countries. These quotas are very high in Finland, Sweden, Norway and the Czech Republic with over 80 per cent of graduates reporting regular employment. The lowest proportion was the graduates from Italy (47%), France (45%) and Spain (44%). Many graduates from these three countries embarked on further study or professional training: Italy (41%), France (60%) and Spain (46%). Altogether,

- 69 per cent quoted regular employment,
- 21 per cent further education and training,
- 11 per cent various temporary jobs,
- 5 per cent more than one single job,
- 4 per cent unemployment,
- 3 per cent child rearing and family care, and
- 8 per cent other activities as predominant activities after graduation.

As Table 6.1 shows, unemployment was predominant for only one or two per cent of the graduates in the majority of countries during the first three to four years after graduation. In Spain, however, the respective quota was 18 per cent, in Italy 9 per cent and in France as well as in Austria 7 per cent. Differences according to field of study were substantially smaller than according to country.

Table 6.1: Predominant Activities Since Graduation in 1994/1995, by Country (per cent; multiple responses)

	Country													Total
	IT	ES	FR	AT	DE	NL	UK	FI	SE	NO	CZ	EUR	JP	
I have spent most of the time on a regular job	47	44	45	73	70	66	75	81	85	83	87	69	78	69
I embarked on further study/professional training	41	46	60	17	12	9	12	9	5	7	17	22	14	21
I had various temporary jobs	20	23	17	18	11	15	8	9	4	2	7	12	3	11
I had more than one job at the same time	13	8	4	7	4	5	2	6	0	3	14	6	1	5
I was mainly unemployed	9	18	7	7	2	2	2	2	1	1	3	5	1	4
I was predominantly engaged in child rearing or family care	6	3	2	4	2	2	2	5	2	1	11	4	1	3
Other	13	20	13	8	11	8	5	1	3	3	8	9	2	8
Total*	150	161	149	134	111	107	106	113	100	100	148	125	100	123

Question C9: How would you characterise and summarise your predominant activities since graduation in 1994 or 1995?

* Count by Country: IT (3056); ES (2992); FR (3033); AT (2274); DE (3451); NL (3054); UK (3386); FI (2606); SE (2576); NO (3291); CZ (3082); EUR (32799); JP (3313); Total (36113).

Source: CHEERS survey data.

6.3 Job Mobility

It should be noted that professional mobility is relatively high during the first years after graduation. Some graduates only obtain short-term contracts initially and quickly have to seek for new ones. Others take an early employment in order to have some income and seek regular suitable employment. Others are not satisfied with their first employment and seek better solutions. Obviously, mobility is more often strived for and implies lesser risk during these early years after graduation than at later career stages. Of all the graduates who were employed for some time during the first four years after graduation

– 42 per cent did not change employers during the first few years after graduation,
– 29 per cent changed employers (including self-employment) once,
– 22 per cent were mobile twice, and
– 6 per cent changed three times or more.

As Table 6.2 indicates, job mobility during the first four years after graduation was most frequent amongst graduates from British, Dutch and Italian higher education institutions. Altogether, however, the differences amongst Western European countries were relatively small. But mobility was exceptional amongst Japanese graduates (27%) and also relatively rare amongst Czech graduates (47%), as compared to over 60 per cent amongst the Western European graduates surveyed.

Table 6.2: Number of Employers After Graduation in 1994/1995 (means and per cent of all employed graduates)

	Country												Total
	IT	ES	FR	AT	DE	NL	UK	FI	SE	NO	CZ	EUR	JP
1 employer	37	39	48	37	43	31	33	39	31	37	53	39	73	42
2 employers	26	29	28	31	32	32	29	32	35	34	29	31	18	29
3-4 employers	26	24	18	26	21	27	27	23	27	25	16	24	8	22
5+ employers	10	8	6	6	4	10	11	6	7	4	2	7	1	6
Total*	100	100	100	100	100	100	100	100	100	100	100	100	100	100
Arithmetic mean	2.5	2.3	2.1	2.3	2.1	2.5	2.6	2.3	2.3	2.2	1.7	2.3	1.4	2.2
Median	2.0	2.0	2.0	2.0	2.0	2.0	2.0	2.0	2.0	2.0	1.0	2.0	1.0	2.0

Question D3: How many employers (including self-employment) did you work for in the period after graduation in 1994 or 1995 (including your present employer)?
* Count by Country: IT (2428); ES (2519); FR (2160); AT (2164); DE (3301); NL (2991); UK (3251); FI (2559); SE (2562); NO (3211); CZ (2948); EUR (30094); JP (3228); Total (33321).
Source: CHEERS survey data.

Differences by field of study were relatively small in this respect. Graduates in the humanities and medical fields were somewhat more frequently mobile than those in other fields of study.

6.4   Transition to a Permanent Job?

The long-term perspective of an employment is often taken as a criterion of the quality of employment. Having a permanent contract can be seen as an indicator of normal employment conditions, whilst temporary contracts can indicate a kind of precarious employment.

As can be seen in Figure 6.17, a gradual increase in permanent employment over the first years after graduation is the dominant pattern in most European countries and in Japan. But there are some exceptions. The process is quite long in Italy and France, whilst in Spain and in Finland permanent employment conditions are relatively rare. In contrast, nearly all graduates were employed on a permanent contract in Japan.

Figure 6.17: Graduates with a Permanent Contract in the First 42 Months After Graduation, by Country (per cent of employed graduates)

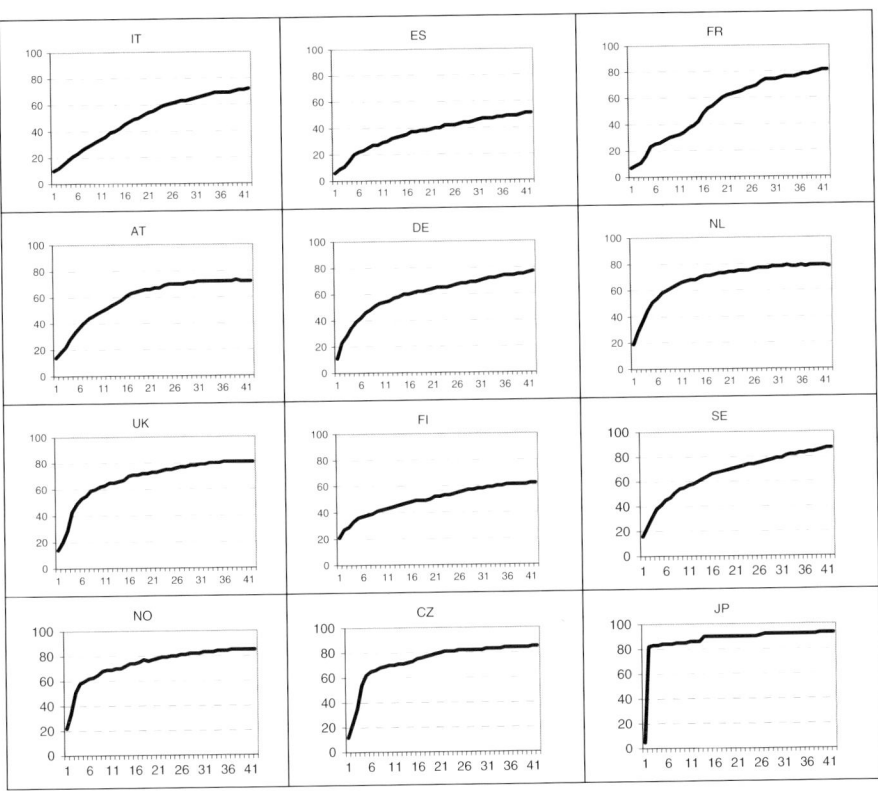

Source: CHEERS survey data.

6.5 Impact of First Job on Subsequent Employment

The available data suggest - although not in every respect - that those who are unemployed or in precarious employment about one year after graduation are also more likely to face labour market problems 3½ years after graduation than those who had a smooth career start. This confirms that the majority of those with a shaky career start do not see this time as an intermission without consequences or as taking time to seek for a good job. Rather, in most cases, late transition to regular employment predicts a less impressive career.

7 EMPLOYMENT SEVERAL YEARS AFTER GRADUATION

7.1 Major Activity

When the survey on higher education and graduate employment was conducted, i. e. three to four years after graduation (we will use "some four years after graduation" in the text),
- 84 per cent of the respondents were professionally active (employed or self-employed),
- 3 per cent were unemployed,
- 7 per cent continued to learn (professional training or advanced academic study), and
- 6 per cent undertook other activities including child rearing and family care (see Table 7.1).

Table 7.1: Kind of Major Activity Some Four Years After Graduation, by Country (per cent)

	Country												Total
	IT	ES	FR	AT	DE	NL	UK	FI	SE	NO	CZ	EUR	JP
Employed	60	65	67	79	79	88	83	89	80	85	76	77	87	78
Self-employed	18	9	2	8	8	5	4	3	3	2	9	6	2	6
Not employed, seeking employment	5	10	7	4	2	2	3	1	1	1	2	3	4	3
Professional training	6	2	6	1	1	0	2	0	2	0	0	2	1	2
Advanced academic studies	8	3	14	2	4	1	5	2	6	5	3	5	4	5
Child rearing, family care	2	0	1	4	3	2	2	3	6	2	9	3	2	3
Other	1	10	3	1	2	3	1	1	1	5	1	3	1	3
Total*	100	100	100	100	100	100	100	100	100	100	100	100	100	100

Question C10: Please inform us about your current major activity.
* Count by Country: IT (3012); ES (2875); FR (3032); AT (2297); DE (3458); NL (3063); UK (3382); FI (2640); SE (2571); NO (3318); CZ (3092); EUR (32740); JP (3411); Total (36151).
Source: CHEERS survey data.

7.2 Unemployment

The highest proportions of unemployment as the major activity some four years after graduation were reported in Spain (10%) and France (7%). In calculating an unemployment rate based on the labour force (i.e. not including those in education and undertaking other activities), we note graduate unemployment rates of 13 per cent in Spain, 10 per cent in France and 6 per cent in Italy (see Figure 7.1). In most of the countries surveyed, however, this rate is not higher than 4 per cent with only 1 to 2 per cent in the Netherlands, Finland, Sweden, Norway and the Czech Republic.

*Figure 7.1: Unemployment of Graduates Some Four Years After Graduation, by Country
(per cent of graduates in the labour market)*

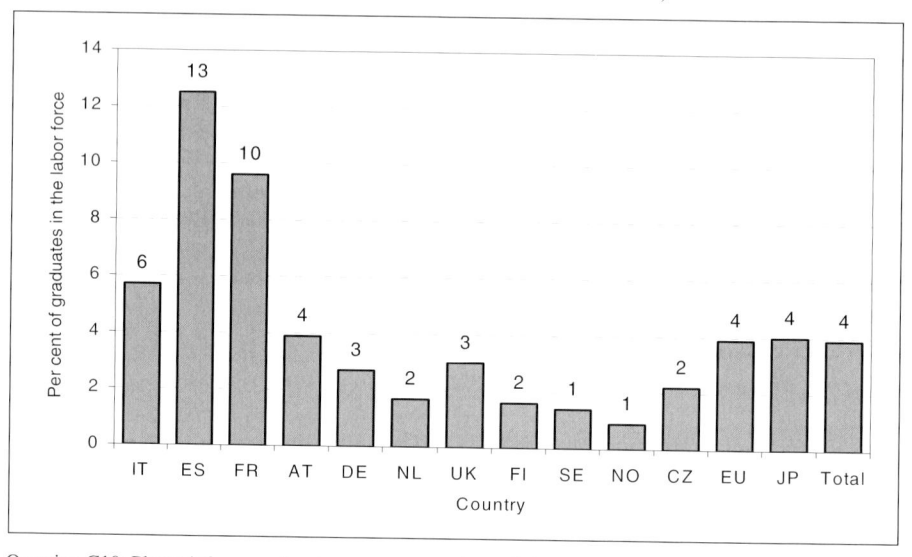

[Bar chart showing per cent of graduates in the labor force by country:
IT: 6, ES: 13, FR: 10, AT: 4, DE: 3, NL: 2, UK: 3, FI: 2, SE: 1, NO: 1, CZ: 2, EU: 4, JP: 4, Total: 4]

Question C10: Please inform us about your current major activity.
Source: CHEERS survey data.

*Figure 7.2: Unemployment of Graduates Some Four Years After Graduation, by Field of Study
(per cent of graduates in the labour market; 12 countries)*

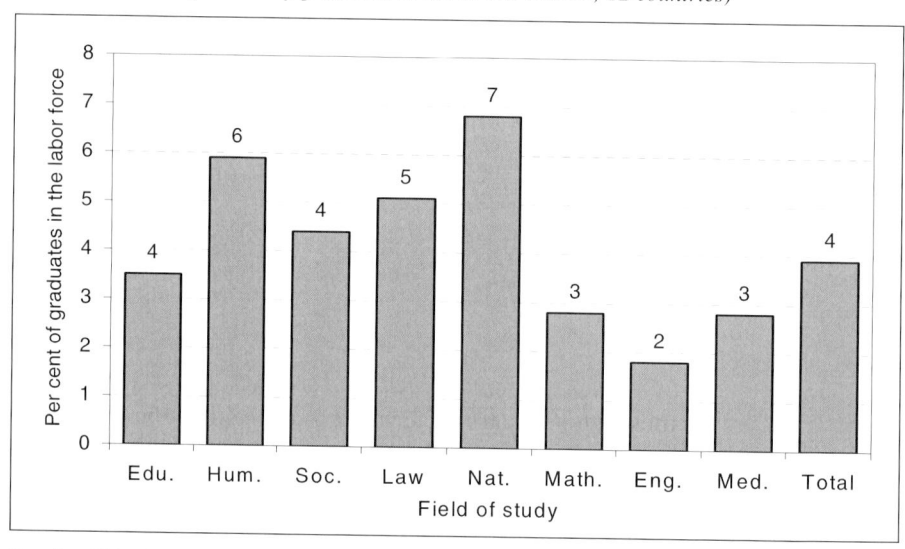

[Bar chart showing per cent of graduates in the labor force by field of study:
Edu.: 4, Hum.: 6, Soc.: 4, Law: 5, Nat.: 7, Math.: 3, Eng.: 2, Med.: 3, Total: 4]

Question C10: Please inform us on your current major activity.
Source: CHEERS survey data.

Educational activities also varied substantially by country: they were most frequent amongst French (20%) and Italian graduates (14%), as Table 7.1 shows.

Educational activities also varied substantially according to field of study. Professional training and advanced academic studies were major activities for:
- 18 per cent of the graduates in natural sciences (mostly in doctoral studies),
- 10 per cent in the humanities,
- 9 per cent each in law (mostly professional training) and medicine, as compared to
- 3-6 per cent of graduates in other fields (see Table 7.2).

Table 7.2: Kind of Major Activity Some Four Years After Graduation, by Field of Study (per cent)

	Field of study								Total
	Educ.	Hum.	Soc.sc	Law	Nat.sc	Math.	Engin.	Med.sc	
Employed	81	69	82	68	67	85	84	76	78
Self-employed	3	9	5	13	4	4	6	6	6
Not employed, seeking employment	3	5	4	4	6	2	2	2	3
Professional training	1	3	1	6	2	1	0	2	2
Advanced academic studies	2	7	3	3	16	5	4	7	5
Child rearing, family care	7	4	3	2	2	1	2	4	3
Other	3	3	2	4	3	2	1	4	3
Total	100	100	100	100	100	100	100	100	100
Count	3553	4598	10488	2743	2312	1404	7048	3383	35529

Question C10: Please inform us on your current major activity.
Source: CHEERS survey data.

7.3 Working Time

Graduates reported that they worked 44 hours per week on average (including paid or unpaid overtime and additional jobs). The working hours differed more strongly by country than by field of study. Japanese (49 hours) and Austrian graduates (47 hours) reported the highest number of hours and French graduates the lowest (40 hours).

Of those employed, 11 per cent worked part-time. As can be seen in Figure 7.3, the proportion of those in part-time jobs was highest in Italy (19%), but it was also above average in Spain, the Netherlands, Germany, Austria and Norway, and below the 5 per cent mark in the Czech Republic, Japan and Finland. Often, the part-time quota is high in countries with problematic labour market conditions, but facilitating part-time employment policies also plays a role (notably in Norway and the Netherlands).

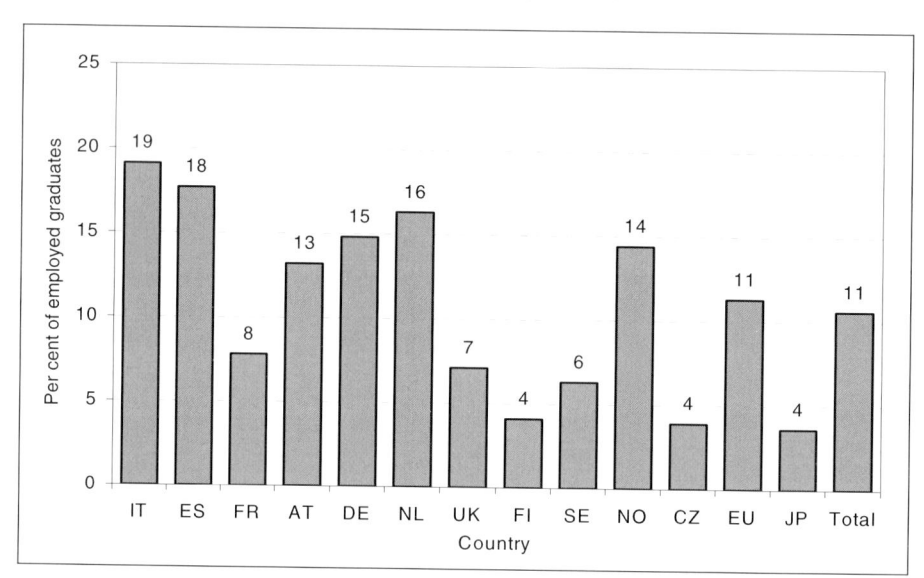

Figure 7.3: Part-time Work of Graduates Some Four Years After Graduation, by Country (per cent of employed graduates)

[Bar chart showing per cent of employed graduates by country:
IT 19, ES 18, FR 8, AT 13, DE 15, NL 16, UK 7, FI 4, SE 6, NO 14, CZ 4, EU 11, JP 4, Total 11]

Question C10: Please inform us on your current major activity. Part-time or full-time.
Source: CHEERS survey data.

Part-time work is most frequent amongst graduates in the humanities, education and medical fields (17-19%), i.e. those with high proportions of women. It is about average (8-12%) in fields with a balanced gender composition (natural sciences, social sciences and law), and it is lowest in engineering and mathematics, i.e. male-dominated fields. Obviously, the differences in part-time employment by field of study are largely due to the much more frequent part-time employment of women (16%) than of men (6%).

7.4 Temporary Contracts

Some four years after graduation, 22 per cent of the employed graduates had a temporary contract. This was most common in Spain (50%) and Finland (35%) and least common in Sweden (13%) and Japan (9%).

Figure 7.4 shows that the proportion of temporary contracts is by far the highest in Spain where it applies to more than half of the active graduates some four years after graduation. This is due to the fact that the temporary contract became the general pattern of employment as a consequence of a reform of employment conditions in the mid-1990s. Temporary contracts were the second most frequent in Finland (35%). In contrast, Japan is the country where temporary contracts represent by far the smallest percentage (9%); they were uncommon at the time the graduates surveyed became employed.

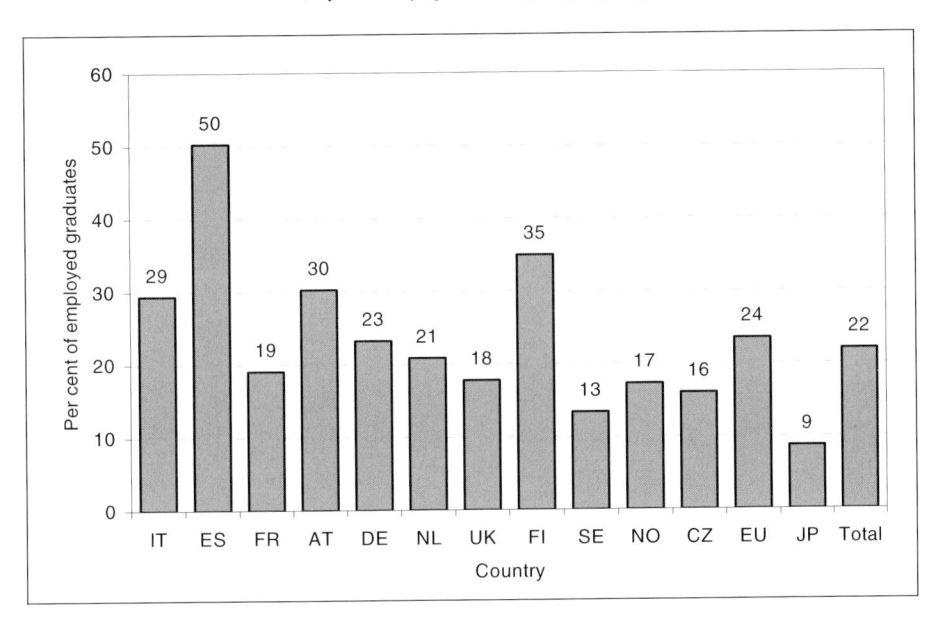

Figure 7.4: Temporary-Contract Employment of Graduates Some Four Years After Graduation, by Country (per cent of employed graduates)

[Bar chart showing per cent of employed graduates with temporary contracts by country: IT 29, ES 50, FR 19, AT 30, DE 23, NL 21, UK 18, FI 35, SE 13, NO 17, CZ 16, EU 24, JP 9, Total 22]

Question C10: Please inform us about your current major activity. Temporary or permanent contract.
Source: CHEERS survey data.

More than 30 per cent of graduates in medical sciences, natural sciences and the humanities have a temporary contract some four years after graduation while, in contrast, those in engineering and mathematics have the lowest proportion (under 16%). The high proportion in the former fields of study is largely a career stage phenomenon: many graduates in natural sciences embark on a regular position with a permanent contract for only a few years after graduation, notably because they intend to return to advanced academic studies and professional training after graduation, and medical doctors have to undergo various years of professional training together with professional practice before they are fully qualified and professionally settled.

7.5   *Economic Sector of Employment*

Some four years after graduation the major economic sectors of the graduates surveyed were
– education (18%),
– mining and manufacturing (15%),
– health (10%) and
– public administration (9%).
About half the graduates were active some four year after graduation in these four economic sectors. Other sectors that absorbed about five or more per cent of

graduates each were trade, financial intermediation, computer and related activities, other business activities and other service activities.

The highest concentration of graduates in the education sector can be found in Finland (35%) and Sweden (23%) and in mining and manufacturing in Japan (20%). Similarly, the highest proportion of those employed in the health sector could be found in Norway (26%) and in public administration in Germany (13%) (see Table 7.3).

Table 7.3: Graduates' Economic Sector Some Four Years After Graduation (per cent of employed graduates)

	Country													Total
	IT	ES	FR	AT	DE	NL	UK	FI	SE	NO	CZ	EUR	JP	
Agriculture, hunting, forestry, fishing	0	0	1	0	1	0	1	0	0	0	3	1	1	1
Mining & manufacturing	18	13	17	13	17	11	12	17	14	11	16	14	20	15
Electricity, gas and water supply	0	1	1	1	1	0	1	1	1	1	2	1	2	1
Construction	1	4	1	2	2	2	3	1	1	2	7	2	5	3
Trade	7	7	9	5	3	6	8	3	5	2	7	6	11	6
Transport, storage and communication	4	4	6	2	3	4	5	6	3	2	4	4	4	4
Financial intermediation	5	9	6	7	5	7	5	3	3	1	7	5	8	5
Computer and related activities	3	4	10	4	6	8	5	2	5	3	5	5	3	5
Research & development	3	2	1	2	3	2	1	4	4	2	2	2	5	3
Legal activities	9	0	3	3	3	1	3	1	1	1	5	3	2	3
Architecture & Engineering consultants	7	0	1	3	4	5	1	1	3	5	1	3	1	3
Other business activities	11	13	6	8	7	12	7	5	7	2	2	7	1	7
Public administration	8	5	8	6	13	7	8	6	9	10	7	8	12	9
Education	11	18	20	19	18	14	18	35	23	14	18	19	10	18
Health	8	14	2	13	8	9	10	8	10	26	7	11	5	10
Social work	2	0	2	3	3	5	1	2	3	15	1	4	1	3
Other service activities	4	5	5	7	4	4	7	6	6	2	8	5	8	6
Other	0	0	0	0	0	0	1	0	0	0	0	0	1	0
Total*	100	100	100	100	100	100	100	100	100	100	100	100	100	100

Question D5: In which economic sector are you currently working? (NACE classification)
* Count by Country: IT (2498); ES (2025); FR (1918); AT (2018); DE (2833); NL (2877); UK (3100); FI (2396); SE (2434); NO (3028); CZ (2575); EUR (27703); JP (2846); Total (30549).
Source: CHEERS survey data.

Graduates in education had the highest proportion of employment in the education sector (68%). In the case of those in the humanities the weight of the education sector was also very high (33%), together with other service activities. There was greater variation with respect to the economic sector amongst the graduates in social sciences. There were five sectors that comprised more than 10 per cent of these graduates: mining and manufacturing, financial intermediation, other business activities, trade and public administration (see Table 7.4).

Graduates in natural sciences tended to work in the education sector (26%), in mining and manufacturing (20%) and in the research and development sector (13%). The largest proportions of law graduates concentrated around legal activities (27%) and public administration (28%). Mathematics graduates were mainly active in the computer and related sector (35%) and, less frequently, in the education sector. Engineers worked most frequently in the mining and manufacturing sector (34%) as architecture and engineering consultants (10%) and in construction (9%). Obviously, medical science graduates worked mostly in the health sector (79%).

Table 7.4: Graduates' Economic Sector Some Four Years After Graduation, by Field of Study (per cent of employed graduates)

	Field of study								Total
	Educ.	Hum.	Soc.sc	Law	Nat.sc	Math.	Engin.	Med.sc	
Agriculture, hunting, forestry, fishing	0	0	0	0	1	0	2	0	1
Mining & manufacturing	2	10	14	5	20	11	34	2	15
Electricity, gas and water supply	0	0	1	1	2	0	3	0	1
Construction	0	1	2	1	1	0	9	0	3
Trade	2	8	10	4	4	4	4	4	6
Transport, storage, and communication	1	4	5	3	3	7	6	0	4
Financial intermediation	1	2	12	10	1	9	1	0	6
Computer and related activities	1	2	4	1	7	35	7	0	5
Research & development	0	1	1	1	12	3	5	1	3
Legal activities	0	1	1	27	1	0	0	0	3
Arch. & eng. consultants	0	1	1	0	3	1	10	0	3
Other business activities	1	7	13	9	4	5	4	0	7
Public administration	3	7	12	28	5	5	5	2	9
Education	69	33	9	5	26	17	6	5	18
Health	2	3	4	2	5	1	2	79	10
Social work	12	1	5	1	1	0	0	4	3
Other service activities	4	18	6	4	4	1	2	1	6
Other	0	1	0	0	0	0	0	0	0
Total	100	100	100	100	100	100	100	100	100
Count	3027	3544	9039	2235	1723	1249	6205	2957	29979

Question D5: In which economic sector are you currently working? (NACE classification).
Source: CHEERS survey data.

7.6 Public or Private Sector

37 per cent of the graduates were employed in the public sector and 6 per cent by non-profit-organisations. Altogether, more than half the graduates in Nordic countries are employed in these sectors, as compared to only about a quarter in Italy and Japan (see Table 7.5).

Table 7.5: Kind of Graduates' Employer/Institution Some Four Years After Graduation, by Country (per cent of employed graduates)

	Country												Total
	IT	ES	FR	AT	DE	NL	UK	FI	SE	NO	CZ	EUR	JP
Public employer	23	30	34	33	37	27	36	55	50	61	30	38	22	37
Non-profit organisation	3	4	6	11	5	20	6	6	2	3	6	7	4	6
Private employer	53	57	55	45	45	42	52	36	44	32	47	46	68	48
Self-employed	16	9	2	9	10	5	4	3	3	3	8	7	3	6
Other	4	1	3	3	3	6	2	0	1	1	9	3	3	3
Total*	100	100	100	100	100	100	100	100	100	100	100	100	100	100

Question D4: Please state your kind of current employer/institution (if several, please refer to main employer)? Please mark one single item only.
* Count by Country: IT (2516); ES (2175); FR (2073); AT (2043); DE (3193); NL (2837); UK (3001); FI (2463); SE (2367); NO (2923); CZ (2643); EUR (28235); JP (2972); Total (31207).
Source: CHEERS survey data.

Not surprisingly, the type of employer varied more strongly according to field of study than according to country, as Table 7.6 shows. Most education and medical graduates were employed in the public sector. In contrast, most graduates in engineering, mathematics and social sciences were active in the private sector.

Table 7.6: Kind of Graduates' Employer/Institution Some Four Years After Graduation, by Field of Study (per cent of employed graduates; 12 countries)

	Field of study								Total
	Educ.	Hum.	Soc.sc	Law	Nat.sc	Math.	Engin.	Med.sc	
Public employer	69	42	29	33	40	26	18	66	36
Non-profit organisation	11	8	8	4	5	3	3	7	6
Private employer	14	38	56	43	48	67	70	17	48
Self-employed	3	8	5	15	4	3	6	7	6
Other	4	3	3	4	4	1	3	3	3
Total	100	100	100	100	100	100	100	100	100
Count	2990	3684	9283	2277	1788	1262	6460	2918	30661

Question D4: Please state your current kind of employer/institution (if several, please refer to main employer)? Please mark one single item only.
Source: CHEERS survey data.

7.7 Self-employment

Six per cent of all the graduates who were surveyed and who were professionally active four years after graduation chose self-employment. Men (7%) had a slightly higher propensity to self-employment than women (5%).

Figure 7.5: Self-Employment of Graduates Some Four Years After Graduation, by Country (per cent of employed graduates)

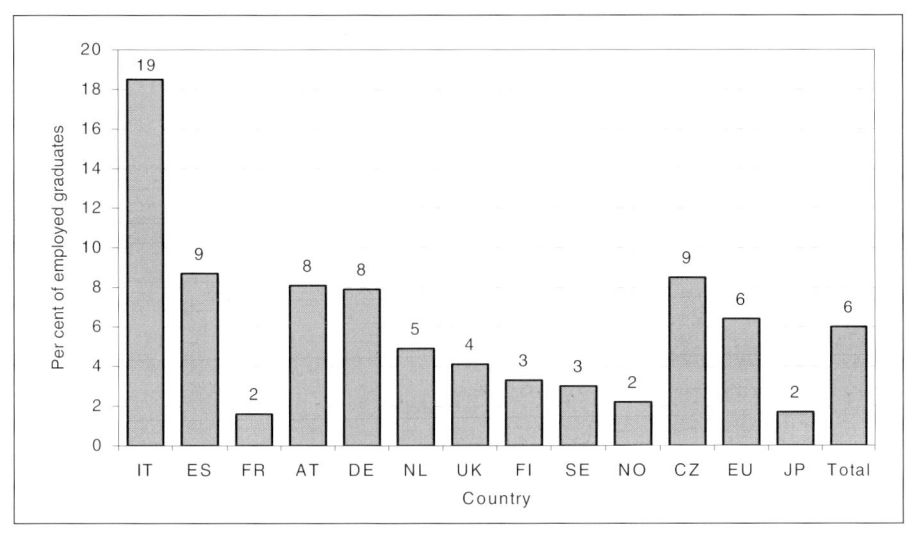

Question C10: Please inform us about your current major activity.
Source: CHEERS survey data.

The most striking differences can be observed by country. As can be seen in Figure 7.5, self-employment was by far the most frequent amongst graduates from Italy (19%) and second most frequent amongst those from Austria (8%). Self-employment was also above average amongst graduates in Spain, Germany and the Czech Republic (8-9%) and below average (ranging from 2-5%) in the remaining countries. The highest proportion was found in countries where graduates faced substantial problems in transiting to employment and embarking on a professional career.

As regards field of study (see Figure 7.6), we note that the proportion of self-employed graduates is highest in law (13%), which reflects the status of independent legal professionals, and above average for those in the humanities (8%). In contrast, relatively low levels of self-employment are observed amongst graduates in education, natural sciences and mathematics (3-4%).

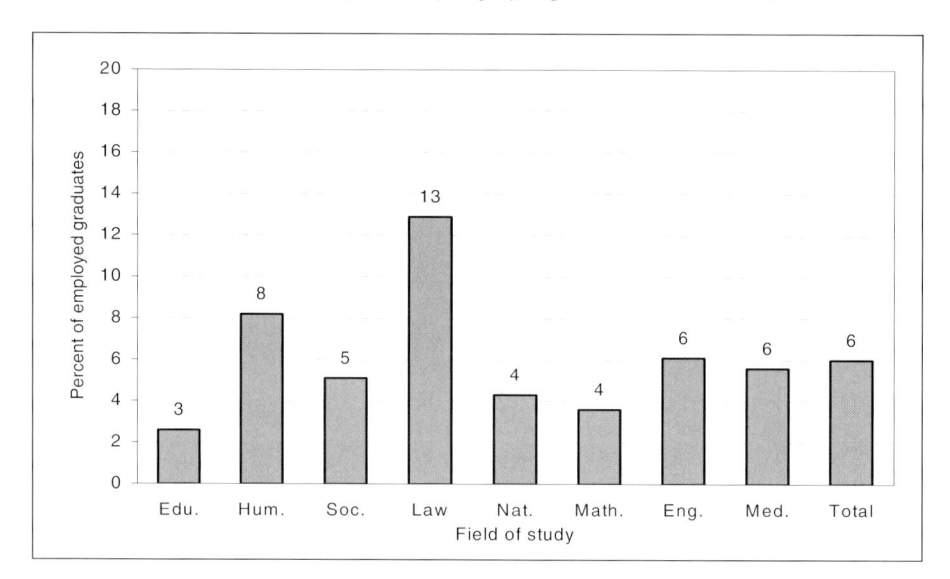

Figure 7.6: Self-Employment of Graduates Some Four Years After Graduation, by Field of Study (per cent of employed graduates; 12 countries)

[Bar chart showing percent of employed graduates by field of study: Edu. 3, Hum. 8, Soc. 5, Law 13, Nat. 4, Math. 4, Eng. 6, Med. 6, Total 6]

Question C10: Please inform us about your current major activity.
Source: CHEERS survey data.

7.8 Job Title

70 per cent of the employed graduates were employed some four years after graduation in the three occupational areas which tend to be seen as typical for graduates from higher education institutions:
– professionals (60%) and
– legislators, senior officers and managers (10%).
A further 18 per cent (see Table 7.7) were employed in middle-level positions, i. e. as technicians and associate professionals. In many of the countries that were surveyed, these positions are viewed as typical for short or applied programme graduates.

The percentage of graduates in the first two categories was higher than 90 per cent in Austria and Finland. In contrast, less than half the graduates from Norwegian and Japanese higher education institutions were employed in the first two categories. Employment in middle-level positions was reported most frequently by Norwegian graduates (40%). This is no doubt due to the fact that Norway went further than other European countries in upgrading former vocational schools to three-year higher education programmes at the time.

Finally, 12 per cent were employed in other occupations (clerks, service workers and manual workers). In most analyses, it is taken for granted that graduates employed in these occupational areas could be seen as a clear indication of a mismatch.

The proportion of those in other occupations (clerks, service workers and manual workers) was above average only in Spain (23%), where many graduates faced employment problems, and in Japan (50%). One should bear in mind, though, that some of the positions of clerks and service workers that were frequently mentioned by Japanese graduates could be similar to those of technicians with respect to status and income. Moreover, these could be entry positions leading to managerial positions.

Table 7.7: Occupations Some Four Years After Graduation, by Country (per cent of employed graduates)

	Country													Total
	IT	ES	FR	AT	DE	NL	UK	FI	SE	NO	CZ	EUR	JP	
Legislators, senior officials and managers	4	10	16	2	5	25	22	7	m	5	8	10	5	10
Professionals	57	63	50	93	78	44	52	86	m	41	74	63	40	60
Technicians and associate professionals	30	4	24	3	12	25	15	5	m	53	16	20	4	18
Clerks	7	17	5	2	4	4	7	1	m	0	1	4	28	7
Service workers and shop and market sales workers	2	5	3	0	1	1	3	0	m	0	1	1	18	3
Skilled agricultural and fishery workers	0	0	0	0	0	0	0	0	m	0	0	0	0	0
Craft and related trades workers	0	0	1	0	0	1	1	0	m	0	0	0	1	0
Plant and machine operators and assemblers	0	1	1	0	0	0	0	0	m	0	0	0	1	0
Elementary occupations	0	1	1	0	0	0	1	0	m	0	0	0	1	0
Total*	100	100	100	100	100	100	100	100	m	100	100	100	100	100

Question C10: Please inform us about your current major activity. Here: Job title according ISCO88 classification.
* Count by Country: IT (2356); ES (1533); FR (2070); AT (2019); DE (2747); NL (2578); UK (2990); FI (2439); SE (2634); NO (3080); CZ (2616); EUR (24428); JP (2797); Total (27226).
m = data missing.
Source: CHEERS survey data.

The proportion of those employed in other occupations (clerks, service workers and manual workers) was higher among graduates in the humanities, social sciences and law than that from the various areas of natural sciences. Again, one should bear in mind that many sales and service occupations taken up by the former graduates in the humanities and social sciences are similar in status and salary as those of technicians which are often taken up by the latter. Therefore, these statistics cannot be interpreted as a clear indication that the former face more frequent employment mismatches than the latter.

7.9 Income

In 1999, full-time working graduates in Western Europe had an annual gross income of about 30,000 euros on average some four years after graduation. The same holds true for Japanese graduates, while Czech graduates earned substantially less. In most

Western European countries, the average income ranged from about 38,000 € in Germany to 25,000 € in France, with Italian (20,000 €) and Spanish graduates (16,000 €) having substantially lower incomes (see Table 7.8). These data do not take into consideration taxes, social security costs and purchasing power.

Table 7.8: Annual Gross Income Some Four Years After Graduation (Thousand euros; means and percent of graduates employed full-time)

Income (1,000 €)	Country													Total
	IT	ES	FR	AT	DE	NL	UK	FI	SE	NO	CZ	EUR	JP	
1 through 5	6	5	4	1	1	1	2	0	5	0	60	7	2	6
6 through 10	14	20	3	1	1	2	2	1	1	0	30	6	1	5
11 through 15	27	31	17	4	3	5	7	2	2	0	6	8	3	8
16 through 20	16	21	21	8	4	16	11	14	8	1	1	10	9	10
21 through 25	18	13	16	16	7	34	18	24	26	8	0	16	18	17
26 through 30	8	5	21	19	13	21	25	22	17	31	1	18	19	18
31 through 35	4	1	8	16	17	10	11	15	18	20	0	12	26	13
36 through 40	2	2	5	13	16	4	8	8	9	17	0	8	10	8
41 through 45	1	1	2	9	13	2	8	5	5	9	0	6	8	6
46 through 50	1	0	1	4	9	1	3	3	4	6	0	3	2	3
51 through 60	1	0	1	6	10	2	3	2	2	4	0	3	1	3
61 and more	2	0	1	3	6	2	4	2	2	3	1	3	1	2
Total	100	100	100	100	100	100	100	100	100	100	100	100	100	100
Count	1692	1448	1916	1669	2616	2359	2757	2279	2146	2618	1986	23486	2810	26296
Arithmetic mean	20.5	16.3	24.7	33.3	38.3	28.4	30.6	30.7	29.9	35.4	6.0	28.0	30.2	28.2
Male	21.8	18.4	26.9	35.5	40.9	30.8	34.2	34.4	35.1	40.1	6.8	30.7	31.8	30.8
Female	18.7	13.7	22.0	29.6	33.1	25.0	27.7	27.3	25.0	31.2	4.8	24.8	26.1	24.9

Question D11: What is your approximate annual gross income? (Thousand €).
Source: CHEERS survey data.

As already shown above, women are more often unemployed than men, and have more temporary contracts, more part-time jobs and earn less than men. The average annual gross income of full-time working women is as an average of the 12 countries only 81 per cent that of men's. Even if we take into consideration men and women's different choice of field of study, an income difference of about 10 per cent can be observed.

8 COMPETENCES AND WORK ASSIGNMENTS

8.1 Recruitment Criteria

Graduates were already indirectly confronted with their prospective future assignments in their job search. Therefore, they were asked to state the aspects their employers took most into consideration when recruiting them (for their first employment). One must bear in mind, however, that recruitment criteria are by no means a perfect mirror of the competences that are expected of graduates, since they may reflect, for example, scarcity or abundance of competences on the labour market, decisions to screen on the basis of a few criteria while taking others for granted, views about the opportunities and difficulties in identifying competences in the recruitment processes, and finally views about the continuity or discontinuity of these competences in education and subsequent employment or about the opportunities and limitations of acquiring them on the job.

Altogether, we note that:
- field of study (and sometimes areas of specialisation within that field) and
- personality

were mentioned most frequently by the graduates as aspects which were decisive for their employers to recruit them. In addition,
- practical experience during the course of study (sometimes in addition practical experiences prior to study),
- computer skills and
- recommendations from third persons

were mentioned as important aspects by about one third of the graduates or more. According to them, the following aspects played a lesser role:
- examination results and grades,
- the reputation of the higher education institution,
- foreign language proficiency and
- experience abroad.

It is obvious that most employers seem to put emphasis on the area of expertise in the field of study, on the level or quality of this expertise, on the graduates' personality and sometimes on some other areas of knowledge and competences which are not necessarily developed in the course of study.

Among European countries, the United Kingdom is known for laying a strong emphasis on breadth of knowledge and less emphasis on specialisation. This leads to a less clear articulation – or greater flexibility – concerning the link between field of study and occupational area. British graduates believe that their employers take the field of study into consideration less frequently than graduates from other European countries. Table 8.1 also shows that Japanese employers are even less concerned with the field of study and the area of specialisation.

Table 8.1: Importance of Recruitment Criteria According to the Graduates' Perception, by Country (per cent of graduates seeking for a job perceiving it as 'very important' and 'important'*)

	\multicolumn{12}{c}{Country**}	Total
	IT	ES	FR	AT	DE	NL	UK	FI	SE	NO	CZ	EUR	JP
Personality	58	61	74	80	78	84	81	75	81	m	57	73	80	74
Field of study	70	68	69	77	77	68	54	85	78	m	78	72	37	68
Main subject/specialisation	38	62	66	46	51	36	45	73	57	m	28	49	32	47
Practical/work experience acquired during the course of study	21	20	52	49	55	50	41	54	29	m	31	40	16	38
Computer skills	35	42	40	47	44	36	40	37	19	m	57	40	17	37
Recommendations/references from third persons	21	29	26	29	27	28	45	32	49	m	29	32	27	32
Exam results	37	25	8	17	42	11	39	34	24	m	25	28	28	28
Foreign language proficiency	25	26	27	31	24	20	9	40	23	m	42	26	13	24
Reputation of the higher education institution	19	16	19	17	16	15	23	24	23	m	26	20	41	22
Practical/work experience acquired prior to the course of study	10	29	18	16	29	17	30	22	23	m	15	22	5	20
Experience abroad	11	11	21	16	13	13	10	17	17	m	15	14	8	13

Question C8: How important, in your eyes, were the following aspects for your employer in recruiting you for your first employment after graduation, if applicable?
* 1 and 2 on a scale of answers from 1 = 'Very important' to 5 = 'Not at all important'.
m = data missing
** Count by Country: IT (1991); ES (2036); FR (1195); AT (1724); DE (2718); NL (2569); UK (2938); FI (2059); SE (2146); NO (m); CZ (2307); EUR (21683); JP (2503); Total (24186).
Source: CHEERS survey data.

One could have expected that exam results and grades would play a major role in countries where the higher education institutions are seen as similar in quality, but that the reputation of the higher education institution would be more important in countries where there is a strong hierarchy of reputation amongst the higher education institutions. These assumptions are confirmed by the important role attributed to the reputation of the higher education institutions in Japan and by the strong emphasis on exam results and grades on the part of German employers. Yet the findings only match these assumptions to a limited degree. For example, the reputation of the higher education institution is not more frequently mentioned as a criterion for recruitment in the United Kingdom and France than elsewhere.

Supplementary skills and experiences seem to be more strongly emphasized by Northern European employers than by Southern European employers. The most striking finding is again that Japanese employers seem to harbour low expectations in those respects, although reports on graduate employment in Japan tend to suggest that employers favour complex recruitment procedures in order to identify those types of competences. Obviously, they trust the subsequent learning and socialisation processes in the course of the career.

Table 8.2: Importance of Recruitment Criteria According to the Graduates' Perception, by Country (per cent of graduates seeking for a job perceiving it as 'very important' and 'important'*; 11 countries)

	Field of study								Total
	Educ.	Hum.	Soc.sc	Law	Nat.sc	Math.	Engin.	Med.sc	
Personality	71	75	80	72	67	73	71	66	74
Field of study	80	52	61	68	66	78	76	86	68
Main subject/specialisation	53	40	43	35	50	62	52	51	47
Practical/work experience acquired during course of study	37	34	40	27	39	39	38	43	38
Computer skills	19	30	41	24	38	79	51	11	37
Recommendations/references from third persons	33	35	31	28	33	28	31	35	32
Exam results	25	32	25	31	32	32	29	23	28
Foreign language proficiency	17	33	28	18	22	21	27	12	25
Practical/work experience acquired prior to course of study	24	20	22	13	14	15	19	18	20
Reputation of the higher education institution	17	19	21	23	21	19	29	22	22
Experience abroad	9	18	16	11	11	8	13	8	13
Count	2416	2982	7537	1622	1254	995	4844	2036	23687

Question C8: How important, in your eyes, were the following aspects for your employer in recruiting you for your first employment after graduation, if applicable?
* 1 and 2 on a scale of answers from 1 = 'Very important' to 5 = 'Not at all important'.
Source: CHEERS survey data.

Aspects taken into consideration by employers in recruitment decisions are one of the few areas addressed in this questionnaire where differences according to field of study outweigh those according to country. As can be seen in Table 8.2,
- the field of study tends to play a stronger role in fields that lead to certain professions than in more open fields and in natural science fields than in the humanities and social sciences.
- But experience abroad is a more frequent criterion for graduates in the humanities and social sciences.
- Foreign languages play a lesser role for positions in education, law and medicine – i.e. fields leading to nationally oriented professions – than in other fields.
- Computer skill requirements dominate in the case of mathematics and engineering graduates.

In contrast, aspects such as exam results, reputation of the higher education institution and practical experiences before or during the course of study are more strongly determined by national cultures than by professional or disciplinary cultures.

8.2 Competences at Time of Graduation

A study on the relationships between higher education and subsequent employment obviously focuses on the knowledge graduates have acquired in the course of study and the extent to which this matches the job requirements. In the framework of a graduate survey, one has to rely on the graduates' self-ratings. Graduates were therefore asked to state in respect to a list of 36 competences the extent to which these were required in their current work as well as the extent to which they had acquired these competences at the time of graduation.

Altogether, many graduates, in retrospect, considered themselves well qualified in many areas at the time of graduation. This did not only hold true for academic knowledge. As can be seen in Table 8.3, more than two-thirds of the graduates considered themselves well equipped as far as power of concentration, working independently, and loyalty and integrity were concerned. More than half of the graduates considered their competences as high in 21 of the 36 domains addressed.

Table 8.3: Perceived Competences at the Time of Graduation, by Country (per cent of all graduates responding 'to a very high' or 'high extent'*)

	Country												Total
	IT	ES	FR	AT	DE	NL	UK	FI	SE	NO	CZ	EUR	JP
Learning abilities	82	79	70	88	82	81	83	86	90	87	81	83	55	80
Power of concentration	73	69	71	80	75	70	67	74	79	68	67	72	62	71
Working independently	57	50	74	77	76	77	77	83	83	78	61	72	31	68
Loyalty, integrity	89	85	81	62	54	72	60	45	65	61	69	68	70	68
Field-specific theoretical knowledge	60	59	60	78	73	69	63	68	78	76	60	67	53	66
Written communication skills	60	65	59	72	69	65	75	71	76	72	0	68	35	65
Getting personally involved	71	71	62	69	61	69	52	68	73	63	59	65	59	64
Adaptability	56	68	66	57	50	70	64	67	81	67	57	64	59	63
Critical thinking	71	65	61	70	62	66	62	64	74	61	51	64	43	62
Tolerance	60	69	60	61	57	64	64	62	72	64	59	63	48	61
Working in a team	53	57	54	50	50	69	68	60	86	73	53	61	46	60
Broad general knowledge	63	59	47	66	54	62	63	60	72	66	54	60	44	59
Accuracy, attention to detail	57	53	58	64	59	64	67	59	73	69	48	61	34	58
Analytical competences	58	56	52	67	62	57	63	65	74	57	41	59	43	57
Fitness for work	50	48	66	59	53	51	49	68	75	58	70	58	51	57
Problem-solving ability	47	51	52	58	59	64	65	59	75	64	41	58	39	56
Oral communication skills	63	52	41	66	56	54	67	57	66	62	48	57	43	56
Working under pressure	51	37	48	59	56	56	67	54	68	62	46	55	36	53
Initiative	49	48	46	48	44	57	64	56	69	57	43	53	49	53
Reflective thinking	57	57	57	55	48	47	63	48	56	66	42	54	31	52
Assertiveness, decisiveness, persistence	66	61	37	56	48	59	44	58	51	47	42	51	45	51

to be continued

Table 8.3 Continued

	IT	ES	FR	AT	DE	NL	UK	FI	SE	NO	CZ	EUR	JP	Total
						Country								
Taking responsibilities, decisions	51	53	38	46	39	61	49	47	62	51	39	48	29	47
Creativity	50	48	34	42	42	54	54	49	62	45	43	47	29	46
Cross-disciplinary thinking/ knowledge	44	45	40	60	54	29	56	47	53	52	33	46	31	45
Documenting ideas and information	39	46	61	42	39	38	61	41	59	47	22	45	33	44
Time management	50	54	45	44	38	49	55	43	32	44	36	45	33	44
Planning, co-ordinating, organising	31	33	35	41	39	37	51	38	54	46	18	39	18	37
Manual skills	32	35	28	29	32	35	27	39	58	47	41	36	37	36
Applying rules and regulations	24	30	40	42	36	32	37	35	37	37	15	33	29	33
Foreign language proficiency	28	22	29	42	29	39	14	54	50	28	28	32	22	31
Computer skills	20	21	24	36	32	39	41	37	29	33	30	31	29	31
Leadership	35	31	21	21	15	29	38	23	42	30	26	28	28	28
Economic reasoning	23	32	25	35	28	29	25	28	41	24	23	28	20	27
Understanding complex social, organisational and technical systems	12	16	15	33	32	25	28	17	32	24	35	24	18	24
Negotiating	26	22	19	16	11	24	26	31	19	19	23	21	18	21

Question E1: Please, state if you had the following competences at the time of graduation in 1994 or 1995 and if they are required in your current work. If you are not employed please answer only (A).

* 1 and 2 on a scale of answers from 1 = 'To a very high extent' to 5 = 'Not at all".

Source: CHEERS survey data.

8.3 Work Requirements

Table 8.4 indicates that graduates, as a rule, considered the job requirements as more demanding than the competences they had acquired before graduation. Most perceived high job requirements in 33 of the 36 domains addressed.

A comparison of the perceived individual job requirements and acquired competences suggests that graduates considered themselves fully qualified or even overqualified in only five of the 36 domains addressed. This holds true for
- field-specific theoretical knowledge,
- broad general knowledge,
- foreign language proficiency,
- learning abilities and
- manual skills.

Table 8.4: Perceived Work Requirements Some Four Years After Graduation, by Country (per cent of all graduates responding 'to a very high' or 'high extent'*)

	\multicolumn{12}{c	}{Country}	Total
	IT	ES	FR	AT	DE	NL	UK	FI	SE	NO	CZ	EUR	JP	
Problem-solving ability	82	80	80	88	88	89	80	90	89	90	85	86	87	86
Working independently	75	45	83	92	94	92	86	92	93	91	91	86	67	84
Oral communication skills	81	77	81	84	84	78	91	89	91	91	81	84	83	84
Working under pressure	81	69	73	84	84	86	91	90	92	88	72	83	81	83
Working in a team	74	74	78	74	73	86	89	82	93	92	76	81	81	81
Taking responsibilities, decisions	80	79	75	82	83	85	85	83	89	85	78	82	66	81
Adaptability	76	79	88	69	65	83	87	83	85	81	76	79	83	80
Accuracy, attention to detail	76	69	67	81	81	86	89	78	85	82	70	79	83	79
Time management	79	74	80	80	81	85	89	86	61	83	71	79	80	79
Initiative	72	69	79	75	74	87	87	83	89	81	73	79	80	79
Assertiveness, decisiveness, persistence	80	72	74	83	82	87	83	75	77	83	75	80	71	79
Planning, co-ordinating, organising	72	68	77	79	83	79	85	82	88	84	58	78	67	77
Power of concentration	74	62	70	80	80	74	78	85	82	76	74	76	80	77
Getting personally involved	75	76	75	84	81	80	68	81	67	77	73	76	66	75
Loyalty, integrity	77	78	76	78	75	80	74	68	63	78	80	75	75	75
Written communication skills	66	63	68	76	76	74	81	80	86	83	0	76	68	75
Learning abilities	75	73	67	75	71	66	75	84	84	85	61	74	76	74
Tolerance	75	72	72	65	64	73	78	77	75	79	73	73	75	73
Reflective thinking	77	70	78	67	67	67	75	77	63	86	66	72	65	72
Analytical competences	73	71	64	74	69	72	67	77	82	64	66	71	77	71
Fitness for work	55	60	71	88	87	33	70	63	90	83	67	70	86	71
Critical thinking	72	59	62	63	64	81	68	74	82	76	62	70	60	69
Documenting ideas and information	72	61	73	68	66	64	76	70	80	69	40	67	77	68
Computer skills	55	55	60	68	66	64	72	71	73	60	71	65	77	66
Creativity	55	49	45	57	59	72	57	71	80	72	65	62	60	62
Negotiating	62	53	55	58	56	63	64	77	58	52	69	61	69	62
Field-specific theoretical knowledge	60	66	60	57	59	63	62	57	63	71	56	61	60	61
Broad general knowledge	54	43	42	51	48	63	61	69	67	78	50	58	77	60
Field-specific knowledge of methods	62	65	61	54	62	62	58	70	62	65	49	61	52	60
Applying rules and regulations	58	56	58	58	61	50	70	57	49	66	45	58	71	59
Cross-disciplinary thinking/ knowledge	59	55	53	70	70	44	66	60	58	75	41	60	43	58
Leadership	57	44	44	55	56	54	67	53	69	61	61	57	56	57
Economic reasoning	60	55	51	65	64	49	44	66	55	40	56	55	72	56

to be continued

Table 8.4 continued

	Country											Total	
	IT	ES	FR	AT	DE	NL	UK	FI	SE	NO	CZ	EUR	JP
Understanding complex social, organisational and technical systems	33	32	36	58	58	44	44	52	57	42	62	48	53	48
Manual skills	30	26	18	24	31	26	32	31	54	67	42	35	47	36
Foreign language proficiency	38	28	27	39	33	35	10	54	47	27	43	34	32	34

Question E1: Please, state if you had the following competences at the time of graduation in 1994 or 1995 and if they are required in your current work. If you are not employed please answer only (A).
* 1 and 2 on a scale of answers from 1 = 'To a very high extent' to 5 = 'Not at all'.
Source: CHEERS survey data.

But they seem to feel deficiencies in most areas. The strongest ones stated were:
− negotiating,
− planning, co-ordinating and organising,
− computer skills,
− time management,
− taking over responsibility, decision-making,
− working under pressure,
− leadership and
− applying rules and regulations.

Figure 8.1 illustrates the differences between the rating of the job requirements and self-rated competences. Figure 8.2 shows the proportions of students who noted a deficit, i. e. rated the job requirements higher than their competences. Similarly, Figure 8.2 shows the proportion of graduates who did not perceive a difference between the job requirements and their competences as well as those who perceived an excess of competences.

It is obvious that graduates on average feel better prepared for their job than the job actually requires in the cognitive domains curricula tend to put emphasis on. In contrast, they often note deficiencies concerning the transfer of knowledge to job tasks. The same holds true for socio-communicative skills, as well as for values and orientations that are relevant for the world of work.

One should bear in mind, though, that the graduates were asked about job requirements and competences acquired at different time points. It may well be that they are expected to acquire many competences during the first few years on the job. In comparing the findings by country, we note that Japanese graduates felt least prepared for the job requirements at the time of graduation because Japanese employers tend to consider graduates as "raw material" and put a strong emphasis on the acquisition of knowledge during off-the-job training and notably during on-the-job training in the initial years of employment.

Figure 8.1: Graduates' Job Requirements and Competences at the Time of Graduation (per cent of all graduates responding 'to a very high' or 'high extent'*)

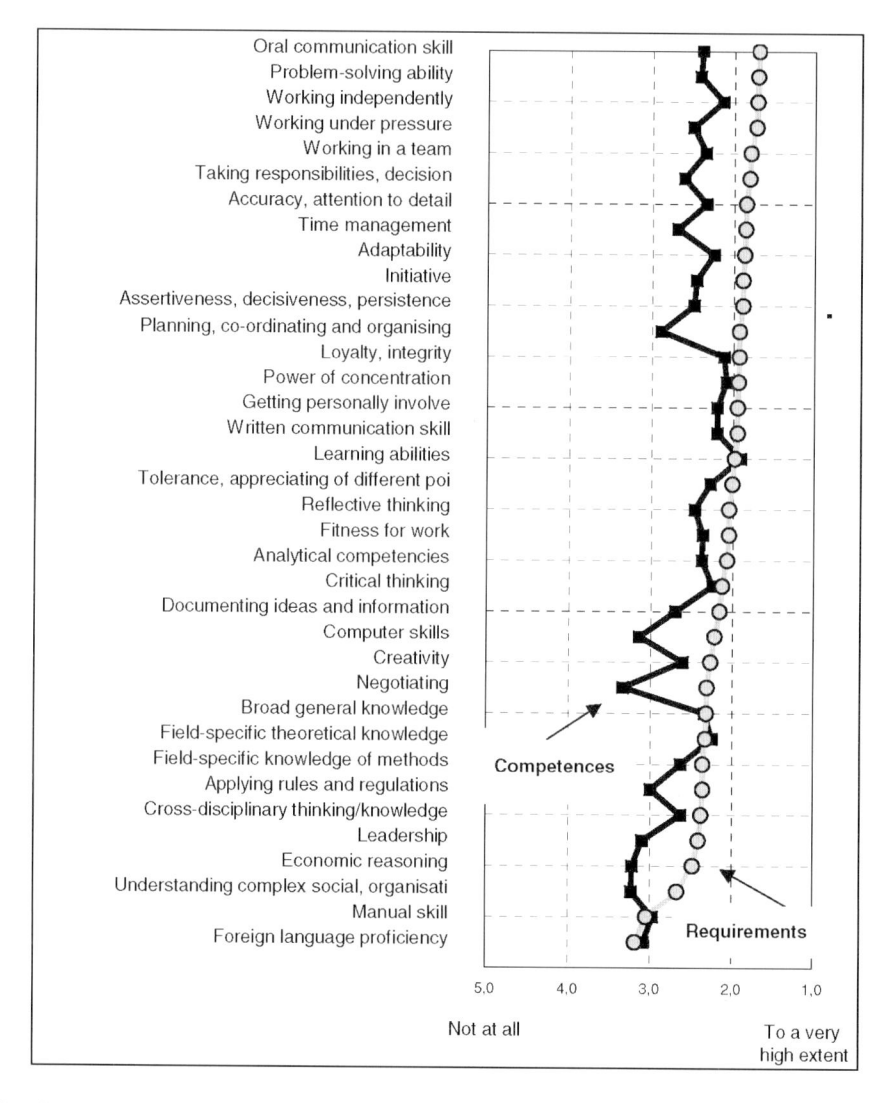

Competence	
Oral communication skill	
Problem-solving ability	
Working independently	
Working under pressure	
Working in a team	
Taking responsibilities, decision	
Accuracy, attention to detail	
Time management	
Adaptability	
Initiative	
Assertiveness, decisiveness, persistence	
Planning, co-ordinating and organising	
Loyalty, integrity	
Power of concentration	
Getting personally involve	
Written communication skill	
Learning abilities	
Tolerance, appreciating of different poi	
Reflective thinking	
Fitness for work	
Analytical competencies	
Critical thinking	
Documenting ideas and information	
Computer skills	
Creativity	
Negotiating	
Broad general knowledge	
Field-specific theoretical knowledge	
Field-specific knowledge of methods	
Applying rules and regulations	
Cross-disciplinary thinking/knowledge	
Leadership	
Economic reasoning	
Understanding complex social, organisati	
Manual skill	
Foreign language proficiency	

Scale: 5,0 (Not at all) — 1,0 (To a very high extent)

Question E1: Please, state if you had the following competences at the time of graduation in 1994 or 1995 and if they are required in your current work.
* 1 and 2 on a scale of answers from 1 = 'To a very high extent' to 5 = 'Not at all'.
Source: CHEERS survey data.

8 COMPETENCES AND WORK ASSIGNMENTS 101

Figure 8.2: Differences Between Perceived Work Requirements and Competences Acquired During Study (per cent of graduates)

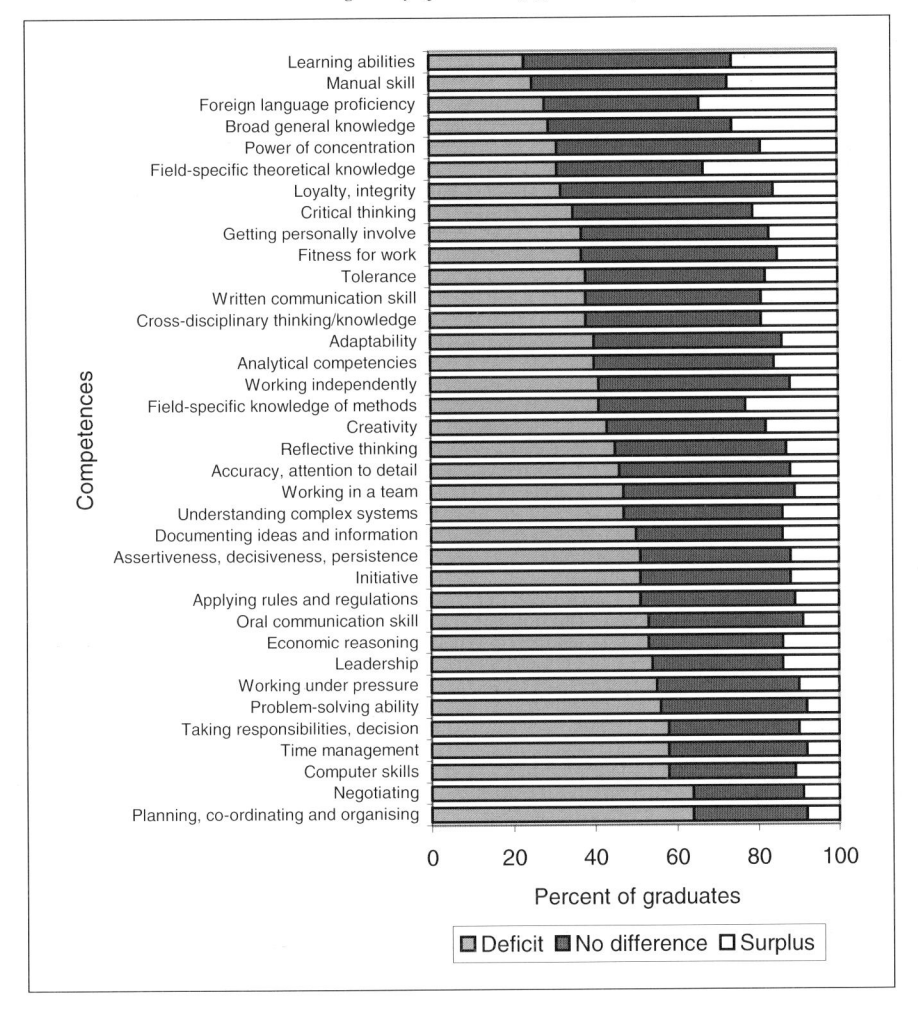

[Bar chart showing Competences (y-axis) vs. Percent of graduates (x-axis, 0-100), with three categories: Deficit, No difference, Surplus. Competences listed from top to bottom:]

- Learning abilities
- Manual skill
- Foreign language proficiency
- Broad general knowledge
- Power of concentration
- Field-specific theoretical knowledge
- Loyalty, integrity
- Critical thinking
- Getting personally involve
- Fitness for work
- Tolerance
- Written communication skill
- Cross-disciplinary thinking/knowledge
- Adaptability
- Analytical competencies
- Working independently
- Field-specific knowledge of methods
- Creativity
- Reflective thinking
- Accuracy, attention to detail
- Working in a team
- Understanding complex systems
- Documenting ideas and information
- Assertiveness, decisiveness, persistence
- Initiative
- Applying rules and regulations
- Oral communication skill
- Economic reasoning
- Leadership
- Working under pressure
- Problem-solving ability
- Taking responsibilities, decision
- Time management
- Computer skills
- Negotiating
- Planning, co-ordinating and organising

Legend: ☐ Deficit ■ No difference ☐ Surplus

Question E1: Please, state if you had the following competences at the time of graduation in 1994 or 1995 and if they are required in your current work. Scale of answers from 1 = 'To a very high extent' to 5 = 'Not at all'.

Source: CHEERS survey data.

8.4 Utility of Studies

Graduates were also asked to assess the usefulness of their studies in preparing them for their current work tasks. 61 per cent of the European graduates (the Japanese graduates were not asked this question) stated that their studies were a very good preparation (1 or 2 on a scale from 1 = "to a very high extent" to 5 = "not as all"). This was most frequent with graduates of higher education institutions in the Nordic countries and in the Czech Republic (three quarters or more). In contrast, slightly less than half the French, German, Italian and British graduates considered their studies prepared them well for their present work tasks (see Table 8.5).

Table 8.5: Utility of Studies for Work Tasks and Other Spheres of Life, by Country (per cent of all graduates responding 'to a very high' or 'high extent'*)

Useful for ...	Country**												Total	
	IT	ES	FR	AT	DE	NL	UK	FI	SE	NO	CZ	EUR	JP	
preparing your present work tasks	46	55	41	54	43	68	49	75	76	79	82	61	m	61
preparing tasks in other spheres of life	35	48	32	32	23	61	42	55	56	53	50	44	m	44

Question E2: How far have your studies (you graduated in 1994 or 1995) been useful for ...?
* 1 and 2 on a scale of answers from 1 = 'To a very high extent' to 5 = 'Not at all'.
m = data missing
** Count by Country: IT (2722); ES (2229); FR (2468); AT (2246); DE (3329); NL (2957); UK (3254); FI (2601); SE (2573); NO (3176); CZ (2909); EUR (30463); JP (m); Total (30463).
Source: CHEERS survey data.

In respect to other spheres of life, 44 per cent of the graduates considered their studies useful. This was most often the case with Dutch graduates (61%) and least often with German graduates (23%).

As regards fields of study, we note that those which prepare for specific professions are considered somewhat more useful than those that prepare for different occupational areas. Yet, mathematics and natural sciences are seen as less useful by their graduates than by graduates from other disciplines in preparing for tasks in other spheres of life. However, these differences are substantially smaller than those by country.

8.5 International Competences

Finally, graduates were asked to assess the importance of those competences for their current work which may have a growing influence on the processes of internationalisation and globalisation.

Table 8.6: Importance of International Competences for Graduates' Work Some Four Years After Graduation, by Country (per cent of all graduates responding 'very important' or 'important'*)

	Country**													Total
	IT	ES	FR	AT	DE	NL	UK	FI	SE	NO	CZ	EUR	JP	
Professional knowledge of other countries***	26	23	24	30	17	23	19	39	26	12	32	24	34	25
Knowledge/understanding of international differences in culture and society, modes of behaviour, life styles, etc.	29	30	42	33	26	43	32	54	53	35	30	37	40	37
Working with people from different cultural backgrounds	47	38	54	35	31	56	54	57	57	50	46	48	29	46
Communicating in foreign languages	47	40	33	41	32	42	11	65	52	34	53	40	41	40

Question E3: How important do you consider the following competences for your current work?
* 1 and 2 on a scale of answers from 1 = 'Very important' to 5 = 'Not at all important'.
** Count by Country: IT (2528); ES (2115); FR (2196); AT (2244); DE (3236); NL (3028); UK (3328); FI (2443); SE (2412); NO (3095); CZ (2982); EUR (29606); JP (3029); Total (32635).
*** E.g. economic, sociological, legal knowledge.
Source: CHEERS survey data.

As Table 8.6 shows,
— almost half the graduates believed that their job required the ability to work with people from different cultural backgrounds,
— almost as many considered communicating in a foreign language as essential for their work,
— more than one third also stated that knowledge and understanding of different cultures, societies, live styles etc. were important, and finally
— one quarter of the graduates believed that professional knowledge of other countries (e.g. the economic, legal, social system) was important for doing their work some four years after graduation.

It is surprising to note how the views differ by country. Finnish graduates saw high requirements in those respects almost twice as often as German and British graduates.

9 MATCH BETWEEN EDUCATION AND EMPLOYMENT

In various respects, the survey on higher education and graduate employment addressed the question of whether the graduates considered their education as matching their employment and work. Some questions mainly addressed the link between educational attainment and occupational status, others the relationship between knowledge and utilisation, and others the extent to which employment and work met their expectations and was viewed as satisfying.

9.1 The Relevance of the Field of Study

Only a minority of graduates believed that their field of study was the only one or the best for their area of work. 38 per cent stated this – exactly as many as those who believed that some other fields of study could prepare them for their occupational area equally well. Only 8 per cent observed that their higher education studies were in no way related to their occupation.

Table 9.1: Relationships Between Field of Study and Area of Work, by Country (per cent of graduates employed; multiple responses)

	Country												Total	
	IT	ES	FR	AT	DE	NL	UK	FI	SE	NO	CZ	EUR	JP	
My field of study is the only possible/by far the best field	51	39	20	47	40	28	37	54	46	51	27	39	23	38
Some other fields could prepare for the area of work as well	31	40	48	26	39	52	35	31	33	43	50	40	25	38
Another field would have been more useful	7	10	12	6	8	9	12	7	7	3	13	9	10	9
The field of study does not matter very much	6	6	11	10	10	10	22	5	3	3	6	9	28	11
Higher education studies are not at all related to my area of work	8	5	15	11	8	3	18	2	0	0	4	7	14	8
Others	1	0	1	1	3	0	3	1	3	1	1	1	0	1
Total*	105	100	107	100	108	102	126	100	192	100	100	105	100	105

Question F2: How would you characterise the relationship between your field of study and your area of work?
* Count by Country: IT (2534); ES (2157); FR (2192); AT (2076); DE (3210); NL (2915); UK (3076); FI (2442); SE (2634); NO (3109); CZ (2628); EUR (26339); JP (2984); Total (29323).
Source: CHEERS survey data.

The views differed substantially according to country, as can be seen in Table 9.1. As will be discussed later, divergent views underlay the debate on a desirable "match" between higher education and employment. When this debate gained momentum in the wake of higher education expansion in the 1960s and 1970s, a close relationship between level of educational attainment and career and between fields of study was often viewed as desirable and even small deviations were considered to be "mismatch", "wastage" etc. In the meantime, more flexible links between the relationships were viewed as normal – partly because it was taken for granted that a perfect "match" could not be achieved, and partly, because softer links between higher education and employment could serve graduates' motives, give rise to the emergence of new occupational areas and reinforce graduates' way of coping with problematic employment conditions. Therefore, the question had to be raised how far not-so-perfect links between higher education and employment could be viewed as desirable or unavoidable "flexibility" and where "mismatch" was the proper description of the state of affairs.

Graduates from Nordic countries, Italy and Austria were convinced that their field of study was the only one or the best for their area of work. In contrast, French, Dutch, British and Czech graduates frequently held the view that their field was not closely linked to their area of work.

Table 9.2: Relationship Between Field of Study and Area of Work, by Field of Study (per cent of graduates employed; multiple responses; 12 countries)

	Field of study								Total
	Educ.	Hum.	Soc.sc	Law	Nat.sc	Math.	Engin.	Med.sc	
My field of study is the only possible/by far the best field	54	33	26	56	29	38	32	76	39
Some other fields could also prepare for the area of work	29	30	46	27	40	48	46	20	38
Another field would have been more useful	6	11	9	6	14	7	10	2	8
The field of study does not matter very much	6	17	14	8	12	6	9	2	10
Higher education studies are not at all related to my area of work	4	15	8	6	11	5	4	1	7
Others	2	2	1	1	1	1	1	1	1
Total	102	109	104	104	107	105	103	101	104
Count	3039	3762	9364	2322	1827	1288	6552	3012	31165

Question F2: How would you characterise the relationship between your field of study and your area of work?
Source: CHEERS survey data.

Moreover, a substantial number of British, French and Japanese graduates believed that their area of work was not linked to their higher education studies. In this case, however, the differences were more substantial by field of study. Graduates in disciplines that were more closely linked to professions – medical fields (76%), law (56%) and education (54%) – considered their field as the only one or the best far more frequently than those in other disciplines (26-38%), as is seen in Table 9.2.

9.2 Use of Knowledge and Skills

Half the graduates surveyed stated that they could make great use of the knowledge and skills acquired in the course of their studies in their job. Only 21 per cent found little use. The differences according to country were more striking in this case than according to field of study.

- As regards country, 74 per cent of Norwegian and 69 per cent of Finnish graduates noted a substantial professional use of their knowledge as compared to 28 per cent of the French and only 22 per cent of the Japanese graduates (see Table 9.3).
- Again, graduates in the fields leading to professions stated a higher professional use (56%-79%) than other graduates (42%-50%).

Table 9.3: *Professional Use of Knowledge and Skills Acquired in the Course of Study, by Country (per cent and arithmetic mean* of graduates employed)*

	Country											EUR	JP	Total
	IT	ES	FR	AT	DE	NL	UK	FI	SE	NO	CZ			
1 To a very high extent	19	21	6	25	14	12	23	35	30	36	23	22	9	21
2	30	27	22	30	29	39	27	34	32	38	31	31	13	29
3	30	27	35	28	34	33	26	19	26	21	30	28	30	28
4	15	19	28	14	20	14	17	10	11	5	13	15	31	16
5 Not at all	6	6	8	3	3	2	8	1	1	0	2	4	16	5
Total	100	100	100	100	100	100	100	100	100	100	100	100	100	100
Count	2550	2166	2197	2081	3239	2914	3133	2455	2415	3116	2628	28893	2927	31821
Arithmetic mean	2.6	2.6	3.1	2.4	2.7	2.5	2.6	2.1	2.2	1.9	2.4	2.5	3.3	2.5

Question F1: If you take into consideration your global current tasks altogether: To what extent do you use the knowledge and skills acquired in the course of your studies (you graduated in 1994 or 1995)?
* Scale of answers from 1 = 'To a very high extent' to 5 = 'Not at all'.
Source: CHEERS survey data.

By and large, the findings are similar to those already reported above on the relevance of the field of study and its utility for the work tasks.

9.3 Appropriateness of Level of Education

More than two-thirds of the graduates considered their employment and work as appropriate to their level of education, and only 13 per cent perceived an inappropriate relationship. Twelve per cent each believed that either a higher or a lower level of higher education would have been more appropriate. Only 8 per cent considered higher education as superfluous for their level of employment and work.

Again, differences according to country were – this time slightly – more striking than according to field of study:
- 82 per cent of the Norwegian and 75 per cent of the Dutch graduates considered the link between educational and occupational level as appropriate as compared to 48 per cent of the Italians and only 43 per cent of the Japanese (see Table 9.4).
- In contrast, the respective shares range from 68 per cent to 81 per cent among the more professional fields and from 55 per cent to 76 per cent among the other fields.

Table 9.4: Appropriateness of Employment and Work for Level of Education, by Country (per cent and arithmetic mean* of graduates employed)

	Country												EUR	JP	Total
	IT	ES	FR	AT	DE	NL	UK	FI	SE	NO	CZ				
1 Fully appropriate	19	30	30	28	22	30	40	46	m	55	56		36	12	33
2	29	34	31	37	39	45	28	36	m	32	27		34	31	34
3	30	20	18	22	24	17	14	11	m	10	10		17	37	19
4	16	11	13	8	11	6	11	5	m	3	5		9	14	9
5 Not at all appropriate	6	5	8	4	4	2	7	2	m	1	1		4	6	4
Total	100	100	100	100	100	100	100	100	m	100	100		100	100	100
Count	2535	2161	2183	2080	3228	2914	3084	2448	m	3115	2624		26372	2984	29355
Arithmetic mean	2.6	2.3	2.4	2.2	2.4	2.0	2.2	1.8	m	1.6	1.7		2.1	2.7	2.2

Question F3a: If you consider all dimensions of your employment and work (status, position, income, work tasks, etc.): How far do your employment and work correspond to your level of education?
* Scale of answers from 1 = 'Fully appropriate' to 5 = 'Not at all appropriate'.
m = data missing
Source: CHEERS survey data.

9.4 Reasons for Inappropriate Position

Those who considered themselves to occupy a job that did not correspond to their level of education were not always compelled to do so because of labour market conditions. The following five reasons were often stated:
- My current job is more interesting,
- I have not been able to find a more appropriate job,
- In doing this job I have better career prospects,
- Preference for the location of my current job,
- My current job offers me more security.

Only one of these five categories suggests that the inappropriate position was not chosen voluntarily.

Table 9.5: Reasons for Taking a Job that Does not Correspond to the Level of Study, by Country (per cent of graduates employed; multiple responses)

	Country*												Total	
	IT	ES	FR	AT	DE	NL	UK	FI	SE	NO	CZ	EUR	JP	
No better job[1]	21	15	16	8	12	7	15	7	10	5	11	11	12	11
Better career prospects[2]	9	8	12	8	11	9	14	7	8	5	19	10	11	10
Preference for this job[3]	2	1	4	3	3	3	5	11	2	1	6	4	7	4
Job promotion[4]	0	0	1	1	1	1	2	1	2	1	8	2	0	2
Higher income[5]	4	3	7	6	5	4	12	5	7	4	20	7	7	7
Greater job security[6]	10	8	9	6	8	5	9	8	2	3	20	8	23	9
More interesting job[7]	8	7	12	10	13	12	12	13	12	5	25	12	22	13
Flexible schedules[8]	11	6	5	9	9	4	5	6	6	4	9	7	4	6
Locality preference[9]	6	7	8	8	11	5	11	8	7	6	22	9	20	10
Family needs[10]	9	4	5	6	7	2	4	5	5	4	17	6	7	6
Beginning of the career[11]	4	5	7	5	5	2	4	8	2	3	12	5	4	5
Other	3	2	6	5	6	7	6	2	6	2	4	5	11	5

* Count by Country: IT (2774); ES (2322); FR (2512); AT (2275); DE (3369); NL (2983); UK (3293); FI (2615); SE (2594); NO (3202); CZ (2915); EUR (30853); JP (3055); Total (33908).

Question F4: If you consider your employment and work as hardly appropriate and not linked to your education: why did you take it up? Multiple reply possible.

[1] I have not (yet) been able to find a more appropriate job.
[2] In doing this job I have better career prospects.
[3] I prefer an occupation which is not closely connected to my studies.
[4] I was promoted to a position that was less closely linked to my studies than my previous position(s).
[5] I can earn a higher income in my current job.
[6] My current job offers me more security.
[7] My current job is more interesting.
[8] My current job provides the opportunity for part-time/flexible schedules etc.
[9] My current job enables me to work in a locality which I prefer.
[10] My current job allows me to take family needs into account.
[11] At the beginning of the career envisaged I have to accept work that does not correspond to my studies.

Source: CHEERS survey data.

9.5   Fulfilled Expectations

Graduates were asked to state if their work situation some four years after graduation met the expectations they had when they began to study. More than 40 per cent rated their current work situation as better than expected, and almost as many saw it as matching their initial expectations. Only just over 20 per cent considered their work situation some four years after graduation as worse than expected. These ratings hardly differed by field of study, but differed considerably by country: again, graduates from Norwegian (69%) and Finnish (49%) higher education institutions (49%) were the most positive, whilst those from Spanish and Japanese higher education institutions more often considered their work situation as worse (see Table 9.6).

Table 9.6: Work Situation Some Four Years After Graduation as Compared to Expectations at Time of Enrolment, by Country (per cent of graduates employed and arithmetic mean*)

	IT	ES	FR	AT	DE	NL	UK	Country FI	SE	NO	CZ	EUR	JP	Total
1 Much better than expected	6	10	8	12	8	7	8	18	7	25	13	11	8	11
2	26	15	31	33	33	35	29	31	33	44	28	31	15	30
3	38	38	37	41	42	48	39	36	37	24	44	39	26	37
4	15	29	12	9	12	8	17	10	16	5	13	13	33	15
5 Much worse than expected	15	8	11	4	5	2	8	5	6	2	2	6	18	7
Total	100	100	100	100	100	100	100	100	100	100	100	100	100	100
Count	2327	2065	1882	2059	2941	2575	2739	2439	2134	2923	2466	26549	2394	28943
Arithmetic mean	3.1	3.1	2.9	2.6	2.7	2.6	2.9	2.5	2.8	2.2	2.6	2.7	3.4	2.8

Question F5: Taking all aspects into account, how far does your current work situation meet your expectations when you started your studies?
* Scale of answers from 1 = 'Much better than expected' to 5 = 'Much worse than expected'.
Source: CHEERS survey data.

9.6 The Proportion of Graduates Facing Problems

Table 9.7 summarizes the findings of seven indicators of the relationship between study and work. It only includes the percentages which reveal problems, such as little use of knowledge and skills, little appropriateness or unfulfilled expectations. For the European graduates, all indicators were below 20 per cent, whilst the percentage of Japanese graduates indicating problems was much higher. Within Europe, problems were more frequently stated by graduates from France and the United Kingdom than by those from Norway and Finland.

Table 9.7: Subjective Indicators of the Relationships Between Study and Work, by Country (per cent of graduates employed)

	IT	ES	FR	AT	DE	NL	UK	FI	SE	NO	CZ	EUR	JP	Total
1) Little use of knowledge and skills	21	25	37	17	23	16	25	12	12	5	16	19	47	21
2) Field of study does not correspond	14	11	25	21	17	13	34	6	4	3	10	14	42	17
3) Little usefulness	23	19	29	18	23	9	24	9	6	5	6	15	m	15
4) Little appropriateness	22	17	22	13	16	8	18	6	m	3	7	13	20	14
5) Lower degree would correspond better	28	29	32	21	26	16	23	12	9	8	13	19	31	20
6) Unfulfilled expectations	30	38	24	13	17	10	24	15	22	7	15	19	51	22
7) Low job satisfaction	18	13	14	10	12	7	18	9	11	4	6	11	28	13

1) Question F1: If you take into consideration your current work tasks: To what extent do you use the knowledge and skills acquired during your studies (you graduated in 1994 or 1995)? Responses 4 and 5 on a scale of answers from 1 = 'To a very high extent' to 5 = 'Not at all'.
2) Question F2: How would you characterize the relationship between your field of study and your area of work? Answers: "The field of study does not matter very much" and "My higher education studies are not at all related to my area of work".
3) Question E2: How far have your studies (you graduated in 1994 or 1995) been useful in preparing you for your present work tasks? Responses 4 and 5 on a scale of answers from 1 = 'Very useful' to 5 = 'Not at all useful'.
4) Question F3a: If you consider all dimensions of your employment and work (status, position, income, work tasks, etc.: How far do your employment and work correspond to your level of education? Responses 4 and 5 on a scale of answers from 1 = 'Fully appropriate' to 5 = 'Not at all appropriate'.
5) Question F3b: What is the most appropriate level of course of studies/degree for your employment and work in comparison with that which you graduated from in 1994 or 1995? Answers: "A lower level of higher/tertiary education" or "No higher/tertiary education at all".
6) Question F5: Taking all aspects into account, how far does your current work situation meet your expectations when you started your studies? Responses 4 and 5 on a scale of answers from 1 = 'Much better than expected' to 5 = 'Much worse than expected'.
7) Question G1: Altogether, to what extent are you satisfied with your current work? Responses 4 and 5 on a scale of answers from 1 = 'Very satisfied' to 5 = 'Very dissatisfied'.
m = data missing
Source: CHEERS survey data.

The mean ranks of the various countries are shown in Figure 9.1. Graduates from Norwegian higher education institutions noted the closest links between studies and subsequent employment.

Positive ratings prevailed also among graduates from Finland, Sweden, the Netherlands and the Czech Republic. Germany, Spain, Italy and the United Kingdom belong to those countries whose graduates often find relatively loose links. Low ratings clearly dominated amongst graduates from Japan and France.

Figure 9.1: Ranking of Countries Regarding the Relationships Between Study and Work in the Opinion of Their Graduates (mean rank of seven indicators*)

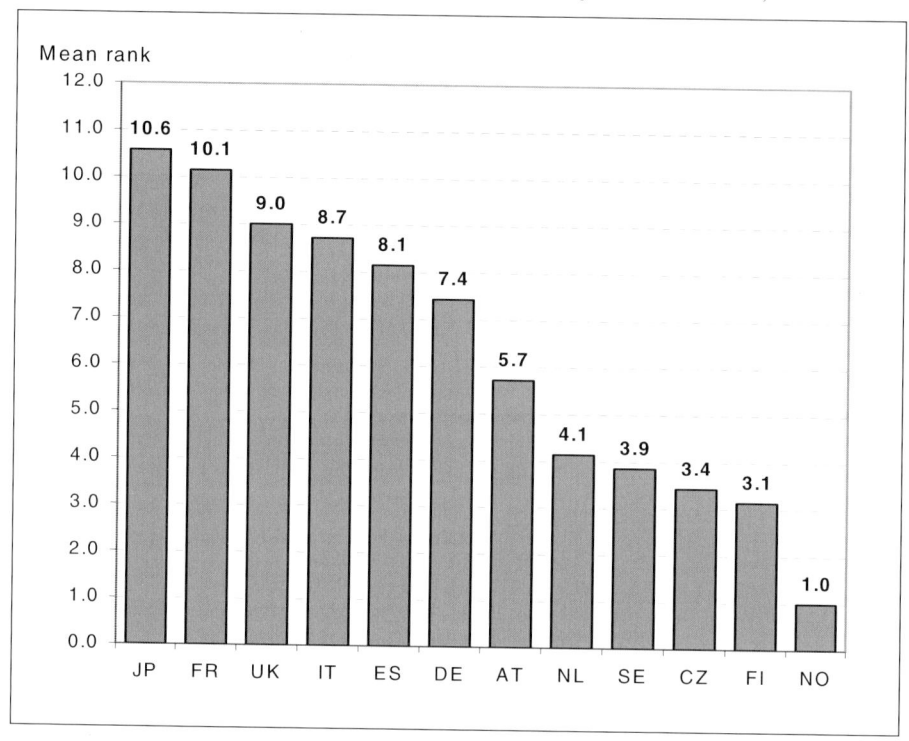

Country	Mean rank
JP	10.6
FR	10.1
UK	9.0
IT	8.7
ES	8.1
DE	7.4
AT	5.7
NL	4.1
SE	3.9
CZ	3.4
FI	3.1
NO	1.0

* See the variables presented in Table 9.7.
Source: CHEERS survey data.

10 ORIENTATION AND JOB SATISFACTION

10.1 Life Goals

At the top of the life goals of graduates four years after graduation are those that could be linked to the concept of post-materialistic orientation (Inglehart): personal development was rated by about 90 per cent of the graduates in all countries as "important" or "very important" (data are not available from the Czech Republic, Finland, Norway and Japan). The differences by country are remarkably low, as Table 10.1 shows. In addition to personal development
- work (77%),
- family (75%),
- "varied social life" (65%),
- "making money" (64%) and
- "academic inquiry" (56%)

were quoted as important life goals.

Only "social prestige" (37%) was emphasized by less than half the graduates.

Table 10.1: Importance of Life Goals Some Four Years After Graduation, by Country (per cent of graduates responding 'very important' and 'important'*)

	Country								Total
	IT	ES	FR	AT	DE	NL	UK	SE	
Personal development	93	90	89	95	91	93	89	95	92
Work	80	84	68	79	76	78	72	83	77
Home/family	82	74	74	73	68	77	72	84	75
Varied social life	59	53	73	66	63	77	55	75	65
Making money	45	68	60	70	71	60	64	71	64
Academic inquiry	87	87	72	29	19	70	48	35	56
Social prestige	35	33	27	49	43	34	35	38	37
Count	3054	2984	2991	2277	3460	3042	3385	2587	23781

Question G2: Please indicate the importance you gave to each of the following life goals - in the past and now.
* 1 and 2 on a scale of answers from 1 = 'Very important' to 5 = 'Not at all important'.
Czech Republic, Finland, Japan and Norway: data missing
Source: CHEERS survey data.

The responses varied most strikingly by country with respect to "academic inquiry": graduates from Italy and Spain underscored this most frequently, as well as those from Austria and Germany. The latter might be because the text in German could have described this as motivation to pursue an academic career.

The high proportion of graduates stating several goals as important in their life indicates that most graduates consider materialistic and post-materialistic orientations as associated. More specifically,

- 59 per cent of the graduates stated that they gave importance to *making money* and *personal development* and
- 49 per cent placed emphasis both on *making money* and *family*.

In contrast, 14 per cent only stated *making money* and 26 per cent *home/family*.

The graduates themselves believe that they greatly change their life goals during the first years after graduation. On average, they did not only become more family-oriented, but also more money-oriented and put more emphasis on work and personal development. In contrast, their goals did not change with respect to social prestige, varied social life and academic inquiry (see Figure 10.1).

Figure 10.1: Importance of Life Goals at the Time of Graduation and Some Four Years After Graduation (arithmetic mean*)

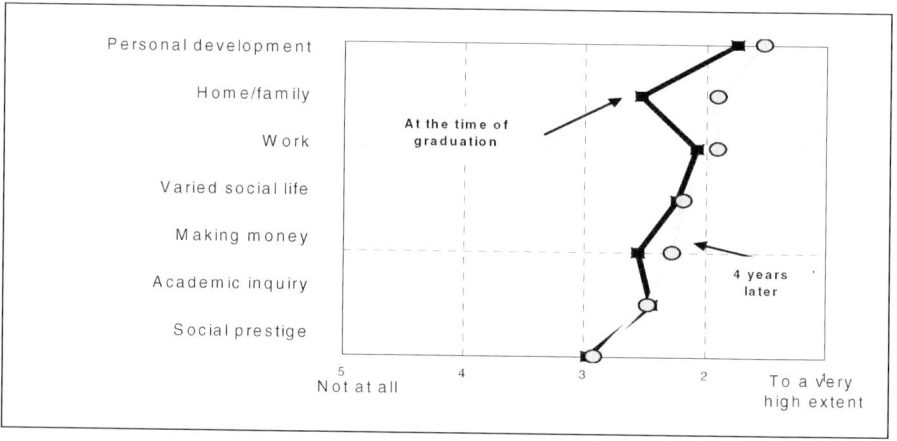

Question G2: Please indicate the importance you gave to each of the following life goals - in the past and now.
* Scale of answers from 1 = 'Very important' to 5 = 'Not at all important'.
Source: CHEERS survey data.

10.2 Work Orientation

Work orientation and job satisfaction are very often viewed as key variables to explain organisational behaviour (see e.g. Luthans 1992; Mortimer, Lorence 1979). In this survey, work orientation was addressed because it could have an influence on the transition process and the subsequent career. In contrast, job satisfaction could be interpreted as an indicator of professional success.

Graduates were asked about the importance of occupational characteristics ("How important are the following characteristics of an occupation for you personally?") The 19 items presented reflected previous similar studies.

As Figure 10.2 and Table 10.2 show, the content and the social context of work were at the top of the list of important characteristics of the professional situation:
- a good social climate (91%) and
- possibilities of using acquired knowledge and skills (84%).

Variety, the opportunity of pursuing personal ideas, opportunity of pursuing continuous learning, challenging tasks and largely independent disposition of work are other aspects that were quoted as important by more than 75 per cent of the graduates surveyed.

These findings support the finding reported above that intrinsic motivation plays a major role amongst professionals and that values are also important: job security (74%), enough time for leisure activities (74%), good career prospects (67%), good chances of combining employment with family tasks (67%) and high income (61%). Of the 19 aspects addressed, only few graduates rate the opportunity of undertaking scientific/scholarly work (37%) and chances of (political) influence (29%) as important.

Figure 10.2: Work Orientations (per cent of graduates responding 'very important' and 'important'*)

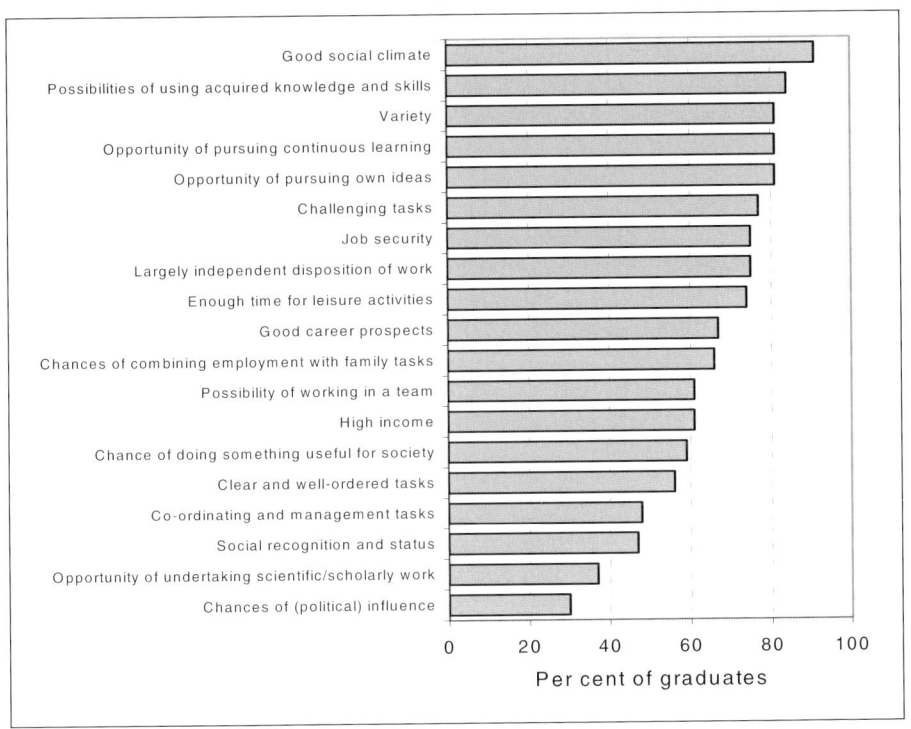

Characteristic	Per cent of graduates
Good social climate	91
Possibilities of using acquired knowledge and skills	84
Variety	81
Opportunity of pursuing continuous learning	81
Opportunity of pursuing own ideas	80
Challenging tasks	77
Job security	74
Largely independent disposition of work	74
Enough time for leisure activities	74
Good career prospects	67
Chances of combining employment with family tasks	67
Possibility of working in a team	62
High income	61
Chance of doing something useful for society	59
Clear and well-ordered tasks	56
Co-ordinating and management tasks	47
Social recognition and status	46
Opportunity of undertaking scientific/scholarly work	37
Chances of (political) influence	29

Question G3: How important are the following characteristics of an occupation for you personally?
* Scale of answers from 1 = 'Very important' to 5 = 'Not at all important'.
Source: CHEERS survey data.

There are noteworthy differences by country, especially with respect to the political motives ("chances of political influence"), whereas professional autonomy ("opportunity of pursuing own ideas") varies only marginally by country (see Table 10.2). Some additional examples of differences by country are: good career prospects were important for 87 per cent of graduates from Spain, but only for 54 per cent from Japan and 56 per cent from both Germany and Norway. Challenging tasks were important for 90 per cent of the graduates from Norway, but only for 49 per cent from France. Work orientations of the Japanese graduates did not differ substantially from those of the European graduates. Similarly to the European graduates, social-communicative and professional values were at the top of the orientations of Japanese graduates. Surprisingly, they were less career-oriented than European graduates: only 54 per cent stated 'good career prospects' as important or very important, compared to 69 per cent on the part of the European graduates.

Table 10.2: Work Orientations, by Country (per cent of graduates responding 'very important' and 'important'*)

	Country**											Total	
	IT	ES	FR	AT	DE	NL	UK	FI	SE	NO	CZ	EUR	JP
Good social climate	89	96	94	94	93	97	79	92	97	95	81	91	90	91
Possibilities of using acquired knowledge and skills	82	91	77	80	70	82	89	96	91	96	78	85	84	84
Opportunity of pursuing personal ideas	83	82	82	85	79	90	71	83	87	76	79	81	78	81
Variety	70	69	73	81	81	90	83	86	87	89	82	81	84	81
Opportunity of pursuing continuous learning	90	93	68	89	82	87	62	92	94	92	63	82	68	81
Challenging tasks	82	74	49	83	78	89	79	87	86	90	61	78	64	77
Largely independent disposition of work	80	66	85	87	85	62	51	88	85	86	65	76	70	75
Job security	69	92	71	68	78	65	77	78	68	79	79	75	71	75
Enough time for leisure activities	68	84	73	70	68	81	76	78	73	79	55	73	83	74
Good career prospects	72	87	69	63	56	69	82	58	64	56	81	69	54	67
Good chances of combining employment with family tasks	78	78	85	58	55	62	56	51	84	77	50	67	60	66
High income	57	69	54	58	55	50	59	74	67	66	68	61	60	61
Possibility of working in a team	53	68	63	73	73	71	62	47	67	71	46	63	43	61
Chance of doing something useful for society	69	78	67	53	43	62	55	43	47	60	58	58	67	59
Clear and well-ordered tasks	63	78	70	50	42	44	49	60	29	58	66	56	60	56
Co-ordinating and management tasks	56	49	38	58	55	51	52	41	48	48	55	50	27	48

to be continued

Table 10.2 continued

	IT	ES	FR	AT	DE	Country** NL	UK	FI	SE	NO	CZ	EUR	Total JP
Social recognition and status	44	44	46	51	44	39	41	52	65	46	60	48	38	47
Opportunity of undertaking scientific/scholarly work	40	54	38	33	24	37	30	29	32	55	18	36	46	37
Chances of (political) influence	52	35	25	19	17	27	15	18	92	24	6	29	32	30

Question G3: How important are the following characteristics of an occupation for you personally?
* 1 and 2 on a scale of answers from 1 = 'Very important' to 5 = 'Not at all important'
** Count by Country: IT (3043); ES (3002); FR (2992); AT (2285); DE (3460); NL (3008); UK (3373); FI (2647); SE (2594); NO (3246); CZ (2993); EUR (32644); JP (3384); Total (36028).
Source: CHEERS survey data.

10.3   Professional Situation

As could be expected, the characteristics of the professional situation did not fully match the motives of the graduates. The characteristics of the professional situation were rated on average 0.4 points lower on a five-point scale than the orientations, i.e. importance given to them by the graduates (see Table 10.3). Their income, career opportunities and the lack of leisure time were least in tune with their orientations. On the other hand, their motives were fully met on average as far as social status and recognition and the opportunity of working in a team were concerned. Italian, Spanish and French graduates perceived the most substantial discrepancies between their orientations and their professional situation.

Table 10.3: Comparison Between Work Orientation and Professional Situation (per cent*)

	Work orientation	Professional situation	Difference (situation-orientation)
Good social climate	91	70	-21
Possibilities of using acquired knowledge and skills	84	66	-18
Challenging tasks	77	64	-13
Largely independent disposition of work	75	64	-11
Variety	81	62	-19
Job security	75	62	-13
Possibility of working in a team	61	61	0
Opportunity of pursuing continuous learning	81	58	-23
Opportunity of pursuing personal ideas	81	57	-24
Chance of doing something useful for society	59	46	-13
Enough time for leisure activities	74	45	-29
Good chances of combining employment with family tasks	66	43	-23
Social recognition and status	47	43	-4

to be continued

Table 10.3 continued

	Work orientation	Professional situation	Difference (situation-orientation)
Clear and well-ordered tasks	56	42	-14
Good career prospects	67	41	-26
Co-ordinating and management tasks	48	39	-9
High income	61	34	-27
Opportunity of undertaking scientific/scholarly work	37	23	-14
Chances of (political) influence	30	22	-8

Question G3: How important are the following characteristics of an occupation for you personally?
Question G3: To what extent do the following characteristics of an occupation apply to your current professional situation (B)?
* Responses 1 and 2 on a scale of answers from 1 = 'Very important' to 5 = 'Not at all important' (work orientation) and from 1 = 'To a very high extent' to 5 = 'Not at all' (professional situation).
Source: CHEERS survey data.

10.4 Job Satisfaction

Almost two-thirds of the graduates stated that they were satisfied with their current work. Satisfaction was most frequently expressed by Norwegian (78%), Finnish and Czech (74%) as well as Dutch graduates (72%). In contrast, only 48 per cent each of the Italian and Japanese graduates seemed to be very satisfied with their professional situation (see Table 10.4). There were hardly any differences in satisfaction average according to field of study.

Table 10.4: General Satisfaction with Current Work, by Country (per cent of employed graduates responding 'very satisfied' and 'satisfied' and arithmetic mean*)

	Country											EUR	JP	Total
	IT	ES	FR	AT	DE	NL	UK	FI	SE	NO	CZ			
1 Very satisfied	11	20	25	26	16	21	19	25	25	33	23	22	10	21
2	37	40	40	42	46	51	38	49	44	45	51	44	38	43
3	34	27	22	21	26	22	25	18	20	18	20	23	24	23
4	14	10	9	7	9	6	13	7	8	3	5	8	22	10
5 Very dissatisfied	4	3	4	3	3	1	6	1	2	1	1	3	6	3
Total	100	100	100	100	100	100	100	100	100	100	100	100	100	100
Count	2538	2221	2401	2104	3254	2908	3157	2438	2404	3109	2630	29165	3023	32187
Arithmetic mean	2.6	2.4	2.3	2.2	2.4	2.2	2.5	2.1	2.2	1.9	2.1	2.3	2.8	2.3

Question G1: To what extent are you satisfied with your current work?
* 1 and 2 on a scale of answers from 1 = 'Very satisfied' to 5 = 'Very dissatisfied'.
Source: CHEERS survey data.

11 CAREER RELEVANT ASPECTS

11.1 Initial and Continuing Professional Education

In some occupations, which vary according to country, graduates must undergo an initial training period after graduation before embarking on regular employment. In other cases, they are regularly employed and must undergo mandatory training periods to obtain a professional qualification. Finally, employers organised off- and on-the-job training for some of their graduates. It is not always possible to make a clear distinction between post-higher education initial professional training and continuing professional education. Hence, in our analysis, no respective distinctions were made. Rather, all post-graduation education other than regular study is treated as "continuing education".

In all countries, *participation* in short courses of professional education are over 50 per cent and about 30 per cent in longer training periods (see Table 11.1). More than 50 per cent of the graduates from Italy, and about 40 per cent of the Austrian and German graduates participated in longer professional training required to obtain a professional qualification. But in Norway, they were only six per cent. Additional further education in short courses or seminars were undertaken most frequently by graduates in Spain and Sweden (more than 70% each). France and Japan showed the lowest participation rate for courses of continuing education.

Table 11.1: Participation in Education and Training Programmes During the First Some Four Years After Graduation, by Country (per cent)

	Country												EUR	JP	Total
	IT	ES	FR	AT	DE	NL	UK	FI	SE	NO	CZ				
Long training	52	39	26	41	39	23	26	22	26	6	21		29	24	28
Short courses	37	71	27	68	64	52	66	56	70	66	60		58	19	54
No training	31	19	52	19	22	35	26	34	21	32	35		30	64	33
Total	119	128	106	128	125	111	118	112	117	105	116		117	107	116
Count	2955	3017	3051	2138	3446	2952	3182	2654	2594	3188	3092		32270	3367	35636

Question H1: Did you undertake compulsory further education and training in order to obtain or keep a professional qualification or another longer professional training period since graduation in 1994 or 1995?
Question H2: After the degree you were awarded in 1994 or 1995 did you undertake other additional/further education/training (short courses, seminars, workshops, self-study, etc., related to your career or to a future career? Do not include professional training programmes stated in response to H1 and what you consider to be unrelated to work and career.
Source: CHEERS survey data.

On average, private institutes were mentioned by half of all graduates of all countries (in Austria and the Czech Republic 60% each, in the Netherlands 57%, and in France only 36%) as *providing institutions*, followed by in-company training (United Kingdom 52%, while in Italy and Spain only about 16% each). Higher education institutions were providers for 28 per cent of attended courses. Only in Finland, did higher education institutions play the most important role as continuing education providers (49%). In Norway, 38 per cent participated in courses of higher education institutions, while in Japan this was the case for only five per cent. In contrast, one fifth of the Japanese graduates participated in distance education, which hardly played any role in Europe, except for Spain with a 13 per cent participation rate.

Table 11.2: Institutions Named Providing Education/Training Courses, by Country (per cent of graduates naming institutions; multiple responses)

	Country												Total
	IT	ES	FR	AT	DE	NL	UK	FI	NO	CZ	EUR	JP	
A higher education institution	27	33	25	29	20	19	23	49	38	18	28	5	27
Private institute offering seminar/training	56	51	36	60	51	58	44	39	50	60	51	49	51
In-company or in-service training	16	17	32	39	44	41	52	39	49	39	38	37	38
Distance education/ written course	2	13	2	1	2	5	3	0	3	0	4	22	4
Other	22	43	27	20	26	13	11	19	22	20	22	13	22
Total	122	157	121	149	143	135	133	145	162	137	143	126	142
Count	1067	2127	795	1561	2171	1512	2105	1461	2067	1835	16701	618	17319

Question H4: Who is (was) responsible for providing this course/these courses?
Sweden: data missing.
Source: CHEERS survey data.

The *costs of continuing education courses* were mainly paid by the employers. This was mainly the case in the Netherlands (85%), Norway, Czech Republic and the United Kingdom, but not in Spain and Italy. In Spain, 61 per cent and in Italy 87 per cent of the graduates mainly paid themselves. In these two countries, public funds are used by more than a quarter of the graduates to finance their continuing education, which in France accounts for 17 per cent of the graduates and in all other countries for ten per cent or less (see Table 11.2).

Consequently, it is not very surprising to note that in Italy and Spain graduates most often *attended continuing education courses* outside their paid working time (see Table 11.3). In the other countries, the courses took place either entirely during working hours (Finland 60%, United Kingdom 59%, France 58%, Germany 45%, the Netherlands and Norway 44% each) or partly during paid working hours (Austria 44% and Czech Republic 43%).

Table 11.3: Sources of Funds for Education/Training Course Participation Named, by Country (per cent of graduates referring to sources of funding; multiple responses)

	Country												Total
	IT	ES	FR	AT	DE	NL	UK	FI	NO	CZ	EUR	JP	
There were no costs	24	10	13	6	7	1	7	8	5	11	7	10	8
Mainly my employer	44	20	54	58	61	85	70	69	78	77	63	56	63
Mainly myself	87	61	19	35	28	12	15	13	9	21	25	26	25
Mainly public funds	27	28	17	6	4	4	5	10	4	4	9	5	9
I don't know	0	1	2	0	0	0	2	0	0	1	1	0	1
Other	21	6	4	5	5	3	5	3	4	4	4	3	4
Total	202	125	108	111	107	106	104	103	100	116	110	100	109
Count	82	2129	803	1590	2175	1515	2124	1458	2025	1839	15740	596	16336

Question H5: Who funded the costs for your participation in this course/these courses?
Sweden: data missing.
Source: CHEERS survey data.

Table 11.4: Education/Training Courses Attendance during Paid Working Hours, by Country (per cent of graduates referring to timing of course attendance)

	Country												Total
	IT	ES	FR	AT	DE	NL	UK	FI	NO	CZ	EUR	JP	
Yes, entirely during paid working hours	20	6	58	28	45	44	59	60	44	39	40	53	40
Yes, partly during paid working hours	12	15	12	44	30	32	17	22	42	43	28	11	28
No, completely outside paid working hours	34	37	11	23	17	22	18	18	11	18	21	25	21
Not applicable, I was not employed	33	42	19	6	8	2	6	0	3	0	11	11	11
Total	100	100	100	100	100	100	100	100	100	100	100	100	100
Count	1063	2050	801	1574	2182	1514	2167	1344	2055	1845	16594	601	17195

Question H6: Did you attend the course(s) during your paid working hours?
Sweden: data missing.
Source: CHEERS survey data.

These results show different conditions and policies regarding the funding of initial and continuing professional education of graduates in the various European countries. However, this difference is largely due to the fact that many Italian and Spanish graduates pay for their professional education because they opt for enhancement of their competences when they are not employed.

Asked about the topics of education and training, the graduates surveyed reported most frequently, that "new scholarly knowledge in my discipline" was addressed in their continuing education programme. Amongst the thirteen topics addressed, "computer skills" and "methodological competences" were also subjects of many continuing education programmes.

In France, "computer skills", "methodological" and "oral or written communication/presentation skills" were mentioned more often than "new knowledge". In the United Kingdom, communication and presentation skills were addressed more often in training programmes than in other countries; also the customer relationships and management competences were topics of education and training for more than 40 per cent. In all other countries, these areas only represented about 20 per cent. "Cross-disciplinary scholarly knowledge" was also an important topic in Norway and in Austria, but not in Italy. Italian graduates most often mentioned "foreign language proficiency" which was least important for those from the United Kingdom and the Netherlands (see Table 11.5).

Table 11.5: Topics of Education/Training Courses Named, by Country
(per cent of graduates referring to topics; multiple responses)

	Country												Total	
	IT	ES	FR	AT	DE	NL	UK	FI	SE	NO	CZ	EUR	JP	
New scholarly knowledge in your discipline	41	63	33	66	70	67	49	42	66	79	71	62	45	61
Computer skills	19	50	45	34	39	31	43	42	49	33	35	39	29	39
Methodological competences	36	22	45	27	32	61	39	34	21	46	41	36	47	36
Cross-disciplinary scholarly knowledge of various fields	13	28	30	35	32	33	26	20	16	42	27	28	21	28
Oral or written communication and presentation skills	17	12	38	28	26	29	41	34	29	27	35	28	26	28
Management/leadership competences	12	10	18	25	22	26	36	24	25	21	27	23	17	23
Relations with customers/clients	13	7	16	24	24	27	38	19	12	10	27	20	17	20
Legal topics	16	19	20	24	27	16	20	0	13	19	28	19	12	19
Foreign language proficiency	47	24	15	22	13	6	4	20	22	5	35	18	16	18
Competences in business administration	9	17	16	21	17	18	21	15	15	13	12	16	12	16
Social/political or philosophical topics	7	11	11	17	13	11	15	14	9	15	11	12	11	12
Manual skills	5	7	4	10	11	9	20	8	10	41	13	14	16	14
Human ecology/ environmental matters	6	10	4	5	6	5	7	7	9	4	9	7	8	7
Other	6	5	10	5	4	9	7	11	11	6	7	7	5	7
Total*	246	284	306	343	335	349	366	288	306	363	378	329	282	328

Question H7: Which of the following topics were covered in the course(s)?
* Count by Country: IT (1072); ES (2095); FR (796); AT (1577); DE (2177); NL (1515); UK (2148); FI (1447); SE (1828); NO (2062); CZ (1843); EUR (18560); JP (619); Total (19179).
Source: CHEERS survey data.

Consequently, the *purpose* of continuing education is predominantly seen as "updating knowledge" (see Table 11.6). Only the British and Spanish graduates underscored slightly more frequently "enhancing career". The training aspect played a greater role only for Spain and Italy – a finding indicating again the occupational situation of graduates in these countries.

Table 11.6: Purpose of Additional/Further Education/Training Named, by Country (per cent of graduates referring to the purpose; multiple responses)

	Country												Total
	IT	ES	FR	AT	DE	NL	UK	FI	NO	CZ	EUR	JP	
Enhancing career, promotion, etc.	12	39	32	33	32	40	54	32	27	11	32	43	32
Updating knowledge	73	33	55	63	77	59	49	68	69	86	63	46	63
Re-training (i.e. preparation for other occupations/careers)	21	28	17	4	4	7	12	3	4	3	10	11	10
Total	106	100	105	100	112	106	115	103	100	100	105	100	105
Count	1084	2020	739	1440	2167	1505	2057	1293	1985	1846	16136	595	16732

Question H8: What was the most important personal purpose of additional/further education/training when you started it?

Sweden: data missing.

Source: CHEERS survey data.

The most important *outcome* of continuing education according to graduates from all countries was helping "to get along with the work tasks" and "to enrich the job" (see Table 11.7). In addition, Spanish graduates (37%) and those from United Kingdom (32%) also reported quite frequently that they obtained employment as a consequence of participating in training programmes.

Finally, graduates were asked about the *need* to participate in additional education. Three replies were given most frequently. Participants considered that continuing education was necessary "in order to cope with tasks which could not be envisaged at the time of initial education" (72%). This is notably true for graduates from the Czech Republic, Finland, Austria, Spain and Germany (see Table 11.8). Continuing education was also viewed as important "in order to acquire knowledge which can be learned better on the job" (71%) with high ratings in the United Kingdom, France, Czech Republic, and Germany.

Table 11.7: Outcomes of Additional/Further Education/Training Named, by Country (per cent of graduates referring to outcomes stating 'to a very high extent' and 'to a high extent'*)

	Country							Total
	IT	ES	FR	AT	DE	NL	UK	
to obtain employment	20	37	25	17	13	10	32	23
to get along with the work tasks	52	56	65	55	53	65	68	59
to enrich the job (e.g. more interesting tasks)	38	37	40	52	48	53	51	46
to raise one's status (e.g. promotion, higher income)	14	20	20	21	15	43	38	25
to cope with requirements from other life spheres than employment and work	29	35	25	25	18	22	24	25
Count	1075	2010	766	1554	2146	1502	2167	11220

Question H9: To what extent did your additional/further education or training actually help you afterwards...?

* 1 and 2 on a scale of answers from 1 = 'To a very high extent' to 5 = 'Not at all'.

Czech Republic, Finland, Japan, Norway and Sweden: data missing

Source: CHEERS survey data.

Table 11.8: Need Felt of Additional/Further Education/Training, by Country (per cent of graduates 'completely agreeing' and 'agreeing'*)

	Country										Total
	IT	ES	FR	AT	DE	NL	UK	FI	SE	NO	CZ
Additional/further education or training is necessary											
... in order to cope with tasks which could not be envisaged at the time of initial education	67	81	71	83	78	55	67	84	56	62	88	72
... because of shortcomings in initial first study	69	60	57	62	50	36	35	44	44	40	57	50
... in order to acquire knowledge which can be learned better on the job	71	71	80	66	77	63	82	76	47	61	81	71
Initial first study provides sufficient training in relevant skill acquisition	8	11	11	16	8	31	26	17	26	27	20	18
Initial first study constitutes a good basis for continuous updating of knowledge and skills	48	70	63	83	70	72	66	83	m	84	74	71
Count	3006	2948	2767	2241	3446	3021	3324	2577	2588	3230	3064	32210

Question H11: To what extent do you agree with the following statements regarding the need for additional/ further education or training?

* 1 and 2 on a scale of answers from 1 = 'Completely agree' to 5 = 'Completely disagree'.

Japan: data missing

m = data missing

Source: CHEERS survey data.

Moreover, graduates emphasized that "initial first study constitutes a good basis for continuous updating of knowledge and skills". Norwegian, Austrian and Finnish graduates stated this most frequently (more than 80%) in contrast with Italian graduates who only shared this view in a few cases. Finally, shortcomings in initial first study were stated as a reason for continuing education by half the respondents. Italian, Austrian and Spanish graduates pointed this out most frequently, as compared with only somewhat more than one-third of the British and Dutch graduates.

11.2 International Mobility

The study addressed international mobility at various stages of the graduates' life. They were asked whether they
- had foreign citizenship at the time of birth,
- had completed secondary education abroad (i.e. not in the country where they graduated),
- found their first employment after graduation in a country that was different from the one where they graduated,
- were professionally active abroad some four years after graduation, and
- resided abroad some four years after graduation.

Table 11.9: Foreign Citizenship, Employment and Living Abroad, by Country (per cent*)

	Country										Total
	IT	ES	FR	AT	DE	NL	UK	FI	SE	NO	
a) Graduating in a foreign country	.6	1.2	5.0	3.3	3.2	2.2	9.2	.5	7.5	3.3	3.6
b) Foreign citizenship at birth	.6	1.2	2.9	1.8	2.0	1.6	2.7	.2	5.0	1.8	2.0
c) Secondary education not in country of graduation	.5	.6	2.2	.8	.5	1.0	2.4	.6	2.0	1.2	1.2
d) First employment after graduation abroad	1.9	2.4	5.3	3.9	2.4	3.0	4.8	2.4	3.7	1.1	3.0
e) Employment abroad some four years after graduation	1.1	1.3	4.1	5.4	2.2	1.9	3.4	4.1	4.5	0.4	2.7
f) Living abroad some four years after graduation	0.9	1.1	3.9	6.0	2.3	m	4.2	4.4	4.2	0.7	2.9

Question I3: Please, provide information about your citizenship and your country of schooling, studies and work.
a): percentage of all graduates; b) to f): percentage of home country graduates only.
Czech Republic and Japan: data missing.
m = data missing
Source: CHEERS survey data.

About two per cent of the graduates who responded *were not citizens* of the country where they graduated. As can be seen in Table 11.9, the share was by far the highest in the United Kingdom. About two per cent of the European respondents who graduated in their home country had another citizenship at their time of birth. This percentage was by far the highest in Sweden (5.0%), as can also be seen in Table 11.9.

1.2 per cent of the graduates who graduated in their home country obtained their secondary education qualification in a foreign country. This was mainly true for French, British and Swedish respondents (about 2% each).

After graduation, 3.0 per cent of the respondents who graduated in their home country (foreign graduates were not included in the subsequent analysis of graduate employment and work) found their first employment abroad. This was most frequent amongst French (5.3%) and British graduates (4.8%).

2.7 per cent of the European respondents who graduated in their home country were employed abroad at the time the survey was carried out, i.e. some four years after graduation. This share was over 4 per cent amongst Austrian, French, Swedish and British graduates.

Finally, 2.9 per cent of the respondents who graduated in their home country lived abroad at the time of the survey, i.e. some four years after graduation. As could be expected, these data were similar to those for graduates who were employed abroad.

The available data suggest that graduates from British, French, and Swedish higher education institutions are more frequently employed abroad both shortly after graduation and about four years later. Graduates from Austrian institutions are as well above average employed abroad four years after graduation. In contrast, international employment is frequent amongst those who graduated in Japan, Italy, and Norway.

But one should bear in mind that this survey may underestimate the proportion of foreign and the proportion of internationally mobile home country graduates. There are endemic difficulties in tracing the most mobile persons. Hence, the internationally mobile graduates may be underrepresented amongst the respondents.

Some 6 per cent of the home country graduates had home country citizenship at birth, but had learning or work experience abroad prior to enrolment. Educational or work experience abroad prior to enrolment were by far most frequent amongst Swedish graduates (22.8%), followed by Finnish graduates (10.1%). In contrast, only about one per cent or less had experience abroad at this stage amongst French, Italian, and Spanish graduates.

17.6 per cent of the respondents had international experiences during their course of study. Of these

– 11.1 per cent reported only study abroad,
– 4.4 per cent study and internship,
– 1.7 per cent only internships, and
– 0.4 per cent other experiences.

Mobility during the study period was highest amongst Dutch graduates (29%), followed by those graduating in Sweden, Finland and Austria (20-22%). It was lowest amongst Japanese (10%) and Spanish graduates (12%).

There are substantial differences according to fields of study: graduates in the humanities (30%) were more often mobile during their course of studies than those in other fields. Those in social sciences (19%), engineering (17%), law (16%) and natural sciences (14%) were close to the average in this respect, whilst graduates in education and mathematics (9-10%) went least to study abroad during their course of studies.

Some four years after graduation, about three per cent of those who graduated in their home country worked abroad – most of them were employed abroad and only a few were commissioned by their home company. During the four-year period after graduation, however, another 16 per cent worked abroad, of whom over two-thirds were commissioned by the home company for some period (see Table 11.10).

Table 11.10: Experiences Abroad After Graduation, by Country
(per cent of home graduates only)

Mobility after graduation	Country										Total
	IT	ES	FR	AT	DE	NL	UK	FI	SE	NO	
Currently working abroad	1.2	1.3	4.0	5.1	2.2	1.8	3.3	4.0	4.4	.4	2.7
Previously employed abroad	2.7	2.8	6.0	4.3	2.8	9.6	11.2	3.3	6.4	2.1	5.2
Occasionally commissioned abroad	9.2	7.7	17.4	8.4	6.6	20.3	10.5	11.0	7.0	8.7	10.7
Non-mobile	86.9	88.1	72.5	82.2	88.4	68.2	75.0	81.7	82.2	88.8	81.5
Total	100.0	100.0	100.0	100.0	100.0	100.0	100.0	100.0	100.0	100.0	100.0
Count	2813	2333	2504	2194	3303	2952	2978	2606	2524	3126	27334

Question I3: Please, provide information about your citizenship and your country of schooling, study and work. Question D15: Have you, since graduation (multiple replies possible) ...a) had regular employment abroad b) been sent abroad by your employer on work assignments.
Czech Republic and Japan: data missing.
Source: CHEERS survey data.

Whereas international student mobility amongst the respondents was highest in the humanities, professional mobility was highest amongst graduates in natural sciences and engineering. Correspondingly, international student mobility was slightly higher amongst the women than amongst the men who were surveyed, but professional mobility was slightly higher amongst the men than amongst the women who were surveyed.

Graduates who were internationally mobile after graduation obviously had more frequent assignments that required foreign language proficiency, international dimensions of their academic knowledge and an understanding of different cultures. But they also seemed to have more frequent rewarding and high-status assignments. Internationally mobile graduates considered their position as adequate and saw closer ties between study and work tasks. They were more satisfied with their job than non-mobile graduates.

11.3 The Family Situation

The graduates were asked to provide information about the aspects of their personal life: whether they lived as singles or together with partners, parents or other persons, and whether they had children in their households. These questions were raised in order to analyse links between the private living situation and career.

Four years after graduation, about half of the graduates lived with a partner. The proportion was clearly below average in Italy (37%), Spain (25%) and Japan (19%), as Table 11.11 shows. In these three countries a substantial proportion of graduates (around half or more) still lived with their parents, while this was true only for less than 10 per cent of the graduates in the Netherlands, Norway, Germany and Austria.

Table 11.11: Living Situation Some Four Years After Graduation, by Country (per cent; multiple responses)

	Country										Total
	IT	ES	FR	AT	DE	NL	UK	NO	EUR	JP	
With a partner	37	25	54	65	65	65	46	70	53	19	49
With parents	50	62	16	6	6	6	16	2	20	47	24
With other persons	5	7	4	6	5	4	26	8	8	5	8
As single	10	10	29	24	28	25	16	23	21	32	22
Total	102	104	103	100	103	100	105	102	103	104	103
Count	3070	2968	2996	2216	3425	3051	3344	3227	24297	3404	27701

Question I6: Did/do you live ... ? Multiple reply possible.
Czech Republic, Finland and Sweden: data missing.
Source: CHEERS survey data.

As one might expect, the percentage of graduates living with a partner has increased during the four years after graduation. But immediately prior to graduation, already 25 per cent, i.e. half, already had lived with a partner

In reverse, living with parents declined from 41 per cent to 24 per cent during the first four years after graduation. To live with parents at the time of graduation was quite common among graduates from Italy (80 %) and Spain (78 %), but exceptional in Norway (9 %), as Table 11.12 shows. These differences can be explained only to a very limited extent by the age of the students and graduates. More strikingly, we observe an independent life of the students themselves or their partners from those of their parents already at a relatively early stage in the northern and middle European countries, while the parents continue to play a strong role for students and graduates during their early career in Southern Europe and Japan.

Table 11.12: Living Situation Immediately Prior to Graduation, by Country (per cent; multiple responses)

	Country										Total
	IT	ES	FR	AT	DE	NL	UK	NO	EUR	JP	
With a partner	9	6	24	40	41	28	23	50	28	1	25
With parents	80	78	43	29	28	24	30	9	40	50	41
With other persons	9	17	9	11	10	20	47	19	18	6	17
As single	4	4	29	20	25	29	8	26	18	46	21
Total	102	105	105	100	105	101	108	104	104	102	104
Count	3063	2946	2994	2226	3440	3062	3300	3283	24315	3406	27722

Question I6: Did/do you live ... ? Multiple reply possible.
Czech Republic, Finland and Sweden: data missing.
Source: CHEERS survey data.

About 30 per cent had a child (or in some cases more than one) in the household about four years after graduation (see Table 11.13). This was by far more common in the Netherlands and quite frequent as well in the Nordic countries, i.e. countries where social norms as well as welfare systems are more favourable to students with children and to young parents in general than in other countries. Actually, 35 per cent of women as compared to 26 per cent of men surveyed reported that they had a child or children in the household.

Table 11.13: Children in the Graduates' Household Some Four Years after Graduation, by Country (per cent)

Children	Country													Total
	IT	ES	FR	AT	DE	NL	UK	FI	SE	NO	CZ	EUR	JP	
Yes	14	11	13	29	22	86	16	44	40	48	30	32	6	29
No	86	89	87	71	78	14	84	56	60	52	70	68	94	71
Total	100	100	100	100	100	100	100	100	100	100	100	100	100	100
Count	3102	2961	3051	2249	3470	3073	3193	2650	2623	3287	3092	32752	3409	36160

Question I7: Are there children in your household?
Source: CHEERS survey data.

Men seldom interrupted study or employment for child rearing and family care. In contrast, some women reserved at least time spans of their study and early career for that purpose. As Table 11.14 shows, 9 per cent of the women surveyed spent some time during the course of study predominantly for child rearing and family care. Over the whole first four years after graduation, this held true only for 6 per cent of the women surveyed, and six per cent as well did so at the time of the survey, i.e. about four years after graduation. Four years after graduation, about one third of women with at least one child in the household were predominantly active in child rearing and family care.

Additional information available suggests that this ratio increased moderately each year after graduation, but the increase remained much smaller than one might have expected. Female graduates frequently opted for part-time employment as a compromise between family and professional tasks: actually, at the time the survey was conducted, 16 per cent of employed women were part-time employed four years after graduation as compared to 6 per cent of men.

Table 11.14: Child Rearing and Family Care some Four Years after Graduation, by Gender and Country (per cent)

	Country													Total
	IT	ES	FR	AT	DE	NL	UK	FI	SE	NO	CZ	EUR	JP	
Some time during period of study														
Female	12	7	8	12	7	4	7	13	10	16	11	0	10	0	9
Male	5	3	1	4	2	1	2	4	5	3	2	0	3	0	2
Total	9	5	5	7	4	3	5	9	8	11	6	0	6	0	6
Predominant activity since graduation														
Female	9	4	4	8	5	3	4	8	4	2	19	2	6	2	6
Male	2	2	1	1	0	0	0	0	0	0	6	0	1	0	1
Total	6	3	2	4	2	2	2	5	2	1	11	1	4	1	3
Four years after graduation														
Female	3	1	2	9	8	3	3	5	11	3	21	8	6	8	6
Male	0	0	0	0	0	0	0	0	1	0	0	0	0	0	0
Total	1	0	1	4	3	2	2	3	6	2	9	2	3	2	3

Source: CHEERS survey data.

11.4 Regional Disparities

To define the regions, we used the current Eurostat NUTS classification (NUTS2). For those regions where Eurostat data were not available, we used national classifications of territorial units (for example the provinces in Japan). In order to measure the impact of regional economic conditions, the regions were classified on the basis of GDP per capita. Four categories were established:

– economically *very strong* regions having a GDP per inhabitant that was higher than one standard deviation above the national mean of GDP per inhabitant;
– economically *strong* regions having a GDP per inhabitant that was between the national average and one standard deviation above;
– economically *weak* regions having a GDP per inhabitant that was between the national average and one standard deviation below;
– economically *very weak* regions having a GDP per inhabitant that was smaller than one standard deviation below the national average.

Since in some countries only a few regions were classified as weak or very weak, these two groups were aggregated.

The survey shows that the employment opportunities of graduates were influenced to some extent by the economic strength of the region they came from and where they graduated. For example, unemployment rates were higher t amongst respondents having graduated in economically weak regions (see Table 11.15). The difference was most striking in Italy where graduates from economically weak regions had an unemployment ratio that was five times as high as those graduating in very strong regions.

Table 11.15: Unemployed Graduates Some Four Years After Graduation, by Economic Strength of Region of Residence and Country (per cent of respondents)

Economic strength of region of residence	Country							
	IT	FR	AT	DE	UK	FI	NO	JP
Very strong	0.8	5.2	0.3	0.2	0.4	0.2	0.5	1.7
Strong	2.0	5.1	0.4	1.0	0.8	-	0.7	3.2
Weak or very weak	5.7	8.5	0.3	1.5	1.9	0.2	0.7	5.2

Czech Republic, Spain, the Netherlands and Sweden: data missing
Source: CHEERS survey data.

The study shows that, in most countries, the transition process – notably the time to find a job – was not linked to the economic wealth of the region of graduation. But the regions mattered regarding various aspects of employment a few years after graduation: full-time employment and employment based on permanent contracts were, in most countries, higher in economically strong regions than in weak regions. Only in Austria, the Netherlands and the United Kingdom, did the study not reveal significant links between graduate employment and regional disparities. Altogether, regional differences affected graduates' careers more strongly in Italy than in all other countries of the survey.

The CHEERS graduate survey enabled the participating researchers to analyse geographical mobility from the region where students studied and were awarded their degree to the region where they lived and were employed some four years after graduation. Therefore, it was possible to examine the extent to which the frequency of mobility varied according to country, field of study and gender as well as the direction of mobility, as far as the economic strength of the region was concerned.

The above named measures of the location of study as well as the location of life and work some four years after graduation provided the opportunity of measuring:
- *"residence mobility"* (graduates living some four year after graduation in another region from that where they graduated) and
- *"employment mobility"* (employed graduates working some four years after graduation in another region from that where they graduated).

Of the graduates surveyed, 59 per cent kept their residence in the region where they studied, and 56 per cent worked in the region where they studied some four years after graduation. By merging the information on both, residence and employment mobility, it is possible to show (Table 11.16) that 54 per cent, that is slightly more than half the graduates, were not mobile in any of the two dimensions. In contrast, 37 per cent were both living and working in another region. The remaining 10 per cent worked in a different region from the one in which they lived. Hence some of them either opted to continue to live or to work in the region of their studies.

Table 11.16: Typology of Regional Mobility Some Four Years after Graduation (per cent)

	Per cent
Non mobile: Living and working in the region of study	54
Mobile	46
Among them:	
Residence mobility while working in the region of study	3
Residence and employment mobility to the same region	37
Residence and employment mobility to different regions	3
Employment mobility while living in the region of study	3
Total	100.0
Count	20,682

Mobility: Graduates, who are employed four years after graduation in a region (NUTS 2) that is different from their study region or are living in a different region; internationally mobile graduates are not included.

Source: CHEERS survey data.

12 MAJOR FINDINGS AND POLICY IMPLICATIONS

12.1 Aims and Methods of the Study

The employment and work of higher education graduates are a major theme that is relevant both for researchers and practitioners in the area of higher education, in terms of understanding the impact of higher education, and for experts in the area of occupations and work, in terms of scrutinizing employment and work of the most highly qualified segment of the labour force. The CHEERS Study (Careers after Higher Education: A European Research Study) aimed to provide information on graduate employment and work in a more comprehensive way than prior research.

First, the study draws in its concepts and in the interpretation of the findings from the often divided domains of higher education and occupational research. Second, it aimed to cross the borderlines of research traditions on the relationship between education and the world of work and thus refers both to the economists' inclinations to collect information on career paths and remuneration and to draw conclusions on that basis on the status of the labour market, the returns to educational investments and mismatches as far as employers' expectations are concerned, as well as to the sociologists' preferences of analysing the impact of values and orientations on behaviour in the course of the career, the perceived use of knowledge and the match between employment and work and educational attainment.

Third, the study aims to fill the gap of international comparability of in-depth information on graduate employment and work. Internationally comparable information is available on employment according to economic sectors, employments' status and remuneration and other statistical categories, but in-depth surveys that address links between competences and job tasks, the impact of orientation on professional behaviour, problems in the transition process etc. were only conducted in individual countries in the past. The CHEERS study succeeded in providing the most thorough comparative information on graduate employment and work and the links between higher education and graduate employment and work so far.

The information presented in this volume is based on responses to a largely standardized questionnaire provided between autumn 1998 and autumn 1999 by about 36,000 people who had graduated from higher education institutions with degrees that were equivalent to Bachelor and Master in the academic year 1994/95. They were surveyed some four years after graduation. A representative selection of higher education graduates in eleven European countries (Austria, the Czech Republic, Finland France, Germany, Italy, the Netherlands, Norway, Spain, Sweden and the United Kingdom) and Japan was addressed, mainly by mail. The response rate of 39 per cent was fairly satisfactory, given the fact that some of the non-respondents may not have been contacted and that it took more than an hour to answer the questionnaire was.

The study by researchers from nine European countries under the lead of the authors of this volume was funded by the European Commission in the framework of the Targeted Socio-Economic Research programme (TSER). Therefore, emphasis was placed on an intra-European comparison. The scope could be widened, however, due to the fact that two other European countries could join subsequently and that Japan also participated thanks to support from the Japan Institute of Labour.

The study provides salient information on:
- the employment situation of higher education graduates in various European countries in the late 1990s,
- the specific conditions and dynamics of transition,
- the diversity of "success" criteria in graduate employment and work,
- the impact of socio-biographical profiles, study conditions and provisions, study behaviour and graduates' transition to employment and work,
- the European diversity and disparity in graduate employment and work,
- specific themes, e.g. employers' views, employment and work of women, regional disparities, international mobility in the course of study and after graduation, etc.

This first volume on the results of the study is descriptive in nature. It aims to provide an account of the major findings in all thematic areas addressed. It is the revised text of the official report presented to the sponsors of the project. The second volume published concurrently, as well as hundreds of already published analyses of specific issues of the relationships between higher education, specific countries and specific fields and professions discuss theoretical frameworks and employ complex modes of data analysis.

Yet, even a presentation of findings that aims to be descriptive is bound to be selective and focused, given the wealth of information available and breadth of conceptual frameworks contributing to the approach of the study. Three questions shaped this volume.

First, we aim to establish how successful graduates were in terms of:
- a smooth transition from higher education to employment, e.g. efforts involved and speed of transition,
- privileged employment, e.g. high remuneration and occupational status and desirable employment conditions,
- a work situation that is desirable for a graduate, e.g. using one's competences on the job, being active in one's area of expertise and having demanding, independent and satisfactory assignments.

This, of course, is discussed in the light of controversial debates on the need for higher education expansion to achieve economic growth and as preparation for the knowledge society on the hand and on the concerns about "over-education" and general labour market problems on the other.

Second, we provide information about the role of higher education in preparing graduates for employment and work: To what extent are fields of study linked to employment areas and work assignments. How far do their competences acquired up to graduation match their job requirement? To what extent do they use what they have learned on the job? What do they do to upgrade their competences during the first years after graduation?

Third, we discuss the extent to which graduate employment and work is similar or varies substantially between the countries included in this study. Did common developments of knowledge, professional work and the economy in economically advanced countries or at least in the countries closely cooperating in Europe lead to a convergence of graduate employment and work? Or is a diversity between different traditions of higher education, professional identity, welfare conditions of employment and work, economic and social conditions in the various countries the prevailing finding?

12.2 Success in Transition, Employment and Work

The CHEERS study shows that higher education graduates in most of the European countries that were analysed and Japan faced relatively positive employment and job prospects in the latter half of the 1990s. This was by no means a matter of procedure. Certainly, a general need was felt for decades to raise the level of competences of the labour force in order to stimulate economic growth and economic well-being. And these arguments gained momentum in the 1990s when a conventional wisdom emerged that the economically advanced countries were on the way to a knowledge society and a knowledge economy. On the other hand, graduates were observed at a historical period in which both many employers and politicians were greatly concerned by a too vast expansion of higher education and tendencies towards over-education. Moreover, many economically advanced countries experienced marginal economic growth rates and increased unemployment during the 1990s.

As regards transition, we note that graduates spent only six months on average on their search for their first job after graduation. Two-thirds were able to complete the search process within three months. In contrast, less than ten per cent were still searching one year after graduation.

One must bear in mind, however, that the search is a complex and time-consuming activity for many graduates. Almost half the respondents had started their job search some time prior to graduation. Many of them opted for various methods. Besides answering advertisements, about half the graduates contacted employers themselves. 22 per cent were supported by career offices of their university and 10 per cent by the academic staff of the university. On average, about 25 contacts between the job seekers and employers were established before a graduate made a final choice.

The timing of the first regular employment varied substantially amongst graduates. This reflects different traditions of transition to employment in the countries included, differences in the "employability" of the graduates, different labour conditions according to country, economic sector and field of study and occupational area, as well as different options and strategies of graduates in the transition period. Overall, about 40 per cent were regularly employed (excluding temporary activities in order to survive the early transition period) immediately after graduation, and about a further 25 per cent up to sixth months after graduation. An additional 10 per cent found employment within the 12 months after graduation, while a quarter who had aimed to be employed had not achieved this within a year after graduation. About four per cent of the latter category remained unemployed most of the first four years after graduation.

In various cases, the career starts with a temporary contract and in some cases with part-time employment. In some countries and economic sectors, short-term contracts are quite common for graduates. Within two years after graduation, most employed graduates were professionally active full-time on a long-term contract.

During the first four years after graduation, more than two-thirds spent most of the time being regularly employed. More than one fifth followed further study and professional training, some of them in addition to regular employment. Less than one sixth were neither predominantly employed nor predominant learners during the first years after graduation, e.g. active in occasional jobs, unemployed, predominantly engaged in child rearing and family care or out of the labour force for other reasons. The majority of those employed changed employers within the first four years after graduation, half of them twice or more.

Four years after graduation, the situation seems relatively settled for many graduates. 84 per cent were employed (including self-employment) and 7 per cent were in graduate education or professional training. Only three percent each were unemployed, primarily engaged in child rearing and family care, or reported other activities. 11 per cent of those employed worked part-time and 22 per cent had short-term contracts.

The women's job search and career start seemed slightly less favourable than those of men in the first two years after graduation. Thereafter, the gap began to widen when a large number of women opted for part-time employment or discontinuation of employment in order to engage in child rearing and family care. Some four years after graduation, 80 per cent were regularly employed, as compared to 89 per cent of men. And of those employed, 16 per cent worked part-time as compared to 4 per cent of men.

Four years after graduation, 70 per cent were active in professional, managerial and other high-level occupations. 18 per cent were in technicians and associate professional positions, and only 12 per cent were employed in occupations that were usually not considered to require advanced levels of educational attainment. The average gross income was just above 28,000 Euros.

In response to questions about the quality of employment and work, most respondents considered their situation as characterized by great use of knowledge, close links between their competences and work tasks, interesting and demanding tasks and overall having a satisfying job. Between 13 and 22 per cent expressed strong reservation in the following respects:
- occupational expectations not fulfilled (22%),
- little use of knowledge and skills (21%),
- a lower educational attainment would fit better (20%),
- field of study does not match the work assignments (17%),
- studies in general had little use for employment and work (15%),
- position did not match level of educational attainment (14%), and
- low overall job satisfaction (13%).

Only 7 per cent believed that higher education was superfluous for their kind of work and employment. Only four per cent would not study if they could choose again. The proportion of graduates who considered their work situation some four years after graduation as being better than they had expected before starting their studies was almost twice as high as those who considered their work situation as being worse than expected.

Most graduates considered themselves as being very strongly motivated. Status, income and employment conditions played a role as well, but were less strongly emphasized. By and large, the motivations and orientations were defined by the graduates as being more ambitious than the actual work situation, but only a small proportion were highly dissatisfied with their employment and work conditions and the discrepancies between their motivations and competences and their actual work situation.

This does not mean that the problems observed in those respects are negligible. But they seem to be smaller on average than debates in the late 1990s about "over-education" and general employment problems had suggested.

12.3 Studies as Preparation for Subsequent Employment and Work

Higher education varies from other levels of educational attainment as being least geared to direct professional preparation. Research and teaching in higher education encourage academics to pursue knowledge for its own sake. Students are not trained for certain job assignments because they should be able to reflect, criticize and revamp established professional practice. It is the innovative function of higher education which precludes a close link. On the other hand, higher education is viewed in some areas as an indispensable prerequisite and in many areas as a very useful preparation for the world of work. A discrepancy between the levels and areas of expertise and the areas of work assignments tends to be viewed as more problematic in the domains of higher education and highly educated professions than in all other areas.

Altogether, the values of students and graduates seem to be so different that any claim for a dominant culture in the relationship between higher education and the world of work remains irrational wishful thinking. The perennial debates on the function of higher education with respect to the world of work could be beneficial because the diversity of higher education is not suppressed by dominant fashions of *Zeitgeist*.

Most graduates surveyed went through 15 to 19 years of schooling up to graduation, of which 12-13 years were spent in primary and secondary education, the latter in more than three cases in academic secondary education programmes, and mostly three to six years of study.

But their life course prior to graduation is often not confined to schooling. Almost one out of three graduates had been employed prior to study, one out of seven had been vocationally trained, and one out of nine was in military service prior to study. The gap between the required period of study (4.1 years of average) and the actual period of study (5.0 years) is often due to extended paid employment during the course of study. Almost half the students reported that they took on paid employment that was not related to their field of study, almost one third of the graduates stated that they worked during their course of studies in assignments that were linked to their studies or future careers and that they participated in internships. Obviously, many students considered acquiring a broad range of experience as being more valuable than believing those who advocated "efficient" study in terms of focus on academic knowledge and a short and smooth "transition".

Most graduates appreciated their studies and believed that learning in higher education was useful for coping with their job tasks. Yet, there was widespread critique of many aspects of higher education – certainly to a varying degree across countries and fields of study. Obviously, many graduates wished that higher education would prepare students to be in the position to transfer knowledge to the work environment and to the job tasks graduates are confronted with.

In addition, graduates were involved in many other experiences and activities prior to graduation that could enhance their potentially relevant competences. Extra-curricular activities, cultural experiences, foreign language learning and international experiences could be quoted in this respect. For example, at the end of their study period, 60 per cent of non-native speakers saw themselves as being capable of reading professionally relevant texts in English. This was the case for 16 per cent in French and 10 per cent in German. The majority had expertise in various software areas. More than one fifth had spent a period of study, internships etc. abroad during their course of study in higher education.

Graduates reported that finding employment required competences and personality traits beyond academic knowledge. Most were convinced that knowledge acquisition in the course of study as well as "personality" were crucial for employers to recruit them.

Some four years after graduation, 80 per cent of the graduates stated that, retrospectively, they felt strong at the time of graduation as regarded general abilities, and about two-thirds each stated a high level of competences as far as power of concentration, working independently, loyalty and integrity, field-specific theoretical knowledge, written communication skills, getting personally involved, adaptability and critical thinking were concerned.

As regards the knowledge and related cognitive abilities, the perceived competences at the time of graduation generally seemed to match the level of job requirements. Yet graduates perceived their assignments as being more demanding than they felt prepared for at the time of graduation. Notably, they stated higher requirements as far as organization-related skills or the transfer of knowledge to practical problem-solving were concerned: notably, negotiating as well as planning, coordinating and organizing time management. In addition, they saw the need to improve their computer skills.

International competences were viewed by many as important for their job. Only a few found an employment abroad, and others were sent abroad on temporary job assignments. But almost half considered it important on their job to work with people from different backgrounds. 40 per cent underscored the importance of foreign language proficiency and almost as many the knowledge and understanding of different cultures and modes of behaviour.

In sum, many graduates who were surveyed did not see close links between study and employment. Only 38 per cent considered their field of study as the only one possible or the best for their area of work, and only half noted a frequent use of their specific area of knowledge. Rather, they perceived a broad range of job requirements which were to a certain extent served by the study programme and by a broad range of experiences prior to and alongside their studies.

To a certain extent, discrepancies between competences at the moment of graduation and subsequent job requirements had to be balanced by formal training or evened out by informal learning and professional socialization. About two-thirds underwent some kind of formal training for initial or continuing professional preparation during the first four years after graduation. These were more often short courses than long training periods. Surprisingly "new scholarly knowledge in my discipline" was quoted very frequently as the theme of professional training.

12.4 European and International Diversity and Disparity

This study on higher education and graduate employment demonstrates a substantial variety between European countries as well as between Japan and the various European countries as far as higher education and its relationship to the world of work is concerned. This variety is fascinating in many respects.

As we already know, there is quite a variety between the countries with respect to the structures of higher education systems, curricular approaches, as well as the desired preparatory function of higher education for professional work. In some countries, long programmes prevailed, whereas in others short ones prevailed. In some countries, one finds a strong professional emphasis of higher education, in others the range of goals is more diverse. In some countries, the reputation of higher education institutions plays a major role, in others it is marginal. Some higher education systems encourage independent learning, others rely more strongly on communication with the teachers.

Similarly, views differ between countries about close links between field of study and occupational areas or more flexible relationships, about the characteristics of a good graduate job, about the extent to which the existing job tasks are accepted or graduates want to contribute to social and political changes.

This variety could be inspiring; for example, the success of the ERASMUS student mobility programme is linked to the fascination of experiences in other countries which contrast with the educational environment at home.

The variety of higher education systems, in contrast, could be seen as a barrier: recent efforts to establish "convergent" structures of study programmes and degrees are based on that assumption. But it is an open question whether economically advanced countries altogether and specifically the European countries that cooperate economically and politically move towards similar situations in areas which tend to be termed universally, such as the move towards a "knowledge society".

By and large, the CHEERS survey demonstrates so striking disparities of graduate employment and work in the 11 European countries and Japan that common elements seem to be at most secondary.

For example, 63 per cent of Norwegian graduates and 97 per cent of Japanese graduates had started their job search prior to graduation. In contrast, only 18 per cent of graduates from French and 16 per cent from Italian higher education institutions started their job search at such an early stage. In the Czech Republic, they contacted only 6 employers on average, but in France they contacted 70 before making a final decision. 37 per cent of the British graduates and 63 per cent of graduates in Japan had sought employment with the help of the career offices of their higher education institution, but this was true for less than ten per cent of graduates in Germany, Norway and Sweden. Family connections were mobilized in the job search process by 54 per cent of Italian graduates, but only by 15 per cent of Norwegian graduates. Eventually, more than three quarters of Norwegian and Japanese graduates were on the job some three months after graduation, whilst more two-thirds of graduates from French higher education institutions took more than a year to be employed on a regular basis. In the majority of countries included in the study, only one or two per cent of the graduates were unemployed most of the first four years after graduation; in contrast, this was true for 18 per cent of the Spanish graduates. And even at the time the survey was conducted, i.e. some four years after graduation, the unemployment quota varied by one and ten per cent.

The average gross annual income of full-time employed graduates in one country is slightly more than 40 per cent of the average income of the country where graduates receive the highest remuneration. Even when differences of purchasing power are taken into consideration income differences according to country remain striking.

Even graduate employment according to economic sector varied substantially. For example, half or more than half of the graduates had public employers in the Nordic countries. This quota was less than a quarter in Italy and Japan and slightly higher than a quarter in the Netherlands. More than 90 per cent of graduates from Austrian and Finnish universities were employed in professional and other high-level occupations. In contrast, about half the Norwegian graduates were active as technicians and associate professionals, and more than 40 per cent of Japanese graduates as clerks and sales workers. Here, a different degree of expansion and diversification of higher education came into play at the time when the graduates surveyed were studying.

The quota of self-employment ranged from an exceptionally high 19 per cent in Italy to less than five per cent in half of the countries, of which two per cent in France, Norway and Japan. Similar differences held true with respect to short-term contracts and part-time employment.

On the one hand, three quarters or more graduates from the Czech Republic considered their studies as very useful in preparing them for their present work tasks. On the other, this was the case for less than half the French, German, Italian and British graduates. Across different measures, Norwegian graduates reported the closest links between study and subsequent work, and graduates of Finnish, Swedish, Czech and Dutch institutions observed a relatively close tie. In contrast, many graduates from Japanese, French, British, Italian and Spanish institutions stated that their knowledge was not very useful for their employment, that they considered their assignments as not matching their level of education or that they were not satisfied with their work situation.

Altogether, the study shows that higher education and the relationship between higher education and employment vary in most respects more substantially by country than by field of study. There are more frequent "national" cultures than "disciplinary" cultures in the relationship between higher education and the world of work; disparities between countries overshadow diversity according to disciplines. One should add that regional differences within countries are moderate in most countries surveyed; they only play a substantial role in a few countries, notably Italy.

It should be added, though, that a more realistic view of the common elements and differences between Western European countries was provided in CHEERS by the inclusion of the Czech Republic and Japan in the project. This made one aware that there were some common elements in Western Europe, despite the visible diversity. For example, the case of Japan shows that the smooth process of study and transition to employment could have its price in providing students with a less great chance of acquiring broad experiences beyond the core domains of higher education. Hence they were equipped with fewer professionally relevant competences upon graduation.

12.5   Strength and Limits of the Study and Prospects

The CHEERS project certainly succeeded in demonstrating the potentials of representative surveys on the relationship between higher education and the world of work across boundaries. It underscored the need to extend the information base on graduate employment and work to issues that were usually covered by education and employment statistics. Surveys that address the competences acquired, the modes of job search, the perceived links between knowledge and work assignments, the extent to which orientations and the realities of the work situation match and finally the retrospective view on the higher education institutions can provide extremely valuable information.

As a practical consequence for research, the authors recommend regular surveys of that kind with a somewhat more centralized organizational structure and a mix of regular core themes and a few additional themes on a rotating basis. In the long term, a generally accepted questionnaire could be developed, and regular surveying could become more efficient than a heterogeneous team spread over various countries.

The authors of this publication deliberately stopped short of discussing at length the practical implications of the research results. They are aware that the practical implications may be differently assessed and that the actors in the field are both knowledgeable in interpreting these findings and inclined – as many highly educated and influential professionals – not to accept that a strong role should be given to researchers on higher education and society in interpreting the practical implications of the research findings. But the authors are convinced that the project provides an extraordinarily valuable source of information for reflection on the future of the relationship between higher education and the world of work.

Moreover, this publication was the first general overview of the findings. Various studies followed that analysed in-depth issues such as the impact of country specifics of higher education or structural options, and the degree of homogeneity or diversification of higher education systems on graduate employment work, differences by fields of study and occupational areas, differences of career success according to graduates' competences, gender disparities in graduate employment and work, the long-term effects of the career starts and other themes. Select issues of that kind analysed by scholars involved in the CHEERS project are presented in the second volume: Ulrich Teichler (ed.): *Careers of University Graduates. Views and Experiences in Comparative Perspective.* Dordrecht, Springer 2006.

Results of the study can be summarized as key "messages": graduate employment and work were less problematic in most of the countries analysed in the late 1990s than public debates about "over-education" and general employment problems had suggested. The links between higher education and the world of work must be more clearly viewed as a multi-facetted pattern of learning, socialization and coping with professional tasks than in the past when often great attention was paid to the use of field-specific knowledge. Finally, differences between countries are more striking features of relationships between higher education and the world of work than we tend to assume in the wake of universal trends towards a "knowledge society" or presumed European and global trends of convergence. But this report aims to make the readers aware of many specific themes and thus hopes to serve as a useful source for many dimensions of the relationships between higher education and the world of work.

LITERATURE

Aamodt, P.O. and Arnesen, C.A. (1995). "The Relationship between Expansion in Higher Education and the Labour Market in Norway." *European Journal of Education*, 30(1), 65-76.

Abbott, A. (1988). *The System of Professions*. Chicago: University of Chicago Press.

Arnesen, C.A. and Egge, M. (eds.) (1992). *Utdanning og arbeidsmarked 1992*. Oslo: NAVFs utredningsinstitutt.

Attewell, P. (1990). "What is Skill?" *Work and Occupations*, 17(4), 422-448.

Berkhout, P.H.G. and Provoost, J.H.C. (1994). "Schoolverlaters op zoek naar een baan: een duuranalyse." Amsterdam: *SEO* (SEO-rapport nr. 339).

Biddle, J. and Roberts, K. (1994). "Private Sector and Engineers and the Transition to Management." *The Journal of Human Resources*, 29(1), 82-107.

Borghans, L. (1992). *A Histo-Topographic Map of Dutch University Studies*. Maastricht: ROA (ROA-W-1992/5E).

Borghans, L. and Willems, E.J.T.A. (1994). *Baanzoekduren van HBO-ers onder de loep*. Maastricht: ROA (ROA-RM-1994/4).

Boys, C.J. et al. (1988). *Higher Education and the Preparation for Work*. London: Jessica Kingsley.

Brandt, E. (ed.) (1993). *Utdanning og arbeidsmarked 1993*. Oslo: Utredningsinstituet for forskning og hoyere utdanning.

Breneman, D.W. (1994). *Liberal Arts Colleges, Thriving, Surviving, or Endangered?* Washington, D.C: The Brookings Institution.

Brennan, J. and McGeevor, P.A. (1988). *Graduates at Work: Degree Courses and the Labour Market*. London: Jessica Kingsley.

Brennan, J. and McGeevor P.A. (1990). *Ethnic Minorities and the Graduate Labour Market*. London: Commission for Racial Equality.

Brennan, J. et al. (1993). *Students Courses and Jobs: the Relationship between Higher Education and the Labour Market*. London: Jessica Kingsley.

Brennan, J. et al. (1994). "The Experiences and Views of Graduates: Messages from Recent Surveys." *Higher Education Management*, 6(3), 275-304.

Brennan, J. et al. (1995). "Employment and Work of British and German Graduates." In Brennan, J., Kogan, M. and Teichler, U. (eds.) *Higher Education and Work*. London: Jessica Kingsley, pp. 47-98.

Brennan, J., Kogan, M. and Teichler, U. (1995). "Higher Education and Work: a Conceptual Framework." In Brennan, J., Kogan, M. and Teicher, U. (eds.) *Higher Education and Work*. London: Jessica Kingsley, pp.1-24.

Bresciani, P.G., et al. (1988). *I contratti di formazione e lavoro. Analisi della domanda*. Milano: IARD.

Burkart, G. (ed.) (1985). *Maturanten, Studenten, Akademiker: Studien zur Entwicklung von Bildungs- und Berufsverläufen in Österreich*. Klagenfurt: Kärtner Druck- und Verlagsgesellschaft.

Buzzi, C. et al. (1988). *I giovani e la condizione lavorativa*. Milano: IARD.

Calanca, A. and Rostan, M. (1993). *Le opinioni e gli atteggiamenti degli studenti della provincia di Como: le zone del Lario Intelvese e delle Alpi Lepontine*. Milano: IARD.

Cappelli, P. (1993). "Are Skill Requirements Rising? Evidence from Production and Clerical Jobs." *Industrial and Labor Relations Review*, 46(3), 515-530.
Carnoy, M. (ed.) (1995). *International Encyclopedia of Economics of Education.* (Second edition), Oxford: Pergamon.
CERI/OECD (1990). *Technological Change and Human Resources Development in the Service Sector.* Paris.
Chiesi, A. (1996). *Quarta indagine nazionale sulla condizione giovanile: Il lavoro. Strategie di risposta alla crisi.* Milano: IARD.
Cockburn, C. (1985). "The Nature of Skill: the Case of the Printers." In Littler, C.R. (ed.) *The Experience of Work.* Aldershot: Gower, 132-140.
Commission of the European Community (1987). *New Technology and Social Change.* Brussels: FAST Report.
Commission of the European Communities, Task Force Human Resources, Education, Training and Youth (1991). *Memorandum on Higher Education in the European Community.* Brussels.
Commission of the European Communities (1993). *The Outlook for Higher Education in the European Community: Responses to the Memorandum.* Brussels.
Copple, C.E. (1991). *Education and Employment Research and Policy Studies: Annotated Bibliography, 1987-1990.* Washington, D.C.: World Bank (Background Paper Series, 26),
Crozier, M. (1993). *L'entreprise à l'écoute: Apprendre le management post-industriel.* Paris: InterEditions du Seuil.
Darrah, C.N. (1992). "Workplace Skills in Context." *Human Organization,* 51, 264-273.
Darrah, C.N. (1994). "Skill Requirements at Work: Rhetoric versus Reality." *Work and Occupations,* 21(1), 64-84.
D' Iribarne, A. (1989). *La Compétitivité: Defí social, enjeu éducatif.* Mesnil-sur-l'Estrée: Presses du CNRS.
Delsen, L. (1995). *Atypical Employment: an International Perspective, Consequences and Policy.* Groningen: Wolters-Noordhoff.
Desmarez, P. and Thys-Clément, F. (1994). "Universities, Students and Employment - Present Position and Prospects." *Higher Education Management,* 6(3), 259-273.
Deutsches Jugendinstitut (ed.) (1993). *Jugend - Wirtschaft - Politik. Lernen und Arbeiten in Europa.* München.
De Weert, E. (1994). "Translating Employment Needs into Curriculum Strategies". *Higher Education Management,* 6(3), 305-320.
De Weert, E. (1995). "Responsiveness of Higher Education to Labour Market Demands: Curriculum Change in the Humanities and the Social Sciences." In Brennan, J., Kogan, M. and Teichler, U. (eds.) *Higher Education and Work.* London: Jessica Kingsley, pp.25-46.
De Weert, E. (1996). *Behoefte aan vorming en opleiding van Wageningse academici na de eeuwwisseling.* 's-Gravenhage: Nationale Raad voor Landbouwkundig Onderzoek.
Esnault, E. (1990). "Les unversités et l'évolution de l'employ." *CREaction,* 92, 23-27.
Estland, G. (1990). *Education, Training and Employment.* Vol. 1, Buckingham: Open University.
Europäische Kommission (1994). *Wachstum, Wettbewerbsfähigkeit, Beschäftigung: Herausforderungen der Gegenwart und Wege ins 21. Jahrhundert.* Luxembourg: Office for Official Publications of the European Communities.
European Commission (1996). *Key Data on Education in the European Union 1995.* Luxembourg: Office for Official Publications of the European Communities.

European Roundtable of Industrialists (1989). *Education and the European Competence: ERT Study on Education and Training in Europe*. Brussels: IRDAC.
Eurostat (1992). *Regions: Nomenclature of Territorial Units for Statistics*. Brussels.
Eurostat (1994). "Le chomage dans les régions de l'Union Européenne en 1993." *Statistiques Rapides*, 2, Brussels.
Ford, G.W. (1990). "Conceptual Changes and Innovations in Skill Formation at the Enterprise Level." In Janssen, J. et al (eds.) *General Report of the Intergovernmental Conference on Technological Change and Human Resources Development*. Zoetermeer: Dutch Ministry of Education and Science, 53-89.
Form, W. (1980). "On the Degradation of Skills." *Annual Review of Sociology*, 13, 29-47.
Freidson, E. (1983). "The Theory of Professions: State of the Art." In Dingwall, R. and Lewis, S. (eds.) *The Sociology of Professions*. London: St Martin's, pp.19-37.
Fulton, O., Gordon, A. and Williams, G. (1982). *Higher Education and Manpower Planning*. Geneve: International Labour Office.
Gallie, D. (1991). "Patterns of Skill Change: Upskilling, Deskilling or the Polarization of Skills?" *Work, Employment and Society*, 5(3), 319-351.
Garcia, P. et al. (1995). "Experimenting Institutional Evaluation in Spain." *Higher Education Management*, 7(1), 101-118.
Gellert, C. (ed.) (1993). *Higher Education in Europe*. London: Jessica Kingsley.
Giffard, A. and Paul, J.J. (1992). "Les politiques régionales de formation professionelles: esquisse d'analyse. " *Document de travail du CEREQ*, 76, 73-92.
Goedegebuure, L. and van Vught, F. (1996). "Comparative Higher Education Studies: The Perspective for the Policy Sciences." *Higher Education*, 32(4), 371-394.
Goedegebuure, L. et al. (eds.) (1996a). *The Mockers and Mocked. Comparative Perspectives on Differentation, Convergence and Diversity in Higher Education*. Oxford: Pergamon Press.
Goode, W.J. (1957). "Community within a Community: the Professions." *American Sociological Review*, 22, 194-200.
Goodlad, S. (ed.) (1984). *Education for the Professions*. Guildford: SRHE & NFER Nelson.
Grip, A. de and Heijke, J.A.M. (1988). *Labour Market Indicators: an Inventory*. Maastricht: ROA (ROA-W-1988/1E).
Guggenberger, H. (1991). *Hochschulzugang und Studienwahl. Empirische und theoretische Ergebnisse von Hochschulforschung*. Klagenfurt: Kärtner Druck- und Verlagsgesellschaft.
Harland, J. and Gibbs, I. (1986). *Beyond Graduation, the College Experience*. Guildford: SRHE & NFER Nelson.
Heijke, H. (ed.) (1994). *Forecasting the Labour Market by Occupation and Education*. Boston, Dordrecht and London: Kluwer Academic Publishers.
Heijke, J.A.M. and Ramaekers, G.W.M. (1992). *Labour Market Position of University of Limburg Graduates*. Maastricht: ROA (ROA-RM-1992/2E),.
"Higher Education and Employment"(special issue) (1995a). *European Journal of Education*, 30(1).
"Higher Education and Employment" (special issue) (1995b) *European Journal of Education*, 30(2).
"Higher Education and the Labour Market" (special issue) (1993). *Higher Education in Europe*, 18(2).
Hughes, G. and O'Connell, P.J. (1995). "Higher Education and the Labour Market in Ireland, 1981-1991." *European Journal of Education*, 30(1), 77-103.

Husén, T. (1987). *Higher Education and Social Stratification: An International Comparative Study.* Paris: Unesco/IIEP.
Industrial Research and Development Advisory Committee (IRDAC) (1992). *Skills Shortages in Europe.* Brussels: Commission of the European Communities.
ISTAT (1994). "Indagine 1991 sugli sbocchi professionali dei laureati." *Collana d'informazione,* 1.
ISTAT (1996). "L'inserimento professionale dei laureat". In *Rapporto sull'Italia.* Bologna: il Mulino, 108-111.
Jablonska-Skinder, H. and Teichler, U. (1992). *Handbook of Higher Education Diplomas in Europe.* München: K.G. Saur.
Jonsson, B. (1991). *Kompetensutveckling pa framtidens arbetsmarknad: en litteraturöversikt, Universitets- och Högskoleämbetet.* Stockholm (UHÄ projekt 1991:3a).
Kaiser, M., Nuthmann, R. and Stegmann, H. (eds.) (1985). *Berufliche Verbleibsforschung in der Diskussion.* 4 vols., Nürnberg: Institut für Arbeitsmarkt- und Berufsforschung der Bundesanstalt für Arbeit (BeitrAB 90.1-90.4).
Karabel, J. and Halsey, A.H. (eds.) (1977). *Power and Ideology in Education.* New York: Oxford University Press.
Kellermann, P. (ed.) (1982). *Universität und Umland: Beziehungen zwischen Hochschule und Region.* Klagenfurt: Kärtner Druck- und Verlagsgesellschaft.
Kellermann, P. (ed.) (1984). *Studienaufnahme und Studienzulassung: Aspekte des Wandels im Zugang zu den Hochschulen.* Klagenfurt: Kärtner Druck- und Verlagsgesellschaft.
Kellermann, P. (ed.) (1994b). *Regionsuniversitäten: Ein transnationaler Polylog zur Bestimmung der Spannung zwischen hochschulischen Funktionen und Standortbedingungen.* Klagenfurt: Kärtner Druck- und Verlagsgesellschaft.
Kellermann, P. (1994a). "Bedürfnis, Arbeit, Geld und Paradigmata: Eine soziologische Collage über handlungsleitende Grundanschauungen in Wirtschaft und Gesellschaft." In Kellermann, P. and Mikl-Horke, G. (eds.). *Betrieb, Wirtschaft und Gesellschaft.* Klagenfurt: Kärtner Druck- und Verlagsgesellschaft, pp.87-117.
Kellermann, P. (1990). "Professions and Expert Labor." *Innovation,* 3(1), 185-194.
Kellermann, P. et al. (1994). *Zum Verhältnis von Studium und Arbeit; Entwicklungen und Bewertungen von männlichen und weiblichen Absolventen der Universitäten Klagenfurt und Salzburg.* Klagenfurt: Universität (mimeo.).
Kellermann, P. (1996). "Ungleiche Beschäftigungschancen von Graduierten vor dem Hintergrund der Entfaltung professioneller Arbeit." In Bolder, A. et al. (eds.) *Die Wiederentdeckung der Ungleichheit.* Jahrbuch '96 Bildung und Arbeit, Opladen, pp.83-103.
Kellermann, P. in cooperation with Lassnig, L. (1996). *Hochschulabsolvent/inn/en und Beschäftigung '96* (Forschungsbericht). Klagenfurt.
Kern, H. and Schumann, M. (1984). *Das Ende der Arbeitsteilung? Rationalisierung in der industriellen Produktion.* München: Beck.
Kivinen, O. and Rinne, R. (eds.) (1992). *Educational Strategies in Finland in the 1990s.* Turku: University of Turku, Research Unit for the Sociology of Education (Research reports, 8).
Kivinen, O. and Rinne, R. (1993a). "Educational Qualifications and the Labour Market: A Scandinavian perspective." *Industry and Higher Education,* 7(2), 111-118.
Kivinen, O. and Rinne, R. (1993b). "The Education Market, Qualifications and European Integration." *Higher Education in Europe,* 18(2), 24-36.

Kivinen, O. and Rinne, R. (1995). *The Social Inheritance of Education.* Helsinki: Statistics Finland (Education 1995/15).
Klerman, J.A. and Karoly, L.A. (1994). "Young Men and the Transition to Stable Employment." *Monthly Labour Review,* August, 31-48.
Kogan, M., and Brennan, J. (1993). "Higher Education and the World of Work: an Overview." *Higher Education in Europe,* 18(2), 2-23.
Lamendola, S. (1995). *Con gli occhi di Caronte: le imprese e i neolaureati.* Bologna: Clueb.
Lancaster, T. (1990). *The Econometric Analysis of Transition Data.* Cambridge: Cambridge University Press.
Levin, H.M. (1994). "Can Education Do It Alone?" *Economics of Education Review,* 13(2), 97-108.
Levin, K. and Rumberger, R. (1989). "Education, Work, and Employment in Developed Countries: Situation and Future Challenges." *Prospects,* 19(2), 205-224.
Lindner, U. et al. (1992). *Higher Education, Industry and Human Resources: The German Experience.* Milano: F. Agnelli.
List, J. (1996). *Grenzüberschreitende Mobilität von Hochschulabsolventen in Europa.* Köln: Deutscher Instituts-Verlag.
Luthans, F. (1992). Organisational Behaviour. Sixth edition. McGraw/Hill 1992.
Lynton, E.A. and Elman, S.E. (1987). New Priorities for the University. San Francisco, Cal.: Jossey-Bass.
Martinelli, D. and Vergnies, J.F. (1995). "L'insertion professionnelle des diplômés de l'enseignement supérieur se dégrade. " *Céreq Bref,* 107, 1-4.
Martinez, R. (1993). "Educacion y empleo en Espana." *Estudios de economia aplicada,* Vol. III, Cadiz: Universidad de Cadiz.
Martinez, R, Mora, J.G. and Vila, L. (1993). "Educacion, actividad y empleo en las Comunidades Autonomas espanolas." *Revista de Estudios Regionales,* 36, 299-331.
Mason, G. (1995). *The New Graduate Supply-Shock: Recruitment and Utilization of Graduates in British Industry.* London: National Institute of Economic and Social Research.
Maurice, M., Sellier, F. and Silvestre, J.-J. (1982). *Politique d'éducation et organisation industrielle en France et en Allemagne.* Paris.
Mayer, K.U. (ed.) (1986). "Lebensverläufe und sozialer Wandel." *Kölner Zeitschrift für Soziologie und Sozialpsychologie* (special issue), 31.
Mora, J.G. (1990). *La demanda de educacion superior: Un estudio analitico.* Madrid: Consejo de Universidades.
Mora, J.G. (1991). "Las enseñanzas universitarias y el mercado de trabajo." In *La Comunitat Valenciana en L'Europa unida.* Valencia: Generalitat Valenciana.
Mora, J.G. (1994). "Educacion y empleo en la Comunidad Valenciana." *Revista de Treball,* 22, 69-96.
Mora, J.G., Palafox, J. and Pérez, F. (1995). *Capital humano: Educacion y empleo.* Valencia: Bancaja.
Mora, J.G. (1997). "Market Trends in Spanish Higher Education." *Higher Education Policy,* 10(3) 187-198.
Mora, J.G. (1997). "Institutional Evaluation in Spain: an On-going Process." *Higher Education Management,* 9(1) 59-70.
Mora, J.G. (1997). "Equity in Spanish Higher Education." *Higher Education,* 33(3), 233-249.
Mortimer, J. T., Lorence, T. and Kumka. D. (1986). *Work, Family and Personality: Transition to Adulthood.* Norwood: N.JAblex Publishing Corporation.

Mortimer J.T. and Lorence, J (1979). "Work Experience and Occupational Value Socialization: A Longitudinal Study." *American Journal of Sociology* 84,1361-1385.
Moscati, R. (1986). "Scuola, mercato del lavoro, professionalità." In Gattulo, M. and Visalberghi, A. (eds.) *La scuola italiana dal 1945 al 1983*. Firenze: La Nuova Italia, pp.229-245.
Moscati, R. (1988). "Quale occupazione per i laureati?" *Università Progretto*, 33-34, 20-26.
Moscati, R. (1993). "Moving Towards Institutional Differentiation: The Italian case." In Gellert, C. (ed.) *Higher Education in Europe*. London: Jessica Kingsley, pp.72-83.
Moscati, R. and Pugliese, E. (1995). "Higher Education and the Labour Market in Italy: Continuities and Changes." In Brennan, J, Kogan, M. and Teicher, U. (eds.) *Higher Education and Work*. London: Jessica Kingsley, pp.118-135.
Nygaard, T. and Vibe, N. (eds.) (1994). *Utdanning og arbeidsmarked 1994*. Oslo: Utredningsinstittuet for forskning og hoyere utdanning.
OECD (1983). *Policies for Higher Education in the 1980s*. Paris.
OECD (1991). *Alternatives to Universities*. Paris.
OECD (1992a). *Education at a Glance: OECD Indicators*. Paris.
OECD (1992b). *From Higher Education to Employment*. (4 volumes), Paris.
OECD (1992c). *Recent Developments in Continuing Professional Education of Highly Qualified Personnel*. Paris, mimeo. (DEELSA/ED/WD(92)10).
OECD (1993a). *From Higher Education and Employment: Synthesis Report*. Paris.
OECD (1993b). *Higher Education and Employment: the Case of Humanities and Social Sciences*. Paris.
OECD (1995). *The OECD Job Study: Evidence and Explanations.* (2 volumes), Paris.
Osterman, P. (1980). *Getting Started: The Youth Labor Market*. Cambridge, Mass.: MIT Press
Oxenham, J. (ed.) (1984). *Education versus Qualification*. London: Allen and Unwin.
Parsons, T. (1968). "Professions." In Shills, E. (ed.) *International Encyclopedia of the Social Sciences*, vol.12, New York: Macmillan, pp.536-547.
Pascarella, E.T. and Terenzini, P.T. (1991). *How College Affects Students*. San Francisco/Cal.: Jossey-Bass.
Paul, J.J. (1989). *La relation formation emploi: un défi pour l'économie*. Paris: Economica.
Paul, J.J. (1992). "Le conge individuel de formation dans les trajectoires professionelles." *Formation Emploi*, 39, 55-76.
Paul, J.J. (1993). "Analyser les trajectoires professionelles: quelques jalongs." In Gazier, B. (ed.) *Emploi; nouvelles donnes*. Paris: Economica, 171-193.
Paul, J.J and Bailly, F. (1992). "Les fondements théoretiques du partenariat Université-Enterprise." *Recruter*, (1), 16-21.
Pearson, R., Andreutti, F. and Holly, F. (1990). *The European Labour Market Review: the Key Indicators*. Brighton: Institute of Manpower Studies.
Pöllauer, W. et al. (1995). *Arbeit und Studium am Beispiel einer Regionsuniversität – Wege und Orientierungen*. Wien.
Psacharopoulos, G. (ed.) (1987). *Economics of Education: Research and Studies*. Oxford: Pergamon.
Raban, A.J. (1991). *Entry of New Graduates into the European Community Labour Market*. Manchester: Central Services Unit.
Raffe, D. (ed.) (1988). *Education and the Youth Labour Market*. London, New York and Philadelphia: The Falmer Press.
Ramaekers, G.W.M. and Heijke, J.A.M. (1995). "Discrepancies in the Labour Market for RL-Educated Economists." In Gijselaers. W.H. et al. (eds.) *Educational Innovation in Eco-*

nomics and Business Administration: the Case of Problem-Based Learning. Dordrecht, Boston and London: Kluwer Academic Publishers, pp.370-381.

Research Centre for Education and the Labour Market (1993). "The Labour Market by Education and Occupation to 1998." *ROA* (ROA-R-1993/10E), Maastricht.

Rostan, M. (1994). "Reticoli imprenditoriali e sviluppo locale: il caso di Santa Nimfa". *Rassegna italiana di sociologia*, (4), 519-568.

Santoro, M. (1994). *Laureati e mondi del lavoro: Condizioni e percorsi in Emilia-Romagna.* Bologna: Istituto Carlo Cattaneo.

Sanyal, B. C. (1987). *Higher Education and Employment: an International Comparative Analysis.* London: The Falmer Press.

Sanyal, B. C. (1991). "Higher Education and the Labor Market." In Altbach, P. G. (ed.) *International Higher Education: an Encyclopedia.* New York and London: Garland, pp.147-168.

Schomburg, H. and Teichler, U. (1993) "Does the Programme Matter?" *Higher Education in Europe*, 18(2), 37-58.

Schomburg, H. and Teichler, U. (1996). "Hochschulabsolventen im Beruf: Ein Sekundäranalytischer britisch-deutscher Vergleich. " In Kehm, B. and Teichler, U. (eds.) *Vergleichende Hochschulforschung: eine Zwischenbilanz.* Wissenschaftliches Zentrum für Berufs- und Hochschulforschung, Kassel, pp.137-163.

Schön, D. A. (1987). *Educating the Reflective Practitioner.* San Francisco, Cal. and London: Jossey-Bass.

Shavit, Y. and Blossfeld, H.-P. (eds.) (1993). *Persistent Inequality: Changing Educational Attainment in Thirteen Countries.* Boulder.

Staufenbiel, J. E. (1993). *Key Information and Jobs for the European Graduate 93/94.* Köln: Institut für Berufs- und Ausbildungsplanung.

Stein, A. et al. (1996). *International Education and Training of Scientists and Engineers and Their Employment in European Industry.* Manchester: PREST.

Teichler, U. (1985). "Higher Education: Curriculum." In Husén, T, and Postlethwaite, T.N. (eds.) (1985). *The International Encyclopedia of Education.* Oxford: Pergamon, pp.2196-2208.

Teichler, U. (1988a). *Changing Patterns of the Higher Education System.* London: J. Kingsley.

Teichler, U. (1988b). "Higher Education and Work in Europe." In Smart, J.C. (ed.) *Higher Education: Handbook of Theory and Research,* Vol. 4. New York: Agathon, pp.109-182.

Teichler, U. (1991). "Towards a Highly Educated Society." *Higher Education Policy*, 4(4), 11-20.

Teichler, U. (1992). "Occupational Structures and Higher Education." In Clark, B. R. and Neave, G. R. (eds.) *The Encyclopedia of Higher Education.* Oxford: Pergamon, pp.975-992.

Teichler, U. (1994). "Higher Education and Employment: Changing Conditions for Diversified Structures of Higher Education." *Higher Education in Europe*, 19(4), 51-59.

Teichler, U. (1996a). "Comparative Higher Education: Potentials and Limits." *Higher Education*, 32(4), 431-465.

Teichler, U. (1996b). "Higher Education and New Socio-Economic Challenges." In Burgen, A. (ed.) *Goals and Purposes of Higher Education in the 21st Century.* London: J. Kingsley.

Teichler, U. (1997). *Higher Education and Employment in Europe: Select Findings from Previous Decades.* Kassel: Wissenschaftliches Zentrum für Berufs- und Hochschulforschung (Werkstattberichte; 52).
Teichler, U., Hartung, D. and Nuthmann, R. (1980). *Higher Education and the Needs of Society.* Windsor: NFER Publ.
Teichler, U., Buttgereit, M. and Holtkamp, R. (1984). *Hochschulzertifikate in der betrieblichen Einstellungspraxis.* Bad Honnef: Bock.
Teichler, U. et al. (1987). *Hochschule – Studium – Berufsvorstellungen.* Bad Honnef: Bock.
Teichler, U. and Winkler, H. (eds.) (1990). *Der Berufsstart von Hochschulabsolventen,* Bad Honnef: Bock.
Teichler, U., Schomburg, H. and Winkler, H. (1992). *Studium und Berufsweg von Hochschulabsolventen. Ergebnisse einer Langzeitstudie.* Bonn: Bundesministerium für Bildung und Wissenschaft (Bildung – Wissenschaft – Aktuell, 18/92).
Teichler, U. and Buttgereit, M. (eds.) (1992). *Hochschulabsolventen im Beruf.* Bad Honnef: Bock.
Teichler, U. and Maiworm, F. (1996). *Study Abroad and Early Career: Experiences of Former ERASMUS Students.* London: Jessica Kingsley.
Topel, R.H., and Ward, M.P. (1992). "Job Mobility and the Careers of Young Men." *The Quarterly Journal of Economics,* 107(2), 439-479.
UNESCO/CEPES (eds.) (1986). *Planning in Higher Education.* Bucharest.
University Competence and Industry (special issue), (1990). *CREaction,* 92.
Utredningsinstittuet for forskning og hoyere utdanning (1994). *Kandidatenundersokelsen 1993.* Oslo.
Vallas, S.P. (1990) "The Concept of Skill: a Critical Review." *Work and Occupations,* 17(4), 379-398.
Veum, J.R. and Weiss, A.B. (1993). "Education and the Work Histories of Young Adults." *Monthly Labour Review,* April, 11-20.
Wende, M.C. van der (1996). *Internationalising the Curriculum in Dutch Higher Education: an International Comparative Perspective.* (doctoral dissertation), University of Utrecht.
Wielers, R. and Glebbeek, A. (1995). "Graduates and the Labour Market in the Netherlands: Three Hyptheses and Some Data." *European Journal of Education,* 30(1), 11-30.
Wijnards Van Resandt, A. (ed.) (1991). *A Guide to Higher Education Systems and Qualifications in the European Communities.* Luxembourg: Office for Official Publications of the Commission of the European Communities.
Williams, B. (1993). *Higher Education and Employment.* University of Melbourne, Centre for the Study of Higher Education, Parkville.
Youdi, R.V. and Hinchliffe, K. (eds.) (1985). *Forecasting Skilled Manpower Needs: The Experiences of Eleven Countries.* Paris: International Institute for Educational Planning.

Higher Education and Graduate Employment in Europe

Survey of Graduates in ... [NatCat]

(Revised Master Questionnaire, 29.10.1998)

[NatCat = where national adaptations are needed]

Dear Graduates,[NatCat the whole cover page is optional]

As heads of the research group, we request your participation in a representative survey of persons graduating in 1994 or 1995 from institutions of higher education in 11 European countries and in Japan.

In reporting the experiences you personally made in the course of your study and after graduation you might contribute to a representative feedback most valuable for those responsible in higher education and as well for those setting the framework conditions for employment and other life spheres.

The survey is undertaken in Austria, Czech Republic, Finland, France, Germany, Italy, Japan, Norway, Spain, Sweden, the Netherlands, and in the United Kingdom. In your country, researchers from the Open University [NatCat] are responsible for the data collection and analysis. The project is financially supported by the European Commission, Directorate General XII through the Targeted Socio-Economic Research Programme.

We assure you that your replies will be used only in the framework of this research project. The results will be published in such a way that identification of individual persons is excluded.

YOUR INFORMATION WILL BE TREATED STRICTLY CONFIDENTIALLY.

If you wish, we will send you a summary of the most important results. Please return the completed questionnaire as soon as possible to the address mentioned below.

Thank you very much for your kind support.

Signature
John Brennan [NatCat]

Signature
Prof. Dr. Ulrich Teichler

Send the questionnaire to:

[NatCat]John Brennan
The Open University, Quality Support Centre
344-354 Gray's Inn Road, WCIX 3BP London

☎ 0171.447.2506 - Fax 0171.837.0290
email j.l.brennan@open.ac.uk [NatCat]

Prof. Dr. Ulrich Teichler
Project Co-ordinator
University of Kassel,
Germany

Explanatory Notes [NatCat this notes are optional]

How long does it take to fill in the questionnaire?

Most of you will need about one hour – less than a movie. It depends of course on the kind of experiences you have made during the last years.

We have developed a high standardized questionnnaire, which mainly expect from you to mark boxes which refer to relevant answers. With this approach we hope that we have made it easy for you to answer the questions.

How to answer the questions?

Please answer <u>all questions applicable to you</u>. In some cases, you will note that the questionnaire suggests you to disregard some questions not applicable to you (e.g. → *GO TO QUESTION ...*).

Since the questionnaire will be <u>captured with the help of a scanner</u>, please fill it in readable.

If questions are itemised, please mark the most appropriate answer like this → ☒.

In some questions we have employed answer scales from 1 to 5 (e.g 1 = *very good* to 5 = *very bad*).

J2 Looking back, if you were free to choose again, how likely would you ...

	Very likely				Not likely at all	
	1	2	3	4	5	
a.	☐	☐	☒	☐	☐	choose the same course of study?
b.	☐	☒	☒	☐	☐	choose the same institution of higher education?

Example of a 5-point-scale:

mark <u>one</u> box for each item (row)

If you would like to <u>correct</u> your answer, make the wrong one black and mark and underscore the right one.

In some cases we ask you for numbers only, e.g. |0|2| / |9|8|

and in others we leave space for you to write an answer (....................).

If you are asked for numbers, please fill in |0|0|, if your answer would be "zero".

If the space for your replies is not sufficient, please include an additional sheet of paper.

Your comments and additional information are welcome

This questionnaire is used in more than 12 countries with a wide range of different fields of study and different institutions of higher education. We could not take into consideration every specific detail of study and work, which might be relevant for the survey. Therefore we would appriciate your comments and additional information.

A. Educational Background Prior to Study

Please provide information on your educational development and your work experiences before your first enrolment in higher education.

A1 What were your entry qualifications when you entered higher education *(full or part-time)* **for the first time? [NatCat]**

☐ School-type qualifications (e.g. A Levels, Highers) [Use national categories, examples here are from UK]
☐ Vocational/professional qualifications (e.g. ONC)
☐ Other qualifications (e.g. access course, entry exam)
☐ Course was "open entry" → *GO TO QUESTION A6*

A2 How would you rate your grades? [NatCat]
[USE NATIONAL CATEGORIES, EXAMPLES HERE ARE FROM UK, REVISE THE HEADLINE OF A2 CORESSPONDINGLY]

☐ High
☐ Medium
☐ Low

A3 When did you get your entry qualification? [NatCat]

|__|__| Month   19 |__|__| Year

A4 How many years of *(primary plus secondary)* **schooling did you spend altogether up to acquiring the entry qualification to higher education** *(include years of repeating classes)*? **[NatCat]**

|__|__| Years of schooling altogether

A5 How many months did you spend on the following activities <u>between obtaining the entry qualification</u> (see A1) [NatCat] and your <u>first enrolment</u> in higher education? *Please state only the major activities.*

Months

|__|__|__| Other education/training/apprenticeship: ....
                                                    (please specify)

|__|__|__| Employment/self-employment

|__|__|__| Child rearing, family care

|__|__|__| Military or civilian service **[NatCat]**

|__|__|__| Not employed, seeking employment

|__|__|__| Other *(please specify)*: ....

A6 Prior to your first enrolment in higher education, have you been employed abroad or have you received any education/training/apprenticeship abroad? *Multiple reply possible*

☐ No → *GO TO QUESTION B1*

☐ Yes, I have been employed abroad: |__|__| Years |__|__| Months   Country: ....
                                                                                  (please specify)

☐ Yes, I received education/training/ apprenticeship abroad: |__|__| Years |__|__| Months   Country: ....
                                                                                                 (please specify)

B. Higher Education Courses Taken

B1 Please, provide information about all higher education courses you have ever taken *(include part-time, post graduate, and courses not completed [NatCat]). If you changed the institution, the field of study or if you took more than one degree, please fill in more than one row. If you studied in more programmes and institutions than this questionnaire provides for, please add a sheet.*

	A. Begin – End *(month/year)*	B. Major(s) studied *(please specify)*	C. Name of institution *(please specify)*	D. Kind of degree earned *(please fill in the number from the list A below)* [NatCat]	E. Class of degree/grade *(if applicable)* [NatCat]
1.	Begin ⎿⎿⎾/⎿⎿⎾ End ⎿⎿⎾/⎿⎿⎾	....	....	⎿⎿⎿⎾ ☐ No degree	☐ First ☐ Upper second ☐ Lower second ☐ Third ☐ Unclassified
2.	Begin ⎿⎿⎾/⎿⎿⎾ End ⎿⎿⎾/⎿⎿⎾ ☐ Not finished (yet)	....	....	⎿⎿⎿⎾ ☐ No degree	☐ First ☐ Upper second ☐ Lower second ☐ Third ☐ Unclassified
3.	Begin ⎿⎿⎾/⎿⎿⎾ End ⎿⎿⎾/⎿⎿⎾ ☐ Not finished (yet)	....	....	⎿⎿⎿⎾ ☐ No degree	☐ First ☐ Upper second ☐ Lower second ☐ Third ☐ Unclassified
4.	Begin ⎿⎿⎾/⎿⎿⎾ End ⎿⎿⎾/⎿⎿⎾ ☐ Not finished (yet)	....	....	⎿⎿⎿⎾ ☐ No degree	☐ First ☐ Upper second ☐ Lower second ☐ Third ☐ Unclassified

List A: Kind of degree [NatCat]

1 BA Hons
2 BA
3 BSc Hons
4 BSC Bachelor of Science
5 Other Bachelor
6 Master of Arts (MA)
7 Master of Science (MSc)
8 Master of Education (MEd), etc.
9 Other Master's
10 PhD
11 Other (please specify in column D)

B2 Did you spend time abroad during the time of your study *(in order to work or to study)*?

☐ No → *GO TO QUESTION B4*
☐ Yes

B3 If you stayed abroad: please state *(for each period abroad, if you have spent more than one)* **the countries, the duration and the activities.**

	A. Country *(please specify)*	B. Duration *(months)*	C. Major activity *(multiple reply possible)*
1	....	⎿⎿⎾ months	☐ Study (classes, self-study, work on thesis etc.) ☐ Work placements/internships ☐ Other *(please specify)*: ....
2	....	⎿⎿⎾ months	☐ Study (classes, self-study, work on thesis etc.) ☐ Work placements/internships ☐ Other *(please specify)*: ....

MASTER QUESTIONNAIRE

B4 How many months between first enrolment in higher education and graduation 1994 or 1995 did you spend predominantly on:

Duration (months)	
|⎵⎵⎵|	Employment/work <u>not related to study</u> or possible future work
|⎵⎵⎵|	Employment/work <u>related to study</u> or possible future work
|⎵⎵⎵|	Work placement, internship (as part of your degree course) [NatCat]
|⎵⎵⎵|	Child rearing, family care
|⎵⎵⎵|	Military or civilian service [NatCat]
|⎵⎵⎵|	Not employed, seeking employment
|⎵⎵⎵|	Other: .... *(please specify)*

B5 How long did you study in higher education for earning the degree you were awarded in 1994 or 1995 (see Question B1) and what period is normally/by law required *(including eventually required lower level diplomas and degrees in higher education and including mandatory periods of work placements/internships; excluding other studies, periods of other activities, etc.)*? **[NatCat years or semester]**

I actually studied	|⎵⎵| Years	|⎵⎵| Months
Normally/by law required are [NatCat]	|⎵⎵| Years	|⎵⎵| Months

→ *Please, notice: The following questions B6 to B9 refer ONLY to the course of study that you graduated from in 1994 or 1995.*

B6 How many hours per week during your study *(that you graduated from in 1994 or 1995)* **did you spend on average on each of the following activities?** *Please estimate*

A. During lecture period (approx. hours per week) [NatCat]

|⎵⎵|	Major subjects: attending lectures
|⎵⎵|	Major subjects: other study activities (inc. self-studies, etc.)
|⎵⎵|	Other subjects
|⎵⎵|	Extra-curricular activities (e.g. societies, drama, sport, student union)
|⎵⎵|	Employment/work (excluding work placements/internships)
|⎵⎵|	Other *(please specify)*: ....

B. Outside lecture period (approx. hours per week) [NatCat]

|⎵⎵|	Attending lectures (e.g. summer school) and other study activities (inc. self-studies, etc.)
|⎵⎵|	Employment/work (excluding work placements/internships)
|⎵⎵|	Other *(please specify)*: ....

B7 To what extent did your work experiences *(employment, internships etc.)* **during study tie up with the content of your studies** *(you graduated from in 1994 or 1995)*?

To a very high extent				Not at all	Not applicable, no work experiences
1	2	3	4	5	6
☐	☐	☐	☐	☐	☐

B8 If you look back to your course of study that you graduated from in 1994 or 1995: to what extent were the following modes of teaching and learning emphasised by your institution of higher education and its teachers? *Please rate each of the applicable options on a 5-point scale*

To a very high extent				Not at all	
1	2	3	4	5	
☐	☐	☐	☐	☐	a. Facts and instrumental knowledge
☐	☐	☐	☐	☐	b. Theories, concepts or paradigms
☐	☐	☐	☐	☐	c. Attitudes and socio-communicative skills
☐	☐	☐	☐	☐	d. Independent learning
☐	☐	☐	☐	☐	e. Regular class attendance
☐	☐	☐	☐	☐	f. Teacher as the main source of information and understanding
☐	☐	☐	☐	☐	g. Freedom to choose courses and areas of specialisation
☐	☐	☐	☐	☐	h. Project and problem-based learning
☐	☐	☐	☐	☐	i. Direct acquisition of work experience
☐	☐	☐	☐	☐	j. Out-of-class communication between students and staff
☐	☐	☐	☐	☐	k. Writing a thesis [NatCat: Thesis or other substantial academic assignment]
☐	☐	☐	☐	☐	l. Detailed regular assessment of academic progress

B9 How do you rate the study provision and study conditions you experienced in the course of study that you graduated from in 1994 or 1995?

Very good 1 2 3 4 5 Very bad

- a. Academic advice offered in general
- b. Assistance/advice for your final examination
- c. Course content of major
- d. Variety of courses offered
- e. Design of degree program
- f. Testing/grading system
- g. Opportunity to choose courses and areas of specialisation
- h. Practical emphasis of teaching and learning
- i. Teaching quality
- j. Chances to participate in research projects
- k. Research emphasis of teaching and learning
- l. Provision of work placements and other work experience
- m. Opportunity of out-of-class contacts with teaching staff
- n. Contacts with fellow students
- o. Chance for students to have an impact on university policies
- p. Equipment and stocking of libraries
- q. Supply of teaching material
- r. Quality of technical equipment (e.g. PC, measuring instruments, etc.)

B10 How do you rate your expertise in selected software areas at the <u>time of graduation</u> 1994 or 1995 and <u>now</u>?

At time of graduation 1994 or 1995
Very good 1 2 3 4 5 No expertise at all

Now
Very good 1 2 3 4 5 No expertise at all

- a. Word processor
- b. Programming languages
- c. Spread sheet
- d. Data base
- e. Subject-related software (e.g. CAD for engineers, SPSS for social scientists)

B11 How do you rate your language proficiency at the time of graduation 1994 or 1995? *Please answer with respect of any listed language and tick the kind of proficiency in each row. Multiple reply possible in each row.*

	Kind of language proficiency				
	A. Capable to <u>write</u> professionally relevant texts	B. Capable to <u>read</u> professionally relevant texts	C. Capable to <u>speak</u> in a professionally relevant context	D. Marginal proficiency	E. No proficiency
a. English	☐	☐	☐	☐	☐
b. French	☐	☐	☐	☐	☐
c. German	☐	☐	☐	☐	☐
e. Other *(please specify):*	☐	☐	☐	☐	☐
f. Other *(please specify):*	☐	☐	☐	☐	☐

C. Job Search and Sequence of Professional Activities

The following questions refer to the period after graduation in 1994 or 1995.

C1 Did you ever seek a job since graduation 1994 or 1995? *Exclude applications for casual and vacation jobs.*

- [ ] Yes ➔ *PLEASE GO TO QUESTION C2*
- [ ] No, I set up my own business/self-employment
- [ ] No, I continued the job I have had before graduation
- [ ] No, I continued to study
- [ ] No, I obtained work without actually searching ➔ *PLEASE GO TO QUESTION C8*
- [ ] Other (please specify): ....

➔ *IF YOU HAVE NOT SOUGHT A JOB PLEASE GO TO QUESTION C9*

C2 When did you start looking for a job? *Exclude search for casual and vacation jobs.*

- [ ] Prior to graduation, |__|__| months earlier
- [ ] Around the time of graduation
- [ ] After graduation, |__|__| months later

C3 Did you intend any of the following during your job search period after graduation in 1994 or 1995? *Multiple reply possible*

- [ ] a. Part-time employment
- [ ] b. To be self-employed (own business, contract work etc.)
- [ ] c. To work abroad
- [ ] d. To be employed/self-employed in the region of my partner/spouse/parents
- [ ] e. None of the above

C4 How did you try to find the first job after graduation? *Multiple reply possible*

- [ ] 1. I applied for an advertised vacancy
- [ ] 2. I contacted employers without knowing about a vacancy
- [ ] 3. I launched advertisements by myself
- [ ] 4. I was approached by an employer
- [ ] 5. I contacted a public employment agency [NatCat]
- [ ] 6. I contacted a commercial employment agency
- [ ] 7. I enlisted the help of the careers/placement office [NatCat] of my institution of higher education
- [ ] 8. I enlisted the help of teaching staff of the institution of higher education
- [ ] 9. I established contacts while working during the course of study
- [ ] 10. I used other personal connections/contacts (e.g. parents, relatives, friends)
- [ ] 11. I started my own business/self-employment
- [ ] 12. Other: .... *(please specify)*

C5 Which method was the most important one for getting your first job after graduation in 1994 or 1995? *Please fill in the item number from question C4.*

|__|__| Most important method

- [ ] Not applicable, I have not found a job after graduation ➔ *PLEASE GO TO QUESTION C9*

C6 How many employers did you contact *(by e.g. letter)* **before you took up your first job after graduation in 1994 or 1995?**

Approx. |__|__|__| number of employers contacted

C7 How many months have you sought all-together *(before or after graduation)* **for your first job after graduation in 1994 or 1995, which you consider not to be a casual job?**

|__|__| Months of job seeking

C8 How important, according to your perception, were the following aspects for your employer in recruiting you for your initial employment after graduation, if applicable?

Very important 1 2 3 4 5 Not at all important

- [ ][ ][ ][ ][ ] a. Field of study
- [ ][ ][ ][ ][ ] b. Main subject/specialisation
- [ ][ ][ ][ ][ ] c. Exam results [NatCat]
- [ ][ ][ ][ ][ ] d. Practical/work experience acquired during course of study
- [ ][ ][ ][ ][ ] e. Practical/work experience acquired prior to course of study
- [ ][ ][ ][ ][ ] f. Reputation of the institution of higher education
- [ ][ ][ ][ ][ ] g. Experience abroad
- [ ][ ][ ][ ][ ] h. Foreign language proficiency
- [ ][ ][ ][ ][ ] i. Computer skills
- [ ][ ][ ][ ][ ] j. Recommendations/references from third persons
- [ ][ ][ ][ ][ ] k. Personality
- [ ][ ][ ][ ][ ] l. Other: .... *(please specify)*

C9 How would you characterise and summarise your predominant activities since your graduation in 1994 or 1995?

- ☐ I have spent most of the time on a regular job
- ☐ I had various temporary jobs
- ☐ I had more than one job at the same time
- ☐ I was most of the time unemployed
- ☐ I embarked on further study/professional training
- ☐ I was predominantly engaged in child rearing or family care
- ☐ Other: ....

C10 Please inform us on your current major activity.

Current situation

Begin (month/year)	Kind of current major activity (please mark one, and inform us about your further major activities in Question C11, if applicable)	Information regarding employment		
		Full-time or part-time?	Type of contract?	Job title and position (please specify)
A	B	C	D	E
Since ☐☐/☐☐ (month/year)	☐ Employed ☐ Self-employed } →	☐ Full-time ☐ Part-time	☐ Permanent ☐ Temporary	**Job title:** (e.g. primary school teacher, production engineer) ....
	☐ Not employed, seeking employment ☐ Professional training ☐ Advanced academic study ☐ Child rearing, family care ☐ Other (please specify):	} → GO TO QUESTION C11		**Position:** (e.g. assistant, team leader, head of department) ....

C11 If your major activity has changed since graduation 1994 or 1995 (e.g. from "unemployed" to "employed") or you experienced a substantial change in your job (e.g. new employer, new position, new work tasks), please provide further information in the following table. Use a new section for each activity whether undertaken sequentially or in parallel. In each section mark one box for the kind of activity only. If you have had many jobs of short duration, please summarise in one or more activities.

	Begin - End (month/year)	Kind of activity (use a new section for each new activity or for activities at the same time)	Information regarding employment		
			Full-time or part-time?	Type of contract?	Job title and position (please specify)
	A	B	C	D	E
1.	Begin ☐☐/☐☐ End ☐☐/☐☐ ☐ Activity not finished yet	☐ Employed ☐ Self-employed } → ☐ Not employed, seeking employment ☐ Professional training ☐ Advanced academic study ☐ Child rearing, family care ☐ Other (please specify):	☐ Full-time ☐ Part-time	☐ Permanent ☐ Temporary	**Job title:** (e.g. primary school teacher, production engineer) ....
			} → GO TO NEXT ACTIVITY		**Position:** (e.g. assistant, team leader, head of department) ....

MASTER QUESTIONNAIRE

	Begin - End (month/year)	Kind of major activity (use a new section for each new activity or for activities at the same time)	Information regarding employment		Job title and position (please specify)
			Full-time or part-time?	Type of contract?	
	A	B	C	D	E
2.	Begin ⊔⊔/⊔⊔ End ⊔⊔/⊔⊔ ☐ Activity not finished yet	☐ Employed ☐ Self-employed } → ☐ Not employed, seeking employment ☐ Professional training ☐ Advanced academic study ☐ Child rearing, family care ☐ Other (please specify):	☐ Full-time ☐ Part-time	☐ Permanent ☐ Temporary → GO TO NEXT ACTIVITY	Job title: (e.g. primary school teacher, production engineer) .... Position: (e.g. assistant, team leader, head of department) ....
3.	Begin ⊔⊔/⊔⊔ End ⊔⊔/⊔⊔ ☐ Activity not finished yet	☐ Employed ☐ Self-employed } → ☐ Not employed, seeking employment ☐ Professional training ☐ Advanced academic study ☐ Child rearing, family care ☐ Other (please specify):	☐ Full-time ☐ Part-time	☐ Permanent ☐ Temporary → GO TO NEXT ACTIVITY	Job title: (e.g. primary school teacher, production engineer) .... Position: (e.g. assistant, team leader, head of department) ....
4.	Begin ⊔⊔/⊔⊔ End ⊔⊔/⊔⊔ ☐ Activity not finished yet	☐ Employed ☐ Self-employed } → ☐ Not employed, seeking employment ☐ Professional training ☐ Advanced academic study ☐ Child rearing, family care ☐ Other (please specify):	☐ Full-time ☐ Part-time	☐ Permanent ☐ Temporary → GO TO NEXT ACTIVITY	Job title: (e.g. primary school teacher, production engineer) .... Position: (e.g. assistant, team leader, head of department) ....
5.	Begin ⊔⊔/⊔⊔ End ⊔⊔/⊔⊔ ☐ Activity not finished yet	☐ Employed ☐ Self-employed } → ☐ Not employed, seeking employment ☐ Professional training ☐ Advanced academic study ☐ Child rearing, family care ☐ Other (please specify):	☐ Full-time ☐ Part-time	☐ Permanent ☐ Temporary → GO TO NEXT ACTIVITY	Job title: (e.g. primary school teacher, production engineer) .... Position: (e.g. assistant, team leader, head of department) ....

D. Current Activities, Employment and Work

D1 If you are at current employed/self-employed: How would you describe your current professional situation? *Multiple reply possible*

☐ I have a regular employment/I am self-employed
☐ I have casual jobs <u>related</u> to my study
☐ I have casual jobs <u>not related</u> to my study
☐ I have more than one job
☐ I am currently doing military or civilian service
☐ Other: ....
   (please specify)

D2 Have you actively tried to obtain (other) paid work in the past 4 weeks?

☐ No → PLEASE GO TO QUESTION D3
☐ No, but I am awaiting the results of earlier job applications
☐ Yes, and I could start working within the next two weeks
☐ Yes, but I could not start working within the next two weeks

D3 How many employers *(including self-employment)* **have you worked for in the period after graduation in 1994 or 1995** *(including your present employer)*?

|___|___| Number of employers

IF YOU ARE NOT EMPLOYED/SELF-EMPLOYED → GO TO QUESTION D15

IF YOU HAVE MORE THAN ONE JOB PLEASE REFER TO YOUR <u>MAJOR JOB</u>.

D4 Please state the kind of your current employer/institution *(if several, please refer to main employer)*? *Please mark one single item only*

☐ Public employer
☐ Non-profit organization
☐ Private employer
☐ Self employed
☐ Other: ....
   (please specify)

D5 In which economic sector are you currently working? *Please state in a specific term (e.g. car manufacturing, primary school, hospital, theatre).*

....
   (please specify)

D6 What is your current major area of work assignment *(e.g. R&D, data processing, sales or teaching)* **and what are your additional area(s) of activities, if applicable?**

Major area of work (please specify)

....

....

Additional area(s) of work (please specify)

....

....

D7 How many hours per week are you working on average? *Multiple reply possible*

Working hours per week

|___|___| Contract hours of my major assignment
|___|___| Additional working hours of my major assignment *(paid and unpaid overtime)*
|___|___| Working hours on other assignments *(second occupation, side jobs, etc.)*
|___|___| Total working hours *(incl. self-employment)*

D8 Do you work in a (big) organisation comprising branches?

☐ Yes, I'm working in a branch
☐ Yes, I'm working in the head office/central unit of an organization comprising branches
☐ No, I'm working in an organization comprising no branches
☐ Not applicable, I am self-employed

D9 Please estimate, to the best of your ability, the approximate number of people who are working in ...

approx. |___|___|___|___| a. the location where you currently work.

approx. |___|___|___|___| b. the <u>entire organisation</u> if there is more than one location.

D10 If you are self-employed: Which of the following characteristics are applicable to you?
Multiple reply possible

- [ ] a. I am serving a single contractor
- [ ] b. I took over an existing firm/office etc.
- [ ] c. I established a new firm/office etc.
- [ ] d. I was asked by my former employer to work self-employed
- [ ] e. I am working at home
- [ ] f. I have no employees
- [ ] g. I have a partnership with friends/relatives
- [ ] e. Other: ....
   (please specify)

D11 What is your approximate annual gross income?[NatCat local currency]:

Thousand [NatCat]

|⎵⎵⎵⎵| a. from your current major job *(excluding overtime and extra payments)?*

|⎵⎵⎵⎵| b. from overtime and extra payments in your major job?

|⎵⎵⎵⎵| c. from other jobs?

D12 Did you undertake business/professional journeys abroad within the last 12 months?

- [ ] No
- [ ] Yes, altogether |⎵⎵| weeks

D13 To what extent do you communicate *(oral and written communication)* **with clients/external partners...**

To a very high extent 1 2 3 4 5 Not at all

- ☐☐☐☐☐ a. in a foreign language?
- ☐☐☐☐☐ b. with foreigners in your language?

D14 What percentage of your work time do you consider to have an international context?

|⎵⎵⎵| Percentage of work time (%)

D15 Have you, since graduation *(multiple reply possible)*

- [ ] a. considered working abroad?
- [ ] b. sought employment abroad?
- [ ] c. actually received an offer to work abroad?
- [ ] d. actually had regular employment abroad since graduation?
- [ ] e. actually been sent abroad by your employer on work assignments?
- [ ] f. None → *GO TO QUESTION E1*

D16 If you have worked abroad: In which country(ies) and how many months (each)?

	Duration	Country *(please specify)*
1	|⎵⎵| months	....
2	|⎵⎵| months	....
3	|⎵⎵| months	....

E. Competencies and Their Application

E1 Please, state the extent to which you had the following competencies at the time of graduation in 1994 or 1995 and to what extent they are required in your current work. *If you are not employed please answer only (A).*

A. Possessed at time of graduation 1994 or 1995	Knowledge, skills and competencies	B. Work requirements
To a very high extent — Not at all 1 2 3 4 5		To a very high extent — Not at all 1 2 3 4 5
☐☐☐☐☐	a. Broad general knowledge	☐☐☐☐☐
☐☐☐☐☐	b. Cross-disciplinary thinking/knowledge	☐☐☐☐☐
☐☐☐☐☐	c. Field-specific theoretical knowledge	☐☐☐☐☐
☐☐☐☐☐	d. Field-specific knowledge of methods	☐☐☐☐☐
☐☐☐☐☐	e. Foreign language proficiency	☐☐☐☐☐
☐☐☐☐☐	f. Computer skills	☐☐☐☐☐
☐☐☐☐☐	g. Understanding complex social, organisational and technical systems	☐☐☐☐☐
☐☐☐☐☐	h. Planning, co-ordinating and organising	☐☐☐☐☐
☐☐☐☐☐	i. Applying rules and regulations	☐☐☐☐☐
☐☐☐☐☐	j. Economic reasoning	☐☐☐☐☐
☐☐☐☐☐	k. Documenting ideas and information	☐☐☐☐☐
☐☐☐☐☐	a. Problem-solving ability	☐☐☐☐☐
☐☐☐☐☐	b. Analytical competencies	☐☐☐☐☐
☐☐☐☐☐	d. Learning abilities	☐☐☐☐☐
☐☐☐☐☐	e. Reflective thinking, assessing one's own work	☐☐☐☐☐
☐☐☐☐☐	f. Creativity	☐☐☐☐☐
☐☐☐☐☐	g. Working under pressure	☐☐☐☐☐
☐☐☐☐☐	h. Accuracy, attention to detail	☐☐☐☐☐
☐☐☐☐☐	i. Time management	☐☐☐☐☐
☐☐☐☐☐	j. Negotiating	☐☐☐☐☐
☐☐☐☐☐	k. Fitness for work	☐☐☐☐☐
☐☐☐☐☐	l. Manual skills	☐☐☐☐☐
☐☐☐☐☐	m. Working independently	☐☐☐☐☐
☐☐☐☐☐	n. Working in a team	☐☐☐☐☐
☐☐☐☐☐	a. Initiative	☐☐☐☐☐
☐☐☐☐☐	b. Adaptability	☐☐☐☐☐
☐☐☐☐☐	c. Assertiveness, decisiveness, persistence	☐☐☐☐☐
☐☐☐☐☐	d. Power of concentration	☐☐☐☐☐
☐☐☐☐☐	e. Getting personally involved	☐☐☐☐☐
☐☐☐☐☐	f. Loyalty, integrity	☐☐☐☐☐
☐☐☐☐☐	g. Critical thinking	☐☐☐☐☐
☐☐☐☐☐	h. Oral communication skills	☐☐☐☐☐
☐☐☐☐☐	i. Written communication skills	☐☐☐☐☐
☐☐☐☐☐	j. Tolerance, appreciating of different points of view	☐☐☐☐☐
☐☐☐☐☐	k. Leadership	☐☐☐☐☐
☐☐☐☐☐	l. Taking responsibilities, decisions	☐☐☐☐☐

E2 To what extent has your study *(you graduated from 1994 or 1995)* **been useful for ...?**

To a very high extent — Not at all
1 2 3 4 5

☐☐☐☐☐ a. preparing you for your present work tasks?

☐☐☐☐☐ b. preparing you for tasks in other spheres of life?

--> *IF YOU ARE CURRENTLY NOT PROFESSIONAL ACTIVE, GO TO QUESTION G2*

E3 How important do you consider the following competencies for doing your current work?

Very important — Not at all important
1 2 3 4 5

☐☐☐☐☐ a. Professional knowledge of other countries (e.g. economical, sociological, legal knowledge)

☐☐☐☐☐ b. Knowledge/understanding of international differences in culture and society, modes of behaviour, life styles, etc.

☐☐☐☐☐ c. Working with people from different cultural backgrounds

☐☐☐☐☐ d. Communicating in foreign languages

F. Relationships Between Higher Education and Work

F1 If you take into consideration your current work tasks altogether: To what extent do you use the knowledge and skills acquired in the course of study *(you graduated from 1994 or 1995)*?

To a very high extent — Not at all
1 2 3 4 5
☐ ☐ ☐ ☐ ☐

F2 How would you characterise the relationship between your field of study and your area of work?

☐ My field of study is the only possible/by far the best field
☐ Some other fields could prepare for the area of work as well
☐ Another field would have been more useful
☐ The field of study does not matter very much
☐ Higher education studies are not at all related to my area of work
☐ Others *(please specify)*: ....

F3 If you consider all dimensions of your employment and work *(status, position, income, work tasks, etc.)*:

a. **To what extent is your employment and work appropriate to your level of education?**

Completely appropriate — Not at all appropriate
1 2 3 4 5
☐ ☐ ☐ ☐ ☐

b. **What is the most appropriate level of course of study/degree for your employment and work in comparison to that which you graduated from in 1994 or 1995?**

☐ A higher level than the one I graduated from
☐ The same level
☐ A lower level of higher/tertiary education
☐ No higher/tertiary education at all
☐ Others *(please specify)*: ....

F4 If you consider your employment and work as hardly appropriate and not linked to your education: why did you take it up? *Multiple reply possible*

☐ a. I have not (yet) been able to find a job more appropriate
☐ b. In doing this job I have better career prospects
☐ c. I prefer an occupation which is not closely connected to my studies
☐ d. I was promoted to a position less linked to my studies than my previous position(s)
☐ e. I can get a higher income in my current job
☐ f. My current job offers me more security
☐ g. My current job is more interesting
☐ h. My current job provides the opportunity for part-time/flexible schedules etc.
☐ i. My current job enables me to work in a locality, which I prefer
☐ j. My current job allows me to take into account family needs
☐ k. At the beginning of the career envisaged I have to accept work hardly linked to my study
☐ l. Other: ....
       (please specify)
☐ m. Not applicable, I consider my job closely linked to my studies

F5 Taking all aspects into account, to what extent does your current work situation meet the expectations you had when you started your study?

Much better than expected — Much worse than expected — Not applicable, I have had no expectations
1 2 3 4 5
☐ ☐ ☐ ☐ ☐   ☐

G. Work Orientations and Job Satisfaction

G1 <u>Altogether</u>, to what extent are you satisfied with your current work?

Very satisfied — Very dissatisfied
1 2 3 4 5
☐ ☐ ☐ ☐ ☐

G2 Please indicate the importance you placed on each of the following life goals - in the past and now.

A. At time of graduation 1994 or 1995 Very important 1 2 3 4 5 Not at all important		B. Now Very important 1 2 3 4 5 Not at all important
☐☐☐☐☐	a. Social prestige	☐☐☐☐☐
☐☐☐☐☐	b. Personal development	☐☐☐☐☐
☐☐☐☐☐	c. Varied social life	☐☐☐☐☐
☐☐☐☐☐	d. Home/family	☐☐☐☐☐
☐☐☐☐☐	e. Making money	☐☐☐☐☐
☐☐☐☐☐	f. Academic inquiry	☐☐☐☐☐
☐☐☐☐☐	g. Work	☐☐☐☐☐

G3 How important are the following characteristics of an occupation for you personally (A) and to what extent do they apply to your current professional situation (B)? *If you are not employed please answer only (A).*

A. Importance Very important 1 2 3 4 5 Not at all important		B. Apply to current situation To a very high extent 1 2 3 4 5 Not at all
☐☐☐☐☐	a. Largely independent disposition of work	☐☐☐☐☐
☐☐☐☐☐	b. Opportunity of undertaking scientific/scholarly work	☐☐☐☐☐
☐☐☐☐☐	c. Clear and well-ordered tasks	☐☐☐☐☐
☐☐☐☐☐	d. Possibilities of using acquired knowledge and skills	☐☐☐☐☐
☐☐☐☐☐	e. Job security	☐☐☐☐☐
☐☐☐☐☐	f. Social recognition and status	☐☐☐☐☐
☐☐☐☐☐	g. Opportunity of pursuing own ideas	☐☐☐☐☐
☐☐☐☐☐	h. Good social climate	☐☐☐☐☐
☐☐☐☐☐	i. Opportunity of pursuing continuous learning	☐☐☐☐☐
☐☐☐☐☐	j. High income	☐☐☐☐☐
☐☐☐☐☐	k. Chances of (political) influence	☐☐☐☐☐
☐☐☐☐☐	l. Challenging tasks	☐☐☐☐☐
☐☐☐☐☐	m. Good career prospects	☐☐☐☐☐
☐☐☐☐☐	n. Enough time for leisure activities	☐☐☐☐☐
☐☐☐☐☐	o. Co-ordinating and management tasks	☐☐☐☐☐
☐☐☐☐☐	p. Possibility of working in a team	☐☐☐☐☐
☐☐☐☐☐	q. Chance of doing something useful for society	☐☐☐☐☐
☐☐☐☐☐	r. Variety	☐☐☐☐☐
☐☐☐☐☐	s. Good chances of combining employment with family tasks	☐☐☐☐☐

MASTER QUESTIONNAIRE

H. Further Education and Training

Please provide us with some more information regarding your further education and training (not including doctoral study or other additional study you have mentioned already in Question B1.

H1 Did you undertake further education and training <u>required in order to obtain or keep a professional qualification</u> or another <u>longer professional training period</u> since graduation in 1994 or 1995 *(e.g. traineeship, Referendariat, Praktikum, "Registered Accountant"; use national terms NatCat)*? **[NatCat]**

☐ No → *GO TO QUESTION H2*

☐ Yes, please specify:

	A. Name/kind of training *(e.g. traineeship, Referendariat, Voluntariat, Praktikum)*[NatCat])	B. Duration *(please specify the number of months)*	C. Kind of certification earned *(if applicable)* [NatCat]
1.	....	⊔⊔ Months ☐ Not finished yet	....
2.	....	⊔⊔ Months ☐ Not finished yet	....
3.	....	⊔⊔ Months ☐ Not finished yet	....

H2 After your degree awarded in 1994 or 1995 did you undertake other additional/further education/training *(short courses, seminars, workshops, self-study, etc.)* **related to your career or to a future career that you might pursue?** *Exclude professional training programmes stated in response to H1 and exclude what you consider to be completely unrelated to work and career.*

☐ No → *GO TO QUESTION H10*

☐ Yes

H3 Please list the most important course(s) and indicate the total duration *(in contact hours of teaching/learning).*

	Name and type of the course/activity *(please specify)*	Duration (hours)
1	....	☐ 1 to 10 hours ☐ 11 to 50 hours ☐ 51 and more hours
2	....	☐ 1 to 10 hours ☐ 11 to 50 hours ☐ 51 and more hours
3	....	☐ 1 to 10 hours ☐ 11 to 50 hours ☐ 51 and more hours

→ *The following questions H4 to H9 apply to your further education activities in general mentioned in H3.*

H4 Who is (was) responsible for providing this course/these courses? *Multiple reply possible*	**H5** Who funded the costs for your participation in this course/these courses *(fees, transportation etc.)*?
☐ a. A higher education institution	☐ a. There were no costs
☐ b. Private institute offering seminar/training	☐ b. Mainly my employer
☐ c. In-company or in-service training	☐ c. Mainly myself
☐ d. Distance education/written course [NatCat]	☐ d. Mainly public funds
☐ e. Other .... *(please specify)*	☐ e. I don't know
	☐ f. Other .... *(please specify)*

H6 Did you attend the course(s) during your paid working time?

☐ Yes, completely during paid working time
☐ Yes, partly during paid working time
☐ No, completely outside paid working time
☐ Not applicable, I was not employed

H7 Which of the following topics were covered in the course(s)? *Multiple reply possible*

☐ a. New scholarly knowledge in your discipline
☐ b. Cross-disciplinary scholarly knowledge of various fields
☐ c. Methodological competencies
☐ d. Manual skills
☐ e. Foreign language proficiency
☐ f. Computer skills
☐ g. Social/political or philosophical topics
☐ h. Competencies in business administration
☐ i. Management/leadership competencies
☐ j. Legal topics
☐ k. Human ecology/environmental matters
☐ l. Oral or written communication and presentation skills
☐ m. Relationships with customers/clients
☐ n. Other: ....
   (please specify)

H8 What was the most important personal purpose of additional/further education/training when you started it? *Please mark only one*

☐ Enhancing career, getting promoted, etc
☐ Updating your knowledge
☐ Re-training (i.e. preparation for other occupations/careers)

H9 To what extent did your additional/further education or training actually help you afterwards ...?

To a very high extent / Not at all
1　2　3　4　5

☐☐☐☐☐ a. to get employed?
☐☐☐☐☐ b. to get along with the work tasks?
☐☐☐☐☐ c. to enrich the job (e.g. more interesting tasks)?
☐☐☐☐☐ d. to raise the status (e.g. promotion, higher income)
☐☐☐☐☐ e. to cope with requirements from other life spheres than employment and work

H10 To what extent do you feel at present a need to update or develop your competencies further through additional/further education or training?

To a very high extent / Not at all
1　2　3　4　5
☐　☐　☐　☐　☐

H11 To what extent do you agree with the following statements regarding the need of additional/further education or training?

Completely agree / Completely disagree
1　2　3　4　5

Additional/further education or training is necessary ...

☐☐☐☐☐ a. ... in order to cope with tasks which could not be envisaged at the time of initial education
☐☐☐☐☐ b. ... because of shortcomings in initial first study
☐☐☐☐☐ c. ... in order to acquire knowledge which can be learned better on the job
☐☐☐☐☐ d. Initial first study provides a sufficient training in relevant skill acquisition
☐☐☐☐☐ e. Initial first study constitutes a good basis for continuous updating of knowledge and skills

H12 How often did you read subject related professional/scientific journals during the last 12 months?

At least once a week / Monthly / About every three months / Seldom / Never
☐　☐　☐　☐　☐

H13 How often did you attend professional relevant meetings/conferences during the last 12 months?

☐ 4 times and more　☐ 1 to 3 times　☐ Never

H14 How often did you use the internet sources for professional relevant information gathering during the last 12 months?

At least once a week / Monthly / About every three months / Seldom / Never
☐　☐　☐　☐　☐

I. Socio-Biographic data

Please provide details about yourself in order to enable us to interpret your work biography as accurately as possible

I1 Gender

☐ Male
☐ Female

I2 Year of birth

19 |__|__| Year

I3 Please, provide some information about your citizenship and your country of schooling, study and work

		X	Other, please specify
a.	Current citizenship	☐	....
b.	Citizenship at birth	☐	....
c.	Country where you completed secondary education	☐	....
d.	Country of first employment after graduation	☐	....
e.	Country of current employment/work	☐	....
f.	Country of current residence	☐	....

✎ [NatCat: x = country in which the survey in undertaken]

I4 In which region have you studied and where do you live today? *Please specify the postal code [NatCat]*

Postal code	
|__|__|	(Main) region during time of studies
|__|__|	Region of current residence
|__|__|	Region of employment, if applicable

✎ [National adaptation of boxes for postal codes or regions]

I5 Parental and partner highest education

Father	Mother	Partner	
☐	☐	☐	Compulsory school or less
☐	☐	☐	Completed (upper) secondary school
☐	☐	☐	Higher education diploma/degree
		☐	Not applicable, I do not have a partner

I6 Did/do you live ... ? *Multiple reply possible*

Immediately prior to graduation in 1994 or 1995	Currently	
☐	☐	with a partner?
☐	☐	with parents?
☐	☐	with other persons?
☐	☐	as single?

I7 Are there children in your household?

☐ No → *GO TO QUESTION I8*

☐ Yes How many? |__|__|

How old are they:

1. |__|__| 2. |__|__| 3. |__|__|

4. |__|__| 5. |__|__| 6. |__|__|

I8 How many hours per week are you *(and eventually your partner)* **working in your household** *(cleaning, cooking, child care, etc.)?*

|__|__| Hours per week myself

|__|__| Hours per week my partner

I9 What is the major activity of your partner, if applicable? *Please tick only one*

☐ Not applicable, I don't have a partner
☐ Employed
☐ Self-employed
☐ Not employed, seeking employment
☐ Professional training
☐ Advanced academic study
☐ Child rearing, family care
☐ Other (please specify): ....

J Retrospective Assessment of Your Studies
(you finished 1994 or 1995)

J1 To what extent did your studies help you ...?

To a very high extent 1 2 3 4 5 Not at all

☐☐☐☐☐   a. finding a satisfying job after finishing your studies?
☐☐☐☐☐   b. for your long-term career prospects?
☐☐☐☐☐   c. for the development of your personality?

J2 Looking back, if you were free to choose again, how likely would you ...

Very likely 1 2 3 4 5 Not likely at all

☐☐☐☐☐   a. choose the same course of study?
☐☐☐☐☐   b. choose the same institution of higher education?
☐☐☐☐☐   c. choose a higher degree level of higher education? [NatCat]
☐☐☐☐☐   d. choose a lower degree level of higher education? [NatCat]
☐☐☐☐☐   e. decide not to study at all?

J3 What kind of improvements in higher education would you suggest according to your experiences?

....
....
....

Thank you very much for completing the questionnaire.

Higher Education Dynamics

1. J. Enders and O. Fulton (eds.): *Higher Education in a Globalising World.* 2002
   ISBN Hb 1-4020-0863-5; Pb 1-4020-0864-3

2. A. Amaral, G.A. Jones and B. Karseth (eds.): *Governing Higher Education: National Perspectives on Institutional Governance.* 2002   ISBN 1-4020-1078-8

3. A. Amaral, V.L. Meek and I.M. Larsen (eds.): *The Higher Education Managerial Revolution?* 2003   ISBN Hb 1-4020-1575-5; Pb 1-4020-1586-0

4. C.W. Barrow, S. Didou-Aupetit and J. Mallea: *Globalisation, Trade Liberalisation, and Higher Education in North America.* 2003   ISBN 1-4020-1791-X

5. S. Schwarz and D.F. Westerheijden (eds.): *Accreditation and Evaluation in the European Higher Education Area.* 2004   ISBN 1-4020-2796-6

6. P. Teixeira, B. Jongbloed, D. Dill and A. Amaral (eds.): *Markets in Higher Education: Rhetoric or Reality?* 2004   ISBN 1-4020-2815-6

7. A. Welch (ed.): *The Professoriate.* Profile of a Profession. 2005 ISBN 1-4020-3382-6

8. Å. Gornitzka, M. Kogan and A. Amaral (eds.): *Reform and Change in Higher Education.* Implementation Policy Analysis. 2005   ISBN 1-4020-3402-4

9. I. Bleiklie and M. Henkel (eds.): *Governing Knowledge.* A Study of Continuity and Change in Higher Education – A Festschrift in Honour of Maurice Kogan. 2005
   ISBN 1-4020-3489-X

10. N. Cloete, P. Maassen, R. Fehnel, T. Moja, T. Gibbon and H. Perold (eds.): *Transformation in Higher Education.* Global Pressures and Local Realities. 2005
    ISBN 1-4020-4005-9

11. M. Kogan, M. Henkel and S. Hanney: *Government and Research.* Thirty Years of Evolution. 2006   ISBN 1-4020-4444-5

12. V. Tomusk (ed.): *Creating the European Area of Higher Education.* Voices from the Periphery. 2006   ISBN 1-4020-4613-8

13. M. Kogan, M. Bauer, I. Bleiklie and M. Henkel (eds.): *Transforming Higher Education.* A Comparative Study. 2006   ISBN 1-4020-4656-1

14. P.N. Teixeira, D.B. Johnstone, M.J. Rosa and J.J. Vossensteijn (eds.): *Cost-sharing and Accessibility in Higher Education: A Fairer Deal?* 2006   ISBN 1-4020-4659-6

15. H. Schomburg and U. Teichler: *Higher Education and Graduate Employment in Europe.* Results from Graduates Surveys from Twelve Countries. 2006
    ISBN 1-4020-5153-0